THE SCIENCE OF VAMPIRES

✠

Titles by Katherine Ramsland

The C.S.I. Effect

The Human Predator: A Historical Chronicle of
Serial Murder and Forensic Investigation

Inside the Minds of Mass Murderers: Why They Kill

A Voice for the Dead: A Forensic Investigator's
Pursuit of Truth in the Grave
(with James E. Starrs)

The Science of Cold Case Files

The Unknown Darkness: Profiling the Predators Among Us
(with Gregg O. McCrary)

The Science of Vampires

The Criminal Mind: A Writer's Guide to Forensic Psychology

The Forensic Science of CSI

Cemetery Stories:
Haunted Graveyards, Embalming Secrets,
and the Life of a Corpse After Death

Ghost: Investigating the Other Side

Bliss: Writing to Find Your True Self

Piercing the Darkness:
Undercover with Vampires in America Today

Dean Koontz: A Writer's Biography

Prism of the Night: A Biography of Anne Rice

The Witches' Companion: The Official Guide to Anne Rice's
Lives of the Mayfair Witches

The Vampire Companion: The Official Guide to Anne Rice's
The Vampire Chronicles

The Anne Rice Reader

The Art of Learning: A Self-Help Manual for Students

Engaging the Immediate: Applying Kierkegaard's
Indirect Communication to the Practice of Psychotherapy

* * *

Novels

The Blood Hunters
The Heat Seekers

THE SCIENCE OF

VAMPIRES

KATHERINE RAMSLAND, PH.D.

BERKLEY BOULEVARD BOOKS, NEW YORK

A Berkley Boulevard Book
Published by The Berkley Publishing Group
A division of Penguin Putnam Inc.
375 Hudson Street
New York, New York 10014

Copyright © 2002 by Katherine Ramsland, Ph.D.
Book design by Kristin del Rosario
Cover design © 2002 by Marc Cohen
Cover photograph by Marty Heitner

PRINTING HISTORY
Berkley Boulevard trade paperback edition / October 2002

Visit our website at www.penguinputnam.com

Library of Congress Cataloging-in-Publication Data

Ramsland, Katherine M., 1953–
The science of vampires / by Katherine Ramsland.—1st Berkley Boulevard
trade pbk. ed.
p.   cm.
Includes bibliographical references and index.
ISBN 978-0-425-18616-9
1. Vampires.   I. Title.

BF1556 .R355 2002
133.4'23—dc21
2002066446

PRINTED IN THE UNITED STATES OF AMERICA

15 14 13 12

For Mom, *who introduced me to Dracula.*

And for Marty Riccardo, Elizabeth Miller,
Mark Spivey, Richard Noll, and Jeanne Youngson,

Through whom I got to know Dracula much better.

CONTENTS

✛

CONTENTS

ACKNOWLEDGMENTS

✦✝✦

This book was born from a conversation with Lance Lionetti and Kim Waltemyer, my editor at Berkley; so the first and most important acknowledgment goes to them. Thanks for inspiring me.

As usual when I venture into the vampire realm, I get suggestions and assistance from all sorts of people. The most enthusiastic this time was Stuart Lee Brown, whose encyclopedic knowledge of horror and science fiction never failed me.

Then there are the people who've discussed different themes, movies, or books with me over the past few years: Poppy Z. Brite, Suzy McKee Charnas, Doug Clegg, Norine Dresser, Chris Golden, Jewelle Gomez, Hespera, Nancy Holder, Jana Marcus, Gorden Melton, Elizabeth Miller, Richard Noll, Lori Perkins, Marty Riccardo, Anne Rice, John Silbersack, David Skal, Mark Spivey, Whitley Strieber, Chelsea Quinn Yarbro, Jeanne Youngson, and the many people in the vampire subculture who shared their experiences and ideas.

Thanks also to people who helped in other ways: Diane Alington, Ruth Osborne, Marie Gallagher, Pelli Wheaton, and Jim Kerr.

I also wish to extend my deep appreciation to the criminalists and investigators who have given me ideas and information about crime scenes, as well as former FBI special agents Gregg McCrary and Robert K. Ressler, both of whom had specific ideas about "vampire crimes."

Without John Silbersack's encouragement several years ago to become an active participant in my book, *Piercing the Darkness: Undercover with Vampires in America Today,* I wouldn't have spotted the patterns that make the present book unique, so many thanks to him for his ideas.

As for the science, I appreciate those experts who humored me in discussions about how certain things apply to vampires.

"He who is not of nature has yet to obey some of nature's laws."
—Dr. Van Helsing on Count Dracula

What Is the Science of Vampires?

✦—I—✦

That's a provocative question, because first we need to know what a vampire is, and that's not so easy. Many ideas about vampires are based in fantasy and superstition, which leaves room for whimsy, vagueness, and contradiction. Narratives about vampires come from many different cultures and many different authors and filmmakers. In addition, the actual origin of vampire folklore is in dispute: Does it derive from mythology that addresses a basic fear of death, a lack of knowledge about body decomposition, an undefined disease, or perhaps the symptoms of a mental illness now known as "clinical vampirism"? That is, do these narratives express some society's need for myth or might a vampire tale be an attempt to explain a frightening phenomenon actually witnessed? Hopefully we can resolve some of this confusion and answer a few questions. No doubt, we'll even raise a few.

To apply science to a mostly fictional creature is nothing new. In science fiction there have been numerous attempts to explain different aspects of the vampire's existence within the physical universe. Sometimes it's because someone wants badly to believe real vampires do exist, and sometimes it's because an author wants to create a new narrative or prove that a powerful myth can be explained within a rational world. Yet few people make this question even more fundamental to consider the notion that the imagination has a biological basis and that even those parts of a story that seem most whimsical may contain inklings of something accessible to the scientific method.

This book isn't so much about the academic study of folklore and of the relationship of folklore to an archetype of popular literature, although such issues will be noted. It has more to do with the idea that our narratives are generated from our physical nature and that many myths do prove to have a psychobiological basis. In that case, if we examine the enduring qualities of the vampire tale in our culture, we may discover scientific truths not overtly articulated within the narratives. For example:

- Does vampire fiction anticipate research on immortalized cells?

- Does emerging work in neurotheology offer ideas on contemporary notions of the vampire as a god?

- Is the vampire culture's preference for a drug called Ecstasy associated with the effect of the vampire's bite on the victim's brain?

- Can the history of science tell us about how the concept of the vampire has changed?

A central thesis of this book is that we may find influences from the unspoken language of our natural bodies within the form and content of our cultural myths. Science can indeed address the vampire, and in more ways than we might expect.

Yet before we go any further, our key task is to pin down a clear understanding of just what a vampire is. This question will turn up again in different forms, but let's deal with its most fundamental form here. We need a starting point for discussion, a common ground from among the many varieties of vampires. That means we need to weed some out. While Richard Matheson's monsters are recognizable as vampires from their nocturnal, bloodsucking aggression in *I Am Legend,* there's another level on which they just aren't what we have in mind. Yet it's also true to say that some of Dracula's many manifestations over the years have undermined his initial disturbing force as the archetypal vampire. Even participants in the "vampire subculture" have refocused the monster to suit contemporary needs, and those needs often involve desire, not fear.

Over years of reading fiction, seeing movies, studying clinical cases, analyzing folklore, and moving among those people who identify so strongly with the vampire that they claim to be Undead, I've seen many different definitions, so I'll try to pin one down—at least to get a start. In a way, when I describe a vampire, what I think we seek is more of a feeling than a creature: the dread of losing control to something that invades us and slowly drains us while holding us enthralled.

In keeping with the most popular notions, then, we may think of a vampire as a preternatural predatory creature in apparent human form that thrives off the resources of others in a way that weakens or kills them. It may be an animated corpse, the person's own soul trapped in an immortalized form, or a demon spirit acting and appearing human. I know this flies in the face of current practitioners of vampire culture who view the vampire as a spiritual symbol, but I'm examining the central vampire traditions that have developed in our culture since the publication of *Dracula.* The "new" vampire that presides over benign spiritual gatherings is a recent manifestation, and we'll get to that, so while I'm proposing this core definition, I will also say that the vampire concept is sufficiently flexible to adapt to many needs. Indeed, both its permanent traits and its elasticity may be the reason for its enduring power.

Looking over the decades, we see that the vampire is indeed malleable. Lestat, Saint Germain, the Ventrues, and Barnabas are definitely unlike Dracula, and the shifts can be linked to a changing culture, so it seems that these creatures operate best as society's shadow. They evolve as we evolve. Still, we need to draw a line somewhere so as to recognize a vampire as a vampire and not merely *as* some satanic or angelic deity with fangs. Thus, I'll stick with a definition that seems most closely to present the core traits of a vampire throughout its shifts and changes.

Let me repeat, then, that the vampire is a preternatural predatory creature in human form that survives by exploiting the resources of others in a way that weakens or kills them. Usually it goes for the primary resource of life—blood or energy—and often drains the victim on which it feeds to the point of death. Sometimes the bite will transform the victim, but sometimes that transformation comes only at the behest of the vampire or by going through some kind of special initiation ritual. It's not always automatic, despite what Professor Abraham Van Helsing would have us believe.

Where did it all begin? According to Thomas Aylesworth, in *The Story of Vampires,* it all began in ancient Greece with tales about entities called *empusas.* They were spirits that could take the form of beautiful women and they seduced young men into joining with them—to the young men's peril. A *lamia,* too, was a female shapeshifting blood drinker, while *strigae* thrived on children's blood. However, the ancient fanged goddess Kali in India was a deity with a powerful and commanding need for blood sacrifice, and creatures with vampiric traits spooked many other non-Western cultures, including Africa and the Polynesian islands. Vampires have also been confused with birth demons, and with incubi and succubi, which come in the night to drink fluids and suck vitality. Sometimes it's a murdered man's spirit, a flying creature made from a murder victim's blood, or a viscera sucker. Whatever the case, the concept of a vampire appears to be a widespread phenomenon, which supports the notion that it's embedded in human consciousness.

Some scholars claim that the word *vampire* has a Hungarian origin in the word *vampir*, although it appears that no one knows for sure. Professor Katharina M. Wilson says that, despite popular ideas, the word is not Hungarian or Romanian. She points out that there are four separate schools of thought on the word's origin, and all of them look at words in some foreign language that appear similar. While one group of scholars insists on Hungarian origins, another writes that it comes from a Turkish word for "witch." Yet a third group says Greek, and a fourth that it is Slavic. Despite the disputes, one thing is clear: in most appearances in European languages, the context used for speaking about vampires is Slavic superstition. There are many other names for these creatures, but since other authors have provided plenty of material on the etymologies, we'll move on.

The first English reference to a vampire is found in a book about churches published in England in 1679, although the word *vampire* is not actually used until 1688, when it appears in some treatises as if readers would be familiar with its meaning. In 1810, an explanation of vampires was published in *Travels of Three English Gentlemen from Venice to Hamburg, Being the Grand Tour of Germany in the Year 1734*. In that book, vampires are thought to be reanimated corpses that arise from their graves at night to suck the blood of the living, which has the effect of killing the living person. Before they die, the victims complain of suffocation and they then become "vampyres" themselves. Generally speaking, this process is drawn out, and the only recourse is to drive a stake through the body of the so-called vampire to make the blood flow out, or else to burn the body to ashes. The anonymous author of this book, a member of the Royal Society, cited eminent scholars who confirmed this phenomenon. (It's quite likely that they did see corpses treated in such ways, but not likely that they saw a vampire in action.)

Some cultures viewed the vampire as a real threat; others saw it as a symbolic way to deal with fears of infection, invasion, and depletion. The English poets romanticized the vampire, while the French devised dramatic stage plays with vampires as lead characters.

Yet our main concern is with the vampires in America.

The precursors to our vampiric traditions were characters from nineteenth-century popular fiction. "Wake Not the Dead," circa 1800, depicts a man who asks a necromancer to restore his dead wife to life, but she returns with a thirst for blood. Lord Byron's doctor, John Polidori, penned a tale in 1819 called simply "The Vampyre." He'd made notes after an evening of storytelling that involved Mary Godwin Shelley, Percy Shelley, and Lord Byron. Even as he witnessed the birth of *Frankenstein*, he wrote down Lord Byron's unfinished story about Lord Ruthven, who appears to die while traveling in the company of a companion, only to show up alive and well and involved with his companion's sister. That narrative inspired several sequels and a play.

Then in 1853, the penny dreadful *Varney, the Vampyre, or The Feast of Blood*, attracted a large following in Britain. Written by James Malcolm Rymer under the pen name of Thomas Preskett Prest, it was sold as a serial in 109 weekly installments. At the end of the series, in a fit of remorse, Sir Francis Varney enters a volcano to commit suicide. Elaborately illustrated, this serial depicts the vampire as a nobleman who attacks women in their beds by sinking his sharp fangs into their necks. He has pale skin (which reddens after feeding), long fingernails, and shimmering eyes. One illustration for the book shows the vampire as a bat in flight, which adds a new dimension to the evolving myth, as does the fact that he survives being shot and that he leaves fang marks as proof of his attack. Drinking blood revives the vampire's physical body, as do the rays of a full moon, and his strength is greater than that of any man. However, in this early tale, he does not avoid the sun. He can walk freely by day and does not have to replenish himself on blood very often—certainly not every day. As the story develops, Varney appears to be more human than do vampires in subsequent fiction. He has feelings and even manages to evoke the sympathy of some humans who recognize that he suffers from a condition that he can't control. In this story, too, those who die from Varney's prolonged feeding turn into vampires, and he thus becomes the hunted himself, a creature that must be destroyed.

Then a female vampire returned to the literary scene, featured in Joseph Sheridan Le Fanu's novella *Carmilla*, which was published in a collection in 1872. She is three hundred years old but appears to be quite young. Manipulating her way into an Austrian household, she seduces a nineteen-year-old-girl named Laura, engaging her in a lesbian relationship, slowly draining the girl of blood. Eventually her true nature is discovered and the typical folklore remedies are applied: she is staked in her blood-filled coffin, beheaded, and cremated.

In terms of truly prominent stories, Bram Stoker's *Dracula* was next, published in 1897. This book has had a more enduring influence on the vampire mythology in America than any other single work of fiction. Set within a Christian context, the vampire was utterly demonized. He was a thing, an infection, a force set apart. A 1927 stage play and 1931 film, both starring Hungarian actor Bela Lugosi, established the vampire firmly as a cultural icon, and thereafter vampire films and comic books into the 1960s followed its lead. After that, *Dark Shadows*, Anne Rice, Chelsea Quinn Yarbro, Whitley Strieber, Mark Rein-Hagen, Poppy Z. Brite, and many other authors created dramatic shifts, and vampire culture was never the same.

In fact, the vampire tale has its own "paradigm shifts" and "paradigm-defining moments" much like those discussed by historians of science. For a while, the Dracula archetype created by Bram Stoker held sway over the popular imagination, but as our culture changed in mid-twentieth-century America, the vampire archetype changed in parallel ways. From one decade to another, people still want the vampire, but they have a different set of needs to which it must speak.

For the most part, the idea of a vampire is that it was once human and is still in possession of a partially human consciousness (or a trapped human consciousness). That makes vampires an extension of ourselves. I think of them as our shadow side, allowing us the vicarious experience of an asocial—even antisocial—inner life. They're associated with darkness, the moon, and the abyss, and they shun whatever symbolizes spiritual redemption from a culturally approved deity. While they've lost the drama of superstition made popular with Bram Stoker's *Dracula*, they're still closely attuned to life's darker side.

Vampires connect to their victims through life energy, which usually means they approach humans for their blood, a symbol for life, birth, and connection. When someone is aroused, the blood pumps hotter, which adds an erotic allure. Added to that, the "mythology of the bite" in our culture overwhelmingly favors pleasure. Some people feel that vampires attract us because they remove the burden of responsibility for choosing such wanton pleasure. They take us against our wills. Thus, no matter what their ultimate intent for us, vampires are undoubtedly exciting.

Now to a more fundamental question. Because vampires seem so close to who we are and because they've been so humanized in recent years, many people ask whether there's such a thing as a "real" vampire?

To simply say no, as rational people would expect, is facile. That's because among those who call themselves vampires today, the definition has changed. The myth involves the immortal creatures that thrive off blood, sleep in coffins, change into bats, and need an invitation to cross a threshold, yet few aside from moviegoers actually do think of vampires that way anymore.

A better question is, *Could* vampires exist?—and the answer might depend on such things as cellular structures, dark energy, and the drug DMT. In other words, on the mechanisms of the physical world.

Scientific explanations for vampires in fiction have ranged from a disease to an infection to the manifestation of an alien race. A vampire might be a doppelgänger projected out from us and given autonomous life or the result of joining two incompatible creatures. The vampire's origins, anatomy, and essential nature have been tackled in all forms of fiction. In *Dracula Unbound*, Brian Aldiss traced the vampire back to a reptilian race, while in *Space Vampires* (1976), Colin Wilson brought them in from outer space as life-sucking parasites. Richard Matheson offered the full range of vampire characteristics as manifestations of a bacterium, and Suzy McKee Charnas developed her vampire from an interest in the medical aspects of synthesized blood.

So here's a brief summary of what I take the "science" part of the science of vampires to be. Scientific knowledge is acquired from relying on systematic, objective observation to make deductions and create formulas from established physical laws, and testing those deductions through articulated hypotheses and controlled experiments that afford replicable results. For example, if you notice on a number of occasions that you see a certain person (let's call him the Subject) only after sunset and never during the day; that whenever he visits a certain other person, that person always seems weakened; and that the Subject always seems to have an earthy odor about him, you can now determine that there are certain apparent regularities about his behavior that are predictable. From that, you can set up a hypothesis to test about those regularities: if the Subject is a vampire and if these traits determine how a vampire behaves (notwithstanding the intrusion of other factors), the Subject will not deviate from these patterns. He will come out only after sunset, smell like dirt, and exert some weakening effect on the person he visits.

You may then continue to observe the patterns under more controlled conditions (but without intruding in a way that alerts the Subject to the conditions) and perhaps note that your initial observations were in error (sometimes he smells like dry cleaning fluid) or you may note even more regularities: the weakened person always looks pale, wears high-collared clothing, and acts defensive when questioned about the Subject's visit. The Subject always grows nervous and excuses himself as dawn approaches. He avoids mirrors and refuses invitations to Italian restaurants. He won't drink . . . wine.

Once you have some patterns established that support your hypothesis, and you lack patterns that contradict it, you can proceed to a more rigorous approach. If your experiment can't be brought into the lab to control for all possible variables, the Subject must be carefully observed in different types of settings and under different conditions. That is, does the weather or season make a difference? Does he deviate from his patterns in a different country? It may also serve your purposes to have other people make observations to get objective agreement. Thus, we might approach the Subject in order to accomplish any of several things:

- determine causes of certain actions

- eliminate all possible explanations but one

- conceptualize a core essence (operational definition) from behavioral regularities

- define specific situations involving vampires, such as a crime scene

- predict what they might do now and in the future

In order to have a population for study, we use an operational definition, which I've offered above but will reiterate here. A vampire thrives off the life resources of others for his or her own benefit, even to the point of killing the host. Even the appearance of offering something only serves the vampire's purpose; he or she does not give altruistically. Obviously, we can find plenty of real-life equivalent of vampirelike predators, notably serial killers, some of whom simply kill and others of whom offer something as enticement before killing. So now we must refine the definition, because while vampires might be serial killers of a sort, not all serial killers are vampires.

So should we say that all vampires drink blood? If we do, that leaves out a whole population of psychic vampires that thrive off the life force or chi energy of their prey, which apparently can be just as destructive as feeding off their blood.

Are all vampires charming and attractive? Not by a long shot. Look at the film *Nosferatu*. That creepy ratlike vampire would have a hard time getting a date. Stephen King's vampire in *'Salem's Lot* likewise, as well as the Eastern European vampires central to early folk superstitions.

Do all vampires avoid the sun? No. Both Lord Ruthven and Varney, two of the early incarnations in literature, could walk in the daytime, as could Dracula, and this was before the multiple-factored sunscreens were invented. Yet it's possible that certain strains of vampire cannot go into the sun without threat of annihilation.

How about the vehicle of vampirism? Can we speak of vampires as being animated corpses? Now we're getting closer, because across cultures and most fictional representations, there seems to be consensus that the vampire is the Undead or the living dead. At one time this night creature was a person who died, and somehow it returned to life looking like that person and inhabiting the very same body.

Obviously we could go on and on with these traits, but the point is that we want to stay focused on stable features so we can say something about vampires from the perspective of science that will have broad applicability. That's the task of this book.

I asked Martin Riccardo, a longtime observer of the evolution of vampire fiction and fact, what he thought an exploration of the science of vampires would cover. Riccardo, who wrote *Liquid Dreams of Vampires* and founded Vampire Studies, a clearing house for information, thought it was an interesting albeit paradoxical question. "*Frankenstein*," he pointed out, "is the classic science-fiction story of science gone wrong. *Dracula*, on the other hand, is the classic horror story in which the modern scientific world of Stoker's time almost fails to recognize true supernatural evil when it appears. In my opinion, Stoker's vampire seems to be a refutation of scientific materialism. However, this is on a purely fictional level, since I think that Stoker himself was a rationalist and a believer in science. It is when the vampire count and Frankenstein monster are brought together in the mid-1940s Universal films *House of Frankenstein* and *House of Dracula* that vampirism is first depicted as a kind of blood disease that might be treated scientifically."

Even so, he went on to say, "While many films, novels, and TV shows seem to feel the need to explain vampirism scientifically as a blood disease, they usually fail to integrate this with the supernatural elements of the vampire which they often also use, such as the lack of reflection in a mirror and the ability to turn into a bat. If my memory serves me, the late Vincent Hillyer once offered ten thousand dollars to anyone who could produce a true vampire, that is, a dead body that would revive at night. As far as I know, no one took up his offer, but that would have been scientific evidence of real vampires."

Regardless of the "evidence," there are plenty of ways to study the vampire—even Dracula—with the tools of scientific analysis. In fact, true scientists desire to know the essence of physical reality, and among them are people who understand that there are more ways of knowing than the methods of observation and articulation. If the universe turns out to be an organic entity with its own intelligence rather than the mechanistic system of forces it once was conceived to be, and if quantum reality implies that scientists create part of their perception as they observe, then examining vampires within the context of science in this broader context is not so far-fetched after all. Our concepts of the universe and our concepts of vampires have gone through dramatic shifts, often in parallel ways. Our fundamental philosophies of reality, then, can contribute quite a lot to our understanding of the vampire tale.

What's in the Book

The science of vampires covers not just the obvious issues, such as the vampire's origin, nature, and procreation, but also the science of the crime scene, the vampire's ability to evolve with a culture, and how vampires have sex. It also includes just what it takes to be a vampire hunter, what it takes to kill a vampire, and the rules for vampire longevity. At times, the different aspects of vampire mythology are described in detail and at other times certain assumptions are made about familiarity with vampire tales in order to get right to the scientific discussion.

The available information would fill many books, so with that in mind, I tried to restrict this presentation to aspects that might interest the scientific mind. There are many different directions in which to go, and each time an author devises a new way to understand the vampire, there's even more material. While it wasn't possible to include all the permutations of vampire biology, anatomy, and psychology, or even to mention all the novels that have been written on vampires and all the films made, most readers will recognize the traditions and tales I do utilize.

With that said, let's open Dracula's coffin.

ONE

Dracula's Shadow

◆━I━◆

Dracula was published in the U.K. in 1897. Written by Bram Stoker, an Irishman, it came out in the U.S. two years later, and it's never been out of print. It has inspired countless plays, fictional spin-offs, critical interpretations, scholarly treatises, films, and imitations. Some say it stands tall as an eternal Christian allegory, while others point to its covert psychosexual anxieties as reflective of the Victorian era. Whatever the case, the original story has spawned derivative versions that promote ideas not true to the actual text, and those ideas, too, have become part of the cultural mythology of Dracula. They may be irrelevant to *Dracula* scholars, but they're significant for any study of how our myths arise from within us.

The Tale

The basic plot of *Dracula* involves an English solicitor's clerk named Jonathan Harker who travels to the Carpathian Mountains of north-eastern Transylvania in 1893 to conduct business with an aristocrat there, Count Dracula. He plans to help the Count purchase a home in England at Carfax Abbey, and Dracula's emissary picks him up and takes him by coach at night to Castle Dracula. Harker has already seen plenty of evidence of the local superstitions, including their belief that he ought not to be traveling on the night designated for his arrival at the castle. Even another coachman attempts to thwart him, but Harker finally reaches his destination.

Dracula welcomes him and tries to make him comfortable, but Harker finds the Count to be rather eccentric and even a bit frightening. Dracula persists in keeping Harker up at night and appears to leave the fortresslike castle by scaling the walls like a spider, upside down. Inside the castle, three women seduce Harker and he soon discovers that Dracula thrives on human blood. When the Count forces him to write letters back to England to the effect that he is already on his way home, Harker realizes that Dracula means to keep him prisoner, and worse. He tries to kill the Count before he himself is killed, but Dracula leaves him imprisoned in the castle while he boards a ship for England with fifty boxes of his native soil. Harker manages to get out, but an attack of brain fever temporarily hinders him. People find him and nurse him back to health.

Meanwhile, a shipwreck off the coast of Whitby, England, attracts the attention of two young women, Mina Murray (Harker's fiancée) and Lucy Westenra. A large dog jumps off the wreck and disappears, and only the body of the captain is found on board, tied to the wheel and holding a crucifix. His log indicates that the rest of the men disappeared one by one and it seemed to him that a gaunt, white-faced stranger aboard ship was responsible. One man had said that he'd put his knife through the figure and it had gone through air.

This proves to be the ship on which Dracula arrived, and it's not long before he claims Lucy as his first victim. Over the course of several weeks back at her home, her health declines and a large bat is seen hovering at her window.

Dr. John Seward, who is caring for her, invites Dr. Abraham Van Helsing, a doctor, lawyer, and brain specialist, to offer another medical opinion. Van Helsing notes the double puncture wounds on Lucy's neck and the inexplicable loss of blood, though there's none on the bedclothes. Despite numerous transfusions from four healthy men, she fails to improve. Van Helsing now knows that their enemy is formidable, so he drapes Lucy's room with garlic, which works until her mother unwittingly removes it. Dracula attacks Lucy once more and she dies.

Yet it's clear that she's still around, as reports surface of a woman in the area attacking young children. It appears that Lucy is now among the Undead, transformed by prolonged contact with a vampire.

Mina and Jonathan, now married, talk with Van Helsing about Jonathan's trip to Transylvania. The information alarms Van Helsing, so he and Lucy's three former suitors open her coffin. They find her corpse too fresh and healthy to have been dead for a week. According to prescribed rituals, they cut off her head, stuff it with garlic, and drive a sharp wooden stake through her heart. From there, they know they must search for the master vampire, Count Dracula, because he's likely to be searching already for another victim. Should he succeed, he will create yet another vampire and that vampire will make more of the same. The scourge must be stopped.

Van Helsing explains that the *nosferatu* has the strength of twenty men and grows stronger from his contact with victims. He also uses necromancy, which involves the use of corpses to acquire special knowledge, and as a mortal had learned every branch of knowledge available in his day. His "brain power" survives his body's death, but his memory is not wholly intact. He exhibits differing levels of emotional and intellectual maturation, but he learns and grows. He's both an animal and a devil, can direct the elements, and can change his form. He also commands rats and other lower animals. He can approach with stealth, vanish into a mist, and see in the dark.

Even as the vampire hunters look for the Count among his various

real-estate holdings in London (throughout which he's distributed his
boxes of native soil), he's begun to work on Mina. Using the bloodthirsty lunatic Renfield, he gains access to the lunatic asylum where
she's staying. The hunters catch him in the act of taking her blood,
but he disappears into a cloud of mist and scoots out by the crack
under the door. Still, he's obviously been driven off by religious items:
the sacred Host and the crucifixes. In fact, Mina also reacts to these
things: when Van Helsing touches the blessed wafer to her forehead,
it burns a mark into her skin. She admits that she was forced to drink
the Count's blood after he supped from her. Clearly the vampire has
claimed her and she's already part of him, though she's not yet dead.

The team locates and destroys forty-nine of Dracula's boxes of
earth, but one has been sent back on a ship to Transylvania, presumably containing the Count. By hypnotizing Mina, who is now "blood
of his blood," they can track him with some accuracy. Though initially
thwarted, they find the one box of earth among some Gypsies, open
it, and discover Dracula helpless inside, so they use knives to stab
through his heart and slice his throat, and he crumbles into dust.

The vampire himself (although since *Dracula*'s publication he has
evolved into many different entities) appears as an energetic and animalistic creature driven by his bloodlust. He's lived for several centuries, and he's clever and calculating. He wears only black, has white
hair, is quite pale, and sports a mustache. His teeth are unusually
sharp, especially the canines, and his eyes are reddened.

In a way, Stoker's characterization of the vampire is more psychologically sound than the vampires of much later fiction. Dracula finds
the most vulnerable and sensitive person in a household, one whose
subconscious may have some kinship with his dark nature, and he
works on that person to gain entrance. He kills by drinking the blood
slowly, in gradual amounts, and leaves behind the seeds of spiritual
infection, ensuring the victim's enslavement in a way that resembles
the progress of other addictions. This is clearly evident in Renfield and

Lucy, both of whom have highly sensitive natures and demonstrate little to no resistance to the monster (although in Renfield's case, it's a psychological addiction, since Dracula has not taken his blood). Yet they don't fully succumb all at once.

In contemporary fiction, as more emphasis is placed on the vampire's inner life and needs, the victim as a person can get lost. For example, Anne Rice often has her thirsty vampires take victims fairly quickly, sucking their blood the way we down a soda on a hot day. They crave the last gasp of the heart as it beats harder to desperately retain life. For them, that's the *pièce de résistance* of the experience, although it can also be dangerous. One exception is Rice's vampire Armand, who gets a kick out of making a game of psychological enslavement. Even so, the victims are more often merely momentary meals rather than people we get to know. In that way, we lose some of the psychological significance of victims selected for traits about which they have no awareness, who are drawn into a death and deviance coherent with the needs of their subconscious. We also lose the sense of a gradually developing addiction for which vampires can serve as a metaphor.

The first feature film of note for Americans to be made from *Dracula* was F. W. Murnau's 1922 silent black-and-white *Nosferatu* (which some say is another word for vampire, although others dispute that). The vampire in this case is Count Orlock. His ratlike appearance, predatory movements, and long fingernails make him truly a horror.

Then came Tod Browning's *Dracula* in 1931, starring Bela Lugosi. That actor portrayed Dracula as an aristocrat in a way that belied his brute compulsions. Suddenly the image of the vampire *became* this charming entity with a Hungarian accent, dressed in a cape and tuxedo. Rather than just attacking his victims, he seduced and commanded them, and his charisma and erotic charm became a hallmark for vampires ever after.

The movie inspired countless others, including the Hammer films of the late 1950s and early 1960s. In Christopher Lee's interpretation, Dracula became more superhuman, more erotic, and more hypnotic. Then, in 1979, Frank Langella took his stage performance of the vampire to film, filling it with masculine dominance. After that, vampire films went off in many directions, including those that presented Dracula as an archetype. A series of lesbian vampire films, starting with the 1936 *Dracula's Daughter*, gave the myth a more feminine spin. Yet throughout the 1990s, more films returned to the Dracula legend for yet another go-round, and some added new theories and research that moved away from Stoker's account.

Drs. Raymond McNally and Radu Florescu, history professors at Boston College, researched the novel's physical terrain and historical sources for their 1972 book, *In Search of Dracula: A True History of Dracula and Other Legends*. They spent another fifteen years documenting other sources for *Dracula: Prince of Many Faces*. Their thesis is that Bram Stoker had known about the fifteenth-century Wallachian nobleman known as Vlad the Impaler, and had been inspired by the details of his life and brutalities.

The name Dracula was actually applied to him, derived from a Romanian word that means "dragon," which was a reference to his father's membership in the Order of the Dragon. Vlad was known to impale his enemies on sharpened stakes outside his castle walls—often alive—which earned him the nickname the Impaler. He also led raids over the borders into other lands, and a woodcut from that time shows him dining among the corpses. There was even a legend that he dipped his bread in the blood of his enemies before eating it. During his six-year reign, he was responsible for killing tens of thousands of people, sometimes merely because they had offended his moral sensibilities, and he refined many methods of torture. When his army was defeated, he escaped over the Carpathian Mountains to Transylvania. There, the king of Hungary arrested and imprisoned him for several years for his renowned cruelties. Although he eventually reclaimed his throne, an assassin quickly brought him down.

Vlad was buried secretly, but when a tomb thought to be his was opened during the 1930s, it proved to be empty, giving rise to rumors that he'd never died—or that he was some kind of supernatural creature. However, a nearby tomb did hold the body of a man wearing a crown. Vlad appears to bear some similarity to the character of Stoker's vampire, so Florescu and McNally urged the public to believe in the obvious associations.

Yet in Stoker's unpublished notes, other scholars claim, there's no evidence that he knew much about the legendary man apart from the vague reputation mentioned in one passage in *Dracula*. Nevertheless, the connection with Vlad the Impaler is fixed, even to the point of becoming the backbone for the film *Bram Stoker's Dracula*. Many people think of the real man and the fictional character as one and the same, despite attempts by *Dracula* purists to correct the error.

Science or Antiscience?

An analysis of the novel's text indicates that Stoker seems to aim toward contradictory goals: to find scientific explanations for a creature like the vampire and to show that there are things that science just cannot explain—at least not yet. He uses Van Helsing, a learned man with numerous credentials, to make this distinction, giving it more weight as well as making it more ominous. While much that Van Helsing says flies in the face of rationality and state-of-the-art science in 1893, and even appears to revert to ignorant superstition, each of his mysterious rituals has the result that he predicts it will have. There's no arguing with the facts.

Stoker's own ideas seem to be reflected in Van Helsing's speech to Dr. Seward in which he states, "It is the fault of our science that it wants to explain all; and if it explain not, then it says there is nothing to explain." Then he lists for Seward the many wonders of nature that do exist but have no rational explanation. In that way, he prepares the doctor for what he is about to say of the vampire's existence.

David Skal is a scholar of *Dracula* in its many renditions. His book *Hollywood Gothic* traces the evolution of Dracula's image from the novel to the stage and screen, and with Nina Auerbach he coedited the Norton Critical Edition of *Dracula*. Also to his credit are such books as *The Monster Show*, a cultural history of horror, and *Vampires: Encounters with the Undead*, a collector's omnibus that combines both literary and factual accounts. When asked his opinion about Stoker's attitude toward science, he offered the following remarks:

"Stoker certainly gave a lot of thought to making vampires at least *seem* scientifically plausible. In *Dracula*, vampirism manifests itself in quasi-medical terms—a disease echoing familiar nineteenth-century maladies like consumption or a languorous, *La Bohème*–like wasting away, and syphilis or blood contamination and telltale skin lesions. The novel takes great pains to describe Dracula himself along then-popular conceptions about Darwinism, especially the notion of evolutionary 'degeneration' [a throwback to primitive intelligence]. Stoker fills the book with all kinds of up-to-date technology, medical and otherwise, to make the vampire at least half-believable to readers in an age of scientific skepticism. Given the book's longevity, it's clear he succeeded in his strategy."

Yet he also pointed out that the vampire is essentially a metaphoric construction, so attempts to explain it in scientific terms have inevitable limitations. Against Stoker's novel, Skal compared the works of more recent authors who specifically set out to fit the vampire into the natural order. "Two books I thought especially successful in persuading the reader to suspend scientific disbelief," he said, "were Brian

Aldiss's *Dracula Unbound*, which posited vampires as evolutionary descendants of prehistoric reptiles, and Dan Simmons's *Children of the Night*, which rather brilliantly juxtaposes AIDS research, vampires, and political turmoil in modern Romania. But in general I don't think it's a good literary strategy to try to overly rationalize vampires, since they thrive best in the realm of dream logic not science."

Another scholar of note among *Dracula* aficionados is Dr. Elizabeth Miller. For many years a professor of English at Memorial University of Newfoundland, Canada, she specializes in the gothic literature of the nineteenth century. Her books *Reflections on Dracula, Dracula: The Shade and the Shadow, and Dracula: Sense and Nonsense* have gone a long way toward establishing the facts about both the author and the novel. Having organized Dracula '97, a key centennial celebration in Los Angeles, she now lectures widely about Stoker's art and intent. To clear up a few of the many misperceptions, Miller has pointed out that Dracula could walk in the sun (he was just weaker than he was at night) and there's no proof that Stoker was inspired by incidents from the life of Vlad the Impaler.

Addressing the way that Stoker used medical doctors versed in science to discuss an inherently supernatural creature that had its origin in a ceremony with the devil, Miller said, "As a writer of a gothic novel, he may just have been trying for realism, to aid the general reader in the suspension of disbelief. We do know that he had two brothers who were medical doctors, one of whom offered him specific assistance. On a deeper level, either consciously or unconsciously, he may have been tapping into the late-Victorian anxieties about the conflict between science—especially evolutionary theory—and religious faith. That both operate side by side in the novel and that both science and faith must be used to overcome Dracula suggests that the two are not incompatible."

The Vampire's Nature—to Be or Not to Be

Thanks to Stoker's depiction (and a few from the movies), we now have a number of vampire behaviors and traits to examine. Some will be addressed here and others are held for consideration in later chapters. To make this list manageable, I've divided those traits that are clearly part of the religious scenario from those for which we can offer some scientific speculation.

The following characteristics about Dracula appear to involve only superstitions concerning the soul:

- the absence of a reflection in the mirror or shadow during the day

- the genuine (not imagined) inability to cross running water at any time except during high or low tide (because water was considered pure)

- the fact that a crucifix or a branch from a wild rose can keep a vampire in its coffin

- the need for an invitation before crossing a threshold

The following traits, reactions, and abilities may have physical or psychological explanations—or at least give rise to such explanations:

- the animation of a corpse

- immortality and defiance of the cellular aging process

- physical agility and increased strength

- ability to see in the dark

- ability to form a mental connection with victims, created through hypnosis

- ability to shapeshift into certain animal forms, dust, or mist

- ability to thrive exclusively on blood

- teeth that grow sharper as a mortal becomes a vampire

- need for a coffin filled with a certain type of soil

- coldness to the touch

- dread of garlic

- fear of religious symbolism, such as a crucifix and holy water

- skin burns at the touch of something religious

- ability to change form at noon, sunset, or sunrise

- influence on weather patterns, especially storms, and over some animals

- destruction by a stake through the heart, a sacred bullet, decapitation, or fire

- ability to create vampire "children" that make more vampires

- the fact that feeding on the victim alone is sufficient to create another vampire, unless it is destroyed before the victim dies

- ability to hold a human enthralled, who may develop blood-thirst without being a vampire

- destruction by sunlight (added in *Nosferatu* and the Hammer films); alternatively, weakened by day

Surprised? The natural world does indeed have things to show us that at the very least can suggest how certain things may happen.

The next step is to narrow things down by deciding on a particular type of vampire. In folklore, there are dead vampires (reanimated bodies), living vampires (astral forms sent out from the living to meet the dead), or psychic vampires (invading spirits that possess a living person). Generally speaking, the kind of vampire we want to explore (until we get into the postmodern era with its many diverse interpretations) is the dead vampire, or the person who died in a manner similar to Lucy Westenra and was transformed into a vampire.

The idea that some mysterious force can animate a corpse derives from the notion that good and evil have no beginning and no end, as well as from the idea that evil has power over nature. However, as we shall see, there may be some peculiar biological involvement as well. First let's look at how people initially discovered that there was a vampire in their midst, because those "symptoms" speak to the vampire's nature.

Primitive cultures devised routine tests for determining if someone was a vampire, which included the following:

- After he dies, his relatives and livestock begin to die.

- After he dies, a dark figure visits his former home at night.

- After he dies, things turn up missing from his former house.

- A large hole appears next to his grave marker.

- A white horse, black stallion, or female goose refuses to walk over his grave.

- His exhumed corpse shows a reddish color, is in a different position than when buried, has "new" skin or bright red blood, is thicker from bloating, has longer hair and nails, has limp limbs, or shows little or no decomposition.

- He shrieks, moans, or bleeds when staked.

One of the foremost scholars on the subject of superstitious beliefs in vampires is Paul Barber, a research associate at the Fowler Museum of Cultural History at UCLA who wrote *Vampires, Burial, and Death*. He argues that most reports of vampires found in folklore can be matched to the irregularities of decomposition about which ordinary people were likely to be ignorant. He can at least account for the unusual appearance of the buried corpse, even if what he says fails to apply to missing objects, mysterious holes, and spouses ravaged in the night.

First, let's look at what really happens when we die. Then we'll examine some of the ways these things put blood into the vampire myths.

When the heart stops beating, there's no more pressure on the blood to move through the body, so it settles according to the force of gravity into whatever parts are closest to the ground. Without red blood cells in the capillaries, the skin pales and starts to look waxy.

Then, in the state of livor mortis (deoxygenation) eight to twelve hours later, the part of the body where the blood settled discolors into a pink and then purple-red color. At first this area will blanch when touched with pressure, but will eventually fix into place (usually around ten hours after death), and will stay where it is even if the body is moved. The stain will darken until internal rot discolors the entire body.

Soon the eyes flatten and the extremities turn blue. While the body's temperature cools at a rate of about one to two degrees per hour (depending on conditions), the muscles relax, but then stiffen into rigor mortis, first documented scientifically in 1811. That means that the entire body becomes rigid. Rigor generally shows up first in the face and soon spreads visibly from small to larger muscle groups until it reaches the lower limbs. Many people think that the body remains rigid, but after one to three days, it relaxes again as the muscle fibers decompose.

Bacteria multiply in the body, breaking through the intestinal walls to begin their work and the trunk slowly putrefies, as seen in a greenish discoloration over the right lower abdomen and a reddening around the mouth and nose from decomposing lungs. Soon the bacteria will travel through the circulation system and hit the entire body, making the face swell and become swollen, discolored, and unrecognizable. Liquids will come out the nose and ears, and the skin will marble in shades of green and black.

As decomposition spreads, a foul odor develops that is rather unmistakable. Bacteria in the intestines produce gases that bloat the body (once thought to be restless spirits fighting to break out) to nearly twice its normal size and eventually turn the skin mostly black. The bloating also makes the tongue and eyes protrude and the lips curl back to reveal the teeth and gums, while the breasts and genitals expand to a grotesque size.

Soon the skin blisters from these gases, the blisters burst and the skin detaches in sheets, and then the internal organs break open. At this point, these liquefying organs leak from all the body orifices. Skin peels away, revealing new skin beneath it, and contrary to rumor, the hair and nails stop growing. In fact, the hair has been falling out and can easily be pulled out in clumps, and the nails often drop off, leaving fresh skin beneath them, which eventually putrefies.

Okay, now if the reader is still with me, let's look at the superstitions to see how these conditions might suggest a vampire.

First, the obvious. The cadaverish smile on a corpse exhumed at a certain stage when the lips curl back might look like an animalistic snarl, and then red stuff around the mouth and a coffin filled with liquid would also seem mysterious and sinister, especially if mixed with runny blood. In some places, it was the practice to exhume the body at certain points, such as after forty days, to ensure that the soul had resurrected. That means the exhumers got a good look at a variety of corpses, and they didn't all look the same. Decomposition effects vary.

When the skin and nails fall away to reveal "new" skin beneath, and the hairline recedes to give the appearance of longer hair, that's downright spooky. Worse is the disappearance of stiffness (rigor), because that may mean to nonpathologists that corpses have acquired a renewed flexibility that will allow them to get around. Bloating that causes a corpse to shift positions in a box may suggest that it's getting in and out (and that it's well fed), and a bloated or stiffened penis (often enlarged) may look like a vampire with a rather specific need. Add to that certain soil or coffin conditions that may preserve bodies beyond the expected time frame, and you have a phenomenon that contradicts all common wisdom on the subject.

We have corpses today, known as the incorruptibles, which have reportedly lasted hundreds of years with little evidence of necrosis. Construction workers digging in the Chinese city of Nanjing unearthed a corpse that was five centuries old yet still had supple skin and flexible joints, while numerous Catholic saints have shown similar grace in death. A man whose coffin washed into a Kentucky river in a 1927 flood who looked as if he'd been buried the day before proved to have died 113 years earlier. Even the casket lining and his clothes were perfectly preserved, and he was no saint. In *Dead Reckoning*, medical examiner Michael Baden, with decades of experience exhuming corpses, tells of his astonishment when he saw the body of Medgar Evers, a civil-rights leader who was murdered in 1963. Exhumed three decades later to examine the bullet holes, the body surprised everyone in attendance. "When we opened the casket," Baden said, "we were all shocked to find that Medgar Evers looked as though he had died only the day before." Even the pine needles placed in the coffin with him were still green.

Then there's the groaning and shrieking: How can a dead person cry out when the stake is driven through his or her body? It's not possible, so that means the person is still alive.

Not really. Any funeral director will tell you that bodies in the back of the hearse may shift, release gas, and seem to moan as decomposition claims them. It makes for a creepy ride to the funeral home or hospital, but the person is indeed dead (usually). Now, given what's happening inside the body, it's no wonder that driving an object like a stake through it might result in a few loud noises. As Paul Barber states, the vampire tale is an "ingenious folk hypothesis" to explain clearly observed phenomena that otherwise seem impossible.

Yet what can we make of the hesitation of animals to walk over the graves of vampires? It may indicate a stench from a shallow grave, and since animals have a better sense of smell than humans, they object more readily. That different animals are used for this purpose appears to depend on the region—some people preferring a black animal, some a white one, some a horse, some a goose. For this method to work, the animals must have no blemishes, which suggest that peasants believed that uniformly colored animals possessed a purity that caused them to be repelled by a vampire's corruption.

At any rate, sometimes the appearance of a decomposing corpse was quite disturbing, especially one that was immersed in its own liquids, and the idea that this thing was getting out at night and trying to turn everyone else into what *it* was provided sufficient reason to chop it up and burn it. For that, a ritual was needed.

Yet in *Dracula* and other fiction, people looking for vampires don't tend to dig up the graves until after they've seen the signs of a vampire's work on victims. This, too, has some parallels in folklore, taking us back to a time when people knew little about the cause of diseases like consumption or tuberculosis. The symptoms were quite similar to the notion of a vampire's attack:

- failing strength

- increased suffering at night

- a sunken chest, emaciation, and wasting away

- a feeling of heaviness on the chest, as if a demon were sitting on it

- increasingly pale skin

- no appetite

- blood in the sputum and crimson cheeks

- offensive breath

In fact, there are a handful of documented cases, some even in the United States, in which a family or town viewed a person who had died from consumption as a vampire. In *Food for the Dead*, folklorist Michael E. Bell examined twenty-one cases from 1793 to 1892 in eight New England states, based on records and published accounts.

In 1896, the *New York World* reported that belief in vampires was alive and well in Rhode Island. Near Newport, six separate incidents were documented that involved exhuming a recently deceased person, removing the heart, and burning it. This generally occurred when several members of the same family appeared to die from a similar wasting disease. People in that area at that time believed that a vampire fed first on those it was close to before moving on to other people, so it seemed that a family member who died first and became a vampire was now victimizing its kin. There is some evidence that Bram Stoker was influenced by these accounts.

One of the most famous tales took place in Exeter, Rhode Island, in

1892. George Brown lost his wife and then his eldest daughter. One of his sons, Edwin, grew ill but moved away, and then another daughter, Mercy, died. Edwin returned and once again became ill, so George exhumed the bodies of his wife and daughters. The wife and first daughter had decomposed, but Mercy's body—buried for three months—was fresh and turned sideways in the coffin, and blood dripped from her mouth. They cut out her heart, burned it, and dissolved the ashes in a medicine for Edwin to drink. However, he also died, and Mercy Brown became known as Exeter's vampire.

Another theory surfaced about rabies being the basis for vampire lore. A Spanish neurologist, Dr. Juan Gomez-Alonso, claimed that watching *Dracula* on film reminded him of what he knew about rabies sufferers:

- They are hypersensitive to odors and light.

- They're hypersexual.

- They experience enormous thirst.

- They do not like to see themselves in mirrors.

- Their muscle spasms can cause bared teeth.

- They may froth bloody fluid at the mouth.

- They can engage in ferocious, aggressive behavior.

- They can infect others through a bite, because the virus is transmitted through saliva.

Gomez-Alonso also found parallels between the outbreak of rabies in certain regions and the increased popularity of vampire tales.

These accounts provide a fair sense of how folklore developed from observations that as yet had no other explanation. But enough of icky reanimated corpses and harrowing diseases. Let's leave folklore behind and get to the science of fiction. How in the world can a sexy, charismatic, Undead, bloodsucking creature of the night walk among us?

How Did Dracula Become a Vampire?

According to Dr. Van Helsing, an associate of his who researched Dracula's origins reported that he must have been "that Voivode Dracula who won his fame against the Turks," which meant that in life Dracula was a man of great courage and iron will. He was also from a family said to have had dealings with the Evil One, learning his secrets at something called the Scholomance, which was located in the mountains over Lake Hermannstadt, in a Transylvanian town. In those same records, Dracula is referred to as a "wampyr."

Scholar Bacil F. Kirtley claims that in a monastery in northern Russia, a manuscript was found dating to 1490, copied from a document written in 1486 and detailing in anecdotal form the harsh and cruel exploits of Dracula of Wallachia, otherwise known as Vlad Tsepesh. It's not clear, however, how much Stoker actually knew about the fifteenth-century nobleman, but he did have some acquaintance with the folklore of southeastern Europe. According to him, the Dracula family (or just the males) attended the Scholomance, or School of the Dragon. Depending on which source we turn to, the Scholomance was an occult school situated in a labyrinth of underground caves where men would make a pact with the devil to gain occult knowledge.

Elizabeth Miller, aforementioned author of *Dracula: Sense and Nonsense,* indicates that, "The first occurrence of the word *Scholomance* is in Emily Gerard's article 'Transylvanian Superstitions' published in 1885. This is one of the works Stoker definitely consulted while working on *Dracula.* Not only is it listed in his working notes but extensive notes are taken from the article. One of these mentions the Scholomance. Apparently the term is a misnomer, as it appears in no other known source, nor in Romanian folklore. It is possible that what Gerard heard while she was in Transylvania was 'Solomonari' spoken by a local with a German accent—there were many ethnic Germans in Transylvania at that time. One Romanian folklorist has supplied information on the Solomonari. Stoker obviously saw in Gerard's reference an 'explanation' for Count Dracula's vampiric origins—the only such hint he gives anywhere in the novel."

In her papers, folklore researcher Emily de Laszowska-Gerard talks about the Scholomance as a school where people learned "the secrets of nature, the language of animals, and all magic spells," as taught by the devil. "Only ten scholars are admitted at a time, and when the course of learning has expired, and nine of them are released to return to their homes, the tenth scholar is detained by the devil as payment." He's mounted on a dragon and becomes the devil's assistant in preparing harsh weather. It's not known whether the tenth was plucked from the group during the course of their training or taken after the training was completed.

By another account, the nine graduating scholars themselves were known as the Solomonari. They were tall, redheaded men clad in white wool and in possession of several instruments of magic and a book of instruction. They trained for nine years in this dark school, overcoming obstacles and surviving ordeals as part of the initiation process. Their final examination involved copying all that they knew about humanity into the Solomonar's book. Once initiated, they become full-fledged alchemists with the power to maintain the balance of nature and to preserve order. (That would account for Dracula's ability to influence the weather.)

So Dracula was probably changed through some kind of magic known only to the devil. For our purposes, that doesn't get us anywhere. Let's look at a different aspect of folklore to see if we can find some answers there.

In general, people during the Middle Ages had fairly primitive ideas about bodies and souls. Quite a few Eastern European cultures believed that the soul, which was separable from the body, did not actually leave it at the time of death but forty days afterward. As pointed out above, the evidence as to whether this process was accomplished lay in the appearance of a disinterred body. If it was decomposing along the normal course into bone, then all was well. If it retained its ruddy look, and especially if it appeared any more vital, reddish, or thick, it was felt that the soul had not departed.

Interestingly, work in the field of psychoneuroimmunology (PNI) may offer some ideas on the subject. For several centuries, it has been the fashion in Western culture to believe that the mind is a different type of substance from the body. While there's some interaction between them, one is physical (takes up space), and the other is mental or ethereal (doesn't take up space). Yet work done in both psychology and medicine (and even physics) indicates that the mind and body actually form a single unit (like energy and mass in quantum mechanics) that manifests itself in different ways. That is, the mind, or soul, is a form of energy that pervades every cell of the body, and it's also affected by the cell's physical condition.

From that notion, and from work done in labs, it became increasingly clear that our emotional temper is part and parcel of our physical experience, in that the enduring emotions are chemically encoded into the physical makeup of the cells. Let's step back a bit and see how this works.

Much of what we experience in the world is the result of the way thoughts and perceptions are converted into physical information. It's all stored in us as chemicals and electrical energy that then affect our emotions. For example, we experience a threat and it floods our bodies with a chemical that inspires us to defend ourselves or run away—

and possibly even to have nightmares later—and what then happens in the situation affects how we feel about the threat and about ourselves. That can even have an enduring impact.

The more intense the information, the stronger its effect. Each organ in the body processes specific emotional energies, and even if the energy known as consciousness leaves the body at death and continues to exist, that does not negate how intricately linked it is to the body while in the physical realm. In other words, the "soul" may depart, but some residual structure of the personality could remain in the body tissues at a cellular level, along with the memories and manner of processing perceptions.

Dr. Candace Pert, research professor in the department of physiology and biophysics at Georgetown University Medical Center, is one of the PNI pioneers. Her ideas can be found in her book *Molecules of Emotion: Why You Feel the Way You Feel.* As she describes it, our body chemicals form a dynamic information network that links emotional experience with the key physiological systems. Thus, certain long-term or intensely felt emotional states become part of our physical makeup, forming what she calls our "bodymind." Our thoughts enter our bodies as one type of energy and become part of the body as another type.

In this way we develop "body memories." That means our bodies get used to certain emotional states in certain repetitive situations. For example, Joe may always eat breakfast at 7 A.M. If he decides to meet someone for breakfast at eight some morning, he'll still feel hungry at seven and may not feel hungry at all by eight. Or if we always drive a certain route, and then one day we go that same route for a ways but have to take a different turn, we'd better pay attention because otherwise we'll keep driving the way we're used to. Body memories are instrumental in many daily activities, from being able to type without looking to walking through our living space without bumping things.

Similarly, the type of home in which we grow up affects our body memories. We absorb the repetitive emotional energy from anger, depression, fear, tension, and other responses in our daily lives. This kind of energy will then feel comfortable to us no matter how far from home we wander. It's part of who we are, and when we lose it, we may experience grief.

So emotional energy unifies with our body's energy and it happens through this mechanism: the brain sends signals to other parts of the body through information bearers called neurotransmitters. They influence the way we process our emotional experiences. At the micro level, our cells organize a network of actions and reactions, link the various physical systems, and even learn.

Some of the molecules on the surface of our cells act as receptors for the information brought by the neurotransmitters. Each receptor acts as a keyhole, scanning all the incoming information to lock onto the right "key"—the chemical information that will unlock and activate that cell's function. The receptor roots, which reach into the cell, respond to chemical substances by vibrating. A typical nerve cell has many receptors, all functioning as scanners, and each is receptive to only a certain type of substance. A serotonin receptor will only receive the chemical information from serotonin or a serotonin-mimicking substance. That makes the body into one large buzzing network of information processing.

When the message reaches the cell's interior, it gives a command, such as to divide, to build proteins, or to produce more of some chemical. These activities then translate into the larger body as behaviors or moods. For example, if a cell is activated to produce more of the neurotransmitter serotonin, the person may feel calmer.

Thus, if it's true that the moods, emotions, and ways of processing information—otherwise known as a personality—reside in our body tissues, then a corpse still has the *potential* to be that same person. The information is all still there in the cells—the unconscious truth of which may have inspired the idea of the forty-day waiting period observed in some cultures.

To add one more bit of folklore, the dead now resent being dead and hate the living for still being alive, so the person who is aware that he has died (i.e., who has a stored memory of it) and has returned might very well want to attack others. The vampire's personality forms from its body memories, with the added impact of having experienced the emotional trauma of death.

If PNI offers the basis for an explanation of how a dead person can be reanimated as essentially the same person he was in life, then we don't need the idea of possession by a demonic spirit in order to inspire the corpse to make decisions about survival, defense, and prey. Such decisions are already part of his biological composition.

So it might be true that Dracula became a vampire through his initiation in the Scholomance, but the process may well have been carried out through the functioning of the mindbody as well.

What we still don't know, though, is just how cells once dead can be restored to vigor. A corpse can't very well be motivated by anger or hunger if it has no sensibility. Some say that it's when the soul leaves after forty days that the corpse becomes vampirized, because the devil can now enter and possess it. But is it the devil or some activation of a natural cellular process?

To sidestep this issue, some novelists have found a way to make the vampire's body just a different biological system from a human one. In other words, the vampire is not considered human. For example, in *The Vampire Tapestry* (1980), written by Suzy McKee Charnas, Edward Weyland tells a therapist that he has lived several human lifetimes between periods of suspended animation. His body synthesizes vitamins, minerals, and proteins through "intestinal microfauna" that allow him to efficiently "metabolize" blood.

Yet the truly interesting aspect of an immortal vampire is the idea that he or she once was a mortal human—so how could that possibly work?

Cellular Death and Immortality

Dracula first appears as an older man in his castle, but later, in London, Jonathan Harker spots him and is astonished to see that the creature is now much younger. Presumably this has something to do with a fresh blood supply. As Van Helsing puts it, his "vital faculties" are strengthened by blood and he takes no other form of nourishment. That's both a significant factor and an insufficient explanation. Many other fictional vampires find that if no one puts fire or the stake to them, they will live forever, and that their strength grows over time. It seems that the very condition of being a vampire—not just the digestion of blood—positively affects the body's cellular endurance and vitality. That means we need a bit of molecular biology.

All living things—including the Undead—are composed of cells. A cell is the smallest unit of activity necessary for life, and it's where food gets broken down and transformed into energy. There are two distinct types of cells: eukaryotic (which have a nucleus) and prokaryotic (which have no nucleus). We're concerned with nucleated cells.

The nucleus is the cell's executive center. Nearly everything it does depends on transforming food to energy, and the way it all works is coordinated by the cell's DNA, i.e., the genetic blueprint made from the way certain protein molecules fit together. DNA is wrapped up into structures called chromosomes, and what a vampire physically becomes is dependent on the way the DNA directs it. So how does this work?

Each of Dracula's traits—heavy eyebrows, male gender, physical height, fingernail strength—is coded through a pair of heredity factors called genes, which are regions of the DNA, and there are many genes inside each chromosome. Had Dracula's genes coded him to be short and bald, he'd have been less imposing. Presumably, something about his transformation into a vampire (we'll get to that later) affected his genetic coding in such a way that he came out with sharp canines, longevity, and the ability to thrive on human blood. The point is, the genetic codes determine what happens to a physical body and therefore have an impact on the aging process. That gets us to the central issue of cellular aging. There's actually been research done on "immortalized cells," and what scientists have discovered appears to have some relevance to Dracula's ability to last for centuries.

While theories about aging abound, there appear to be two distinct processes to consider in the case of vampires: nourishment and chromosomal activity. Let's look first at the food intake of mortals and compare that to vampires.

To this point, it's believed that there are sixty-one separate genes in the human chromosomes that change during the aging process, and those changes contribute to diseases such as Alzheimer's, arthritis, cancer, and other degenerative conditions. One theory holds that free radicals floating in the body converting food to energy damage certain genes and then mutate them into diseased states. In other words, the more you eat, the more free radicals you have floating around and the more damage may be done to your cells.

According to Dr. Roy Walford, professor of pathology at the School of Medicine at the University of California, Los Angeles, studies with mice indicate that quantity of food consumption has an effect on aging. When mice consumed 30 percent less than usual, their life spans increased from an average of thirty-nine months to an average of fifty-six months. Even so, there's no escaping some degree of gene damage that can harm the body's basic life-serving functions. In other words, for mere mortals, it's all bad news.

So how does this apply to vampires? It's generally accepted that vampires don't consume a lot of food. In fact, their diet is both simple and restricted. Even if they obtain most of their daily blood supply from one person, that would only be about eight pints of fluid. (Stoker had Dracula drinking small amounts and he didn't explore how the vampire expels waste, so presumably it gets absorbed into his system through a special digestive process such as vampire bats might possess.) That means that vampires may have fewer free radicals floating around in their bodies to age their cells, but clearly there's more to Dracula's youthfulness than that. He doesn't just stop growing older, he actually gets younger, and he doesn't just retard the aging process, he stops it. (We may even say, given how he aged several centuries upon being destroyed and crumbled into dust that he literally transforms it.)

So let's look a little closer at the research on "immortalized cells." It may be that vampires possess the very secrets that scientists have only recently begun to crack. It's a bit complicated, but it's the best science we've got to explain how a vampire's body might work.

We have structures in our cells called telomeres that some scientists believe appear to have a significant function in the aging process. Let's look first at what they are and then at how they affect us.

Back to the chromosomes that house the DNA in the nucleus of most body cells (except red blood cells). Remember that DNA is the unique blueprint for the genetic codes that determine what we'll look like. Human cells contain twenty-two pairs of chromosomes and two sex chromosomes, which together contain from fifty thousand to a hundred thousand genes.

On the ends of the chromosomes are sequences of DNA called telomeres. They're like little caps. While they protect and stabilize those ends, they also seem to function as counting mechanisms, or "molecular memory." Aging is in part about cellular division, and they keep track of how many times a cell divides. Each time it does, the telomeres shorten just a little bit until they reach a preset length. That means that each cell may only get a predetermined number of divisions. Then it stops dividing, goes into a state of senescence (aging), and eventually dies. In other words, we're young for as long as those cells continue to divide, and then we get old. However, aging involves a few more factors.

Genes that control the aging process in mortals that are located near the telomeres appear to be inactive in young cells. As the telomeres shorten, the aging genes are activated. Whatever genetic damage has accumulated from heredity and the environment may then mutate the cells and cause molecular disorder. Since the telomeres are now short, they can't protect the chromosomal ends, and that makes them unstable, which means problems such as loss of energy and functional break down that makes us vulnerable to disease. Thus, aging in mortals appears to be a matter of quality control. The cells do still reproduce, but the new cells have diminished function. Eventually they slow down and stop.

So now we've got Dracula, whose cells have stopped aging but who shows vital functions. How did he do it? Scientists know something about this, too.

It seems that through the activity of an enzyme known as telomerase, the youth-preserving activity of the telomeres can be extended. In other words, there's an actual chemical in our cells that may hold the secret to eternal youth, and if so, it may explain how vampires can live forever. Let's see what the scientists have discovered.

In one study, cells of patients suffering from Werner syndrome, a genetic disorder involving premature aging, were treated with telomerase. Generally these cells have a short life span in the lab because they age so fast, but the enzyme-treated cells proved to last indefinitely (at least thus far). That's significant for vampires.

A second study involved treating blood vessel cells in human skin with telomerase. They actually formed new capillaries without the damaging alterations associated with cellular mutations such as cancer. When transplanted into mice under the skin, these cells also fused with the cells already present, and they even carried blood. Thus, telomerase apparently has the capacity to induce the growth of functional cells. That's important if we want to know how Dracula could actually look younger. But this process is only going to work for a vampire, because there's one more thing that the research showed.

While telomerase conveys an unlimited capacity to the human cell to replicate, which means it can retain its youth, it's also active in 90 percent of cancer cells, and there's the rub. While we want the cell to

keep dividing without wearing down the telomeres, it is this very process that may trigger cancer. One recent finding with mice indicated
that when aging was hindered, the mice were more vulnerable to cancer. Apparently nature designed mortal organisms for health during
the reproductive years but not for endless longevity when those years
were over.

At any rate, for our purposes in understanding Dracula, science
appears to have found a way to make normal cells last a lot longer
and perhaps even become immortal. (At least, conceptually speaking,
if they can divide endlessly they're immortal, but of course, no one
has watched these genes long enough to prove it in practical terms.)
This discovery may suggest how an immortal entity is at least possible.

Since vampires appear to be immune to diseases like cancer (we'll
deal with immunity later), Dracula could have telomerase present in
his cells, protecting him from senescence. Thus, if at the molecular
level, a vampire's body can produce the conditions that (1) make the
cells divide indefinitely but remain immune to disease, or (2) stop them
from dividing altogether without death setting in, then the genetic
damage involved in aging is irrelevant; it doesn't occur. Whether it
can be reversed so that Dracula can become younger (making his white
hair dark, presumably, and his wrinkles disappear) is another matter,
and scientists haven't yet accomplished it. But they're trying.

Even immortal beings need nutrition for energy, so we'll move on
to the ingestion of blood.

The Blood Is the Life

Since the beginning of time, blood has been considered a mysterious
and even holy substance, as well as one associated with illness and
death. It's used in religious rituals across cultures, from the sacrifices
in India to the blood goddess Kali to the imbibing of Christ's trans-
muted blood during Christian rituals. It was even believed in ancient

times that deities resided within the blood, which meant that blood made regeneration and immortality possible. Certainly in the folklore, the reanimating factor for the dead-turned-Undead was blood.

It's also metaphorical. Blood has served as an explanation for varying moods. A "hot-blooded" person is passionate or angry. A "cold-blooded" person is calculating or without feeling. "Red-blooded" implies health and vigor, "thin-blooded" means that one gets cold easily, while "bad blood" connotes something amiss between people. "Blood kin" refers to those people who are genetically related and therefore bonded.

The medical practice of bloodletting was used as a way to purify the blood from evil "humors." Sometimes it just meant draining blood from the body, while some cultures applied leeches to suck it out. The cure was not always effective.

Since primitive times, humans have been known to drink blood, often in religious rituals. Mongolian warriors ingested animal blood as a source of food, and even today some Masai of Tanzania do the same. They use it to supply nutrition while they travel. Although a voluminous ingestion of blood by humans tends to provoke vomiting, small amounts of blood do get broken down in the stomach into amino acids, iron, and proteins. Yet people who claim to need to drink blood in order to survive, such as those suffering from the delusion that they're vampires, are generally in error.

However, some sanguinary acts reported in history have nothing to do with nutrition or ceremony. In 300 B.C. a Buddhist monk drank the blood of swine to cure an illness said to be incurable—and it worked. Warriors of many cultures drank the blood of their enemies to symbolically affirm their conquest and enhance their power. Some even did it as an act of communion with their victim. In contrast, the compulsion to drink blood is generally part of a sexual perversion called hematomania. For example, serial killer Peter Kürten, "the Monster of Düsseldorf," claimed to have felt the buildup of erotic tension before he attacked a victim and to have achieved release only after violence that involved licking their wounds or drinking their blood. It seems that blood is a complex symbol that inspires both healing and destruction.

Because we need blood to survive and even a certain amount of depletion can adversely affect us, it's considered our life source and the means through which we are energized. Because we can lose it by a piercing instrument such as a bullet or knife, and thereby terminate our lives, blood is also a source of great vulnerability. Thus, in many cultures, blood was considered sacred. It could be used to cleanse someone of sins, confer guilt (blood on his hands), offer a sacrifice to a deity, fertilize crops, and restore certain vital powers. It may also facilitate magic. Even the blood of executed criminals was believed to be so powerfully laden with energy that it protected against diseases and ill fate. Some cultures used a vampire's blood as an apotropaic, or a means of protecting them from the vampire itself.

Blood seals promises, as in blood oaths—including those made in pacts with the devil. It's used in many initiation rituals, and some people believe that to exchange blood spiritually joins them in an eternal bond. The blood shed by the sexual penetration of virgins and in giving birth gives it an erotic charge.

Vampires that thrive on blood (not all do) acquire a double-edged allure. They hold the threat of stealing our most precious substance, but through that same substance they may also deliver ecstasy and transformation.

While some authors allow their vampires to substitute animal for human blood, the National Heart, Lung, and Blood Institute says, "There is no substitute for human blood. Human blood cannot be manufactured; animal blood cannot replace it. People are the only source of [human] blood."

Crime-scene processing techniques can make this same distinction. German biologist Paul Uhlenhuth designed such a test when he discovered that if he injected protein from a chicken egg into a rabbit, and then mixed serum from the rabbit with egg white, the egg proteins separated from the liquid to form a cloudy substance. This is called precipitin. In the forensic test for human blood, either a sample of the suspect substance is put into a test tube over the rabbit serum or it's placed into a gel on a glass slide next to a sample of antihuman serum. When an electric current is passed through the glass, the protein molecules filter into the gelatin and toward each other. If a line forms where they meet—called a precipitin line—the sample is human blood.

Some people in the vampire subculture claim that the issue is not even about physical properties. They believe that human blood just supplies more energy, tastes better, and has a more pleasing consistency.

So how does blood function in our bodies that makes it so important?

The heart is responsible for keeping our blood circulating. It's pumped in a continuous circuit, from the heart throughout the body and back to the heart. It leaves the heart through a blood vessel called the aorta, which branches into smaller vessels, or arteries. These carry blood away from the heart into arterioles and capillaries. There are thousands of capillaries spread throughout the body, and the red blood cells have to squeeze through them. Because capillaries are part of tissues like skin and organs, they allow for the exchange of nutrients, gases, and waste products. They bring in oxygen and nutrition and take away carbon dioxide and other waste. As the blood moves back toward the heart, it's deoxygenated, so it goes to the heart through blood vessels that increase in size, from venules to veins. Deoxygenated blood enters the heart through the right atrium and then goes out through the right ventricle to get to the lungs to pick up more oxygen and release its load of carbon dioxide. It then returns to the heart to be distributed again through the body.

While it's a long-held idea in our culture that Dracula (and other vampires in his tradition) gets his blood source through the jugular vein (there actually are two, on either side of the neck, an internal jugular and an external jugular), we might expect that he'd prefer the contents of one of the carotid arteries. The carotids, which lie alongside the jugular veins, carry oxygenated and nutrient-rich blood to the brain, while used-up blood flows through the jugular veins back to the heart. The blood in arteries, which ascend on both sides of the neck, ought to have a better taste and a more potent charge, although the arterial walls are thicker and tougher to pierce. There's also the chance of a mess, since the high-pressure arteries spurt when punctured, while the low-pressure veins are less likely to do so. Thus, the choice might simply come down to expediency over taste.

Blood has two basic components, cellular solids (red, white, and platelets) and plasma, which is more than 90 percent water. The blood cells are all made in the marrow in the center of the bones. It's the hemoglobin protein of the red cells that carries the oxygen to the trillions of cells in our bodies that need oxygen for metabolism; the red cells also carry the waste by-products from the metabolism process away from the cells. White blood cells known as phagocytes move around the body seeking out and battling foreign bacteria that might harm it. A different type of white blood cells called lymphocytes enhance immunity to infection. They find antigens, bind them with antibodies, and trigger the immune system to attack. Platelets help stop bleeding at an open wound.

Another function that blood serves is to cool the overheated body by moving to the skin's surface, and to keep a cold body warm for as long as possible by staying deep inside. When a body dies and the heart stops pumping, the blood gradually settles to the lowest gravitational point.

In 1667, in France, blood was considered more seriously as a way to treat illness. Jean-Baptiste Denis wrote about the transfer of blood from one person to another, and not long afterward, William Harvey described the human circulatory system. However, it was not yet known that different blood types don't mix, so sometimes a transfusion killed the patient. There has to be compatibility between donor and recipient.

That means that it's unlikely that giving Lucy Westenra the blood of four brave men would be entirely efficacious (as novelist Fred Saberhagen pointed out in *The Dracula Tape*). It's doubtful that the men shared compatible blood types, so Lucy might have sickened and died as a result of such transfusions.

Different blood types were recognized in 1875, but it wasn't until 1901 that Karl Landsteiner named the four groups and understood their reactive qualities. Red blood cells carry a substance called an antigen, which produces antibodies to fight infection, and there appeared to be several different types. In a centrifuge, he separated red blood cells from plasma. Then, adding red blood cells from other subjects, he found two distinct reactions—clumping and repelling. He labeled the two types as A (antigen A present, anti-B antibody present, but antigen B absent) and B (antigen B present, antigen A absent). Then a third reaction was labeled type C (both antigens A and B absent), but was relabeled later as O. Then another distinct serum behavior was discovered, and this fourth type was labeled AB (both antigens present). It soon became clear that blood type depended on genetic inheritance. Type A and O are the most common in the human population, AB the most rare.

Then, in 1940, Landsteiner discovered the rhesus factor, labeling it Rh+ if the antigen was present in the red blood cells, and Rh− if not. Scientists in Britain found a chromosome-related structure in the nuclei of female blood cells, which they named the Barr body.

Today, blood typing involves many different enzymes and proteins that perform specific activities in the body. More than 150 serum proteins and 250 cellular enzymes have been isolated, as well as more antigens. Having blood types available and understanding how they function made possible the idea of blood banks for transfusions, and the first one in the U.S. was set up in Chicago in 1936. Many authors who don't want their vampires to be brutal rely on blood banks for their sustenance. Or, like Karen E. Taylor in *Blood Secrets*, authors have their vampires take discreet amounts that heighten eroticism but fail to kill a person.

Now for the question of digestion. It seems that a vampire would have to adapt to a specific type of digestive process in order to (1) survive exclusively on blood, and (2) keep it down without vomiting. We can rely on a certain amount of mutation occurring at the point at which the person is transformed into a vampire (more detail on that in chapter 3), and perhaps use our knowledge of the way hematophagous creatures such as leeches and bats digest blood to help us explain the process.

In order to store blood for slow digestion, the bloodsucking leech secretes an antibiotic into its digestive system to prevent the growth of bacteria and retard putrefaction. It then also secretes special enzymes.

Since the vampire bat is both a sanguivore and a mammal, it's probably closer to what we're looking for. It requires an enormous intake of iron, which helps to make hemoglobin for carrying oxygen from the lungs to the body tissues. Yet the iron intake is generally higher than what the bat needs, so it has a special process for excreting the excess. When ingested, the blood goes through a tract that's adapted for extracting nutrients. Research on this system suggests that bats have a mucous membrane along the intestinal tract that acts as a barrier to prevent too much iron from getting into their bloodstreams. They also appear to have numerous capillaries at work absorbing the blood more quickly into the system than humans can.

The hematophagous vampire's body would have to adapt in order to survive, using only the particular proteins, enzymes, and nutrients carried in blood in its digestion.

Growing Fangs

To get the blood, the vampire needs a way to pierce through skin and veins or arteries. While it could as easily have been a sharpened fingernail or a weapon, or even the special pricklike needle hidden under the tongue that Suzy McKee Charnas has her vampire describe in *The Vampire Tapestry*, the convention that arose in literature was the possession of fangs. In part, this was to identify the vampire with predatory creatures like snakes, rats, and wolves. Having protruding, sharp, or elongated teeth, as in both *Varney the Vampyre* and *Dracula*, was a signal of danger. Like wolves, vampires curl back their lips in a snarl to reveal their intent to penetrate and steal the life force. (In the case of a psychic vampire, fangs aren't necessary, and even the idea of penetration is lacking. They merely suck the life energy away from their victims through some form of absorption.)

A few vampires have been depicted with frontal fangs, some with elongated canines, some with numerous sharpened teeth like a shark, and some with both upper and lower fangs. Certain vampires even have retracting fangs, like several species of viper. In all cases, the idea is that they did not have teeth like this as humans, so what is it about becoming a vampire that shapes and changes certain teeth?

It appears to be the case, supernaturally speaking, that the same spirit infusion that allows the mortal cells of the physical body to stop aging also affects the teeth. In that case, there must be some sort of spiritual set of instructions, as with DNA but with more force, not only to produce the change but to build strong enamel where there was none before.

In an effort to duplicate this effect in contemporary culture, some people actually have permanent canines implanted—including gold ones!—while others have learned the orthodontist's trade and can fashion many different sets of fangs that penetrate flesh. These they slip in and out at will, and even have to care for them like dentures. It beats having to await science to devise a way to grow the teeth, since this process may only occur through a genetic mutation—and it's probably not on any researcher's list of priorities. The immortalization of cells relies on certain known processes, but actually adding on layers of cells to grow teeth is another story.

Reflections

While Harker shaves in Castle Dracula, he notices that Dracula's image fails to show up in his shaving mirror. This occurs before he has real suspicions about the man, and Dracula quickly throws the mirror out in a rage against the vanities of man (though he himself sports a mustache). Later, in the 1931 film, Van Helsing uses a mirror to confront Dracula with his obvious lack of a soul. Having no soul, he is surely a creature of the devil.

There's no science to explain this one, aside from some kind of mirror distortion. Anything that takes up space and has visibility ought to show up in a mirror. The idea that only someone possessing a soul that can know salvation would be able to see his or her image in a mirror is clearly a religious superstition. Other authors have recognized the nonsensical nature of this device and discarded it. Anne Rice, for example, shows her vampires preening in front of mirrors, and she explains that putting the reflection back into the mirror was a statement about her agnostic frame of mind. If there's no God and thus no redeemable soul, then the whole mirror issue is irrelevant.

Dracula scholar Elizabeth Miller has also given this issue some thought. "Of course, Dracula is not always a solid entity," she reminds us. "When he chooses, he can become as mist or elemental dust, at which times none of his corporeal frame would show up in a mirror anyway. One could try to explain it by arguing that given the pseudo-solid nature of Dracula's physical body, the mirror does not pick up the image. Neither can he be photographed—though Stoker does not use that in the novel. It was in his original notes but for some reason he discarded it. I suspect that Stoker used the mirror concept with the lack of soul in mind."

Similarly, the use of religious symbols as repellents is useful only in a religious context, along with the fact that a holy wafer can burn a scar into the skin of a vampire or his victim, as was the case with Mina Harker.

Nevertheless, these things were used in a 1992 film *Vampire's Kiss* to introduce a psychological angle. In an example of mind over matter, Nicolas Cage plays a character who believes that he's been bitten by a vampire and thus cannot see himself in a mirror. Yet the audience can see his reflected image, so the problem is clearly in his own head. His perception has been confused by what he believes, and the same could occur to produce a reaction to crucifixes, holy water, and Communion wafers.

Perception is a peculiar thing. In fact, we can develop what's called a perceptual set, which is influenced by culture and habits. If we expect to see something in a certain context, we actually can, even if it's not there. According to Elizabeth Loftus, a professor of psychology and an expert on eyewitness research, having an expectation about an incident before it occurs can influence how we see it and how much attention we pay to specific details. That's because there's an acquisition stage, a retention stage, and a retrieval stage for information, and beliefs affect how things get stored in memory and thus how they get retrieved. If a person believes he is a vampire, that belief is intensified by a strong emotion like fear, and his perceptual set includes an array of corollaries, such as having no reflection and a phobia about crucifixes, he then may perceive these things as grounded in fact. It's even the case that a very strong belief can produce a physical reaction when there's no basis to the stimulus. If a highly suggestible person can react with skin blisters to what he erroneously believes is poison ivy (as has been demonstrated in a laboratory), then people who think they're vampires can manifest a few vampirelike physical reactions as well.

Psychology also plays a part in the idea of vampires being able to cross a threshold only when invited inside. There appears to be no physical reason why they can't just walk in, especially since they can change into things like mist and dust, so something else is at work. "The connection here is to the concept of complicity," says Elizabeth Miller, "allowing evil to enter. Once the commitment is made, it becomes a permanent fixture." So someone with a subconscious attunement to the vampire allows it to enter and then cannot shut it out.

Sleeping Arrangements

For most of this century, the vampire appeared to be dependent on a coffin for its daytime sleep. (Richard Matheson's 1954 *I Am Legend* and other science-fiction books actually dispensed with this device, but they had little effect on the gothic trappings of horror fiction.) Because folklore preceded fiction, and since in folklore vampires were generally the corpses of people who had died and been buried, the coffin seemed a natural place for the vampire to return after his nighttime forays. That was his sanctuary because few people would just dig up a coffin. He went in and out by changing his shape. Generally his means of exit and entrance was a hole in the ground next to his grave.

In *Dracula* and many subsequent vampire tales, the coffin was often filled with the vampire's native soil. If the vampire wanted to transfer its residence, the coffin had to go with it, and this proved to be one of its greatest vulnerabilities. First, if the vampire traveled with a box resembling a coffin, superstitious folks might know what was up, and second, those boxes are pretty heavy. They're also conspicuous, so vampire hunters looking by day for the vampire's hiding place would have a pretty good idea what was inside once they spotted it. Dracula understood this and was prepared: he brought fifty boxes with him to England and placed them in different properties that he purchased, making it more difficult for the vampire hunters to locate him. Even after they found and destroyed forty-nine boxes of soil, there was still one more, and by the time they realized where it was, Dracula was gone.

However, the novel is not clear about the need for the soil. In one place, Stoker says it was because Dracula required consecrated ground, and in another, he says just the opposite. "This is just one of many inconsistencies that permeate the text of the novel," says Elizabeth Miller. "That's due in part to the fact that he wrote it intermittently over a period of several years and apparently did not have a good copy editor. In keeping with traditional associations of vampires with evil and Satan, it would make more sense that the soil in which they rest be unconsecrated. All one need think of is the fact that for centuries, a suicide could not be buried in consecrated ground; committing suicide was considered in many Catholic countries of Europe to be one sure way of becoming a vampire after death. If the soil is unconsecrated, it would then follow that to prevent a vampire from returning to it—and thus entrapping him at his most vulnerable—all the hunter needs to do is consecrate the soil. This is what Van Helsing does on one occasion in *Dracula,* using the eucharistic wafer as the consecrating agent."

In *The Gilda Stories,* Jewelle Gomez keeps the tradition of the soil as a symbolic way for her wandering vampire to retain emotional roots. "The aspect of the lore about the vampire needing to rest in native soil was appealing to me," she explained, "because it was a metaphorical thing about home and family and roots. That seemed crucial to the mythology, because if you create a character who's all-powerful and can live forever, the character has to be rooted in something."

Other authors have responded differently to this poorly explained need.

The coffin itself, besides being a box in which we bury the dead, provides a good way to avoid the sunlight, since it's pretty well enclosed. Barnabas Collins we recall, was chained into a coffin, while Gabrielle, one of Anne Rice's vampires, simply went into the woods and buried herself in dirt.

Vampires and Water

The reason why Dracula (or any vampire) cannot cross water might be that water is a part of the ritual of baptism and a symbol of salvation, and the vampire cannot corrupt the fluid that washes us clean. However, this myth might also point to the fact that bloated bodies tend to float. Folklore described bloated bodies as vampires, and if they did not sink, that meant water would not accept them. Therefore the Undead cannot enter water. In days gone by, bodies sometimes popped out of moist ground, too, and had to be weighted down. (The high water table in New Orleans forced aboveground burials in many places because floods came in and washed bodies out of the soil, floating them—in coffins or out—into places where they did not belong.)

The Potent Herb

Less religious in meaning than the crucifix is the use of garlic to:

- ward off a vampire

- detect a vampire

- keep a vampire in its coffin

In some cultures, a man who could not eat garlic was at least suspect. This means of identifying vampires was used in places as diverse as Mexico, Romania, China, South America, and southern Slavic countries. But why would vampires in particular have such an intense aversion to this everyday herb?

Since ancient times, garlic has been known as a healing agent. It helps to cleanse the blood and it acquired the reputation of an effective treatment against supernatural powers. Distributing garlic throughout a community was thought to protect the people and also to bring out a closeted entity. Garlic flowers or cloves were placed over doorways and around windows, and animals might be rubbed in garlic or given the herb in their food. If a buried body was suspected to belong to a vampire, it might be exhumed and stuffed with garlic.

Supposedly, a vampire contaminated its victim's blood with its own evil nature such that when the victim died, he or she might also become a vampire. Fear of blood contamination is a basic human concern, so whatever appears to purify the blood takes on an aura associated with magical properties.

Garlic also smells to high heaven. Wearing it, eating it, and rubbing it over walls and animals kept other creatures away. In fact, garlic keeps a lot of humans away. We don't need science to explain that.

Shapeshifting

Some Slavs apparently believed that a vampire could come among them in the form of a bat, and this may have been based on horror tales told by seamen about bloodsucking bats in other countries. The bat uses heat sensors in its nose to find capillaries in the skin of a sleeping animal and makes tiny cuts with its sharp incisors. Its saliva numbs the area and then keeps the blood from clotting. The bat licks the wound with its grooved tongue in a quick pulsing manner. In a short amount of time, it can consume several ounces of blood, but it excretes the plasma. When it seemed that vampirism was spreading like a plague in such regions as Eastern Europe, it was logical to attribute it to creatures that could fly.

In *Dracula*, the tiny marks on the necks of the victims of vampire attacks are thought to have been made by rats or bats, and in several cases, a large bat is seen outside the window of the vampire's victim. As Van Helsing explains it, Dracula could transform himself into certain animals, showing up variously as a wolf and bat.

Yet vampire bats only exist in Central and South America, and their wingspan is about eight inches (nowhere near the size that Dracula adopted). There have been some recorded cases of a human host, but vampire bats mostly feed on livestock.

Besides animal forms, some fictional vampires can also dissolve into mist and than seep out of a coffin or grave or enter a locked residence through a keyhole. This process seems sufficiently similar to the act of changing a mortal into a vampire to reserve discussion of it to chapter 3.

First let's examine how the vampire has shapeshifted as a psychological entity in our culture.

TWO

Shapeshifter

✦✝✦

Among American monsters, the vampire has undergone the most change even as it remains recognizable as a vampire. "You either have to follow Stoker's rules," says Christopher Golden, author of a trilogy of vampire novels and *The Monster Book*, "or you have to reinvent that world altogether and come up with something original." That makes for a wide range of vampire phenomena.

To understand how science applies to the narrative, we must do more than speculate on the scientific angles of the vampire's nature. We need to understand as well how the larger frame of explained reality, with its own paradigmatic displacements, has had a sufficiently influential trickle-down effect into the culture to gradually shift our perspectives.

Most relevant to this venture, science has moved away from the definitive ideas of Newtonion physics into the fluid arena of quantum mechanics in much the same way that society has shifted from believing in clear and comforting explanations of the existence of good and evil toward grappling with the disturbing gray areas. The symbols of the imagination that people respond to will reflect such shifts, the vampire among them. The many stages of vampire development reflect the crisis of science that followed the discovery of the behavior of subatomic particles and the realization that things are not always as they had seemed.

Let's first have a look at some of the forms into which the vampire has moved.

The Stir of Change

A dramatic shift in the American vampire mythos occurred in 1954 when Richard Matheson published his science-fiction/horror novel *I Am Legend*. Although comic books retained a Draculean perspective throughout this period, something was happening on the literary and cinematic front. Just a few years before, there had been hints in several Dracula spin-off movies that vampirism was a disease of the blood rather than a supernatural curse, but Matheson was to use this idea more boldly, providing a description propped up by scientific analysis.

In this novel, narrator Robert Neville is the only human left intact among an entire population transformed into vampires (even the dogs). In desperation, he reads *Dracula,* but finds no answers there. Compared with his own encounters with vampires, Stoker's novel seems to him to be full of superstitions about supernatural entities spawned by the devil. Contrary to Stoker's Dracula, Neville knows that vampires can see themselves in mirrors and that they do not change into wolves, mist, or bats. However, they must avoid the sun and garlic, and they can be destroyed with a wooden stake through the heart, so by day Neville proceeds to visit the homes where they sleep in order to dispatch them. This he does for his own survival. He appears to have a unique immunity to becoming a vampire as his family and neighbors have, but that makes him potential prey for the masses of vampires that know where to find him. At night, they stand outside his barricaded house, throwing rocks, beckoning to him, and trying every possible means to get inside or draw him out. He's definitely a man alone.

Everyone he knows has succumbed to what he discovers is a bacterium that infects the blood, causes the canine teeth to elongate, and creates a thirst for blood. It also heals all wounds save those opened by a wooden stake. Neville works hard to try to understand all of this, doing research and testing various hypotheses until he finds enough consistent data to form a tentative theory.

In order for a vampire novel to work as science fiction, the entire thing must be based in physical laws, with explanations of how the transformation occurs, how it works, and how the entities are destroyed. For example, to find out just why garlic is a repellent, Neville experiments with its various ingredients. He also looks up medical material on the lymphatic system and realizes that the bacterium protects itself from the harmful sun by forcing the vampires into a coma by day. (Hence the vampire's fear of the sun is no longer related to its inability to tolerate God's light.)

What drives the plot of this vampire novel is the creatures' desperate need to feed on blood. When they can't get at Neville, they turn on one another.

Once Neville isolates the germ, he searches for a way to combat the plague that destroyed his life. His primary tool is a microscope, which he uses to learn about the behavior of this vampire bacterium under normal and abnormal conditions. He theorizes that it had ridden on the wind to seek out optimal survival conditions and re-created itself into a form that would work best. Thus, the creation of vampires is as much the result of a contagious disease as any other plague. In order to destroy the vampire, Neville must find a way to change the germ into a self-consuming parasite, and he soon gets a break: he discovers that the wooden stake that mysteriously kills the vampires lets air into the body and changes the state of the bacterium from a symbiotic anaerobic system to an aerobic one.

The problem, though, is that bacteria can mutate.

I Am Legend is an involved exploration of vampirism as a natural result of a system gone awry. There's no religious apparatus and nothing supernatural at work. Explanations are offered for the effects of garlic and stakes, and even Neville's immunity is described as the result of early exposure to a weaker strain. It's all quite scientific and coherant with the natural order.

While Matheson's idea had little impact on the vampire of the classic horror novel, barely a decade later the vampire's essential malleability became more obvious. Despite its predatory, animal-like need for human blood, the soulless entity was found to have a soul after all.

The Reluctant Vampire

In 1966, a creepy mansion in New England on a cliff overlooking the ocean—where presumably people had jumped to their deaths on the jagged rocks below—became the setting of a gothic after-school series on the ABC television network known as *Dark Shadows*. Almost a year into the show, a visiting "cousin" from England came calling at the Collinwood estate and took up residence in a cottage on the grounds. He looked exactly like the portrait hanging in the house of a Collins ancestor, right down to the large ring he sported on his finger. Thus was Barnabas Collins introduced—the cursed vampire who searches for a cure to his illness even as it compels him to kill young women to feed off of. Rather than arriving from England as he stated, he'd been chained into a coffin on the estate and was freed by an unwitting caretaker. For the next four years on this series, his origins, doomed love life, and eventual fate were analyzed from every angle.

Barnabas became a vampire after having an affair with a witch, Angelique Bouchard, on the island of Martinique. When Barnabas spurned her, she sent a bat to attack him, and then cursed him. He begged his father to kill him, but instead was chained to the coffin for what was supposed to be eternity.

For a brief time, Barnabas actually does get cured by modern medicine, thanks to the persistent (and infatuated) Dr. Julia Hoffman, but a vengeful Angelique returns him to his supernatural form. She's able to do this because she, too, has been turned into a vampire through the magic of a warlock and can now make a human into a vampire herself. She then dies in flames. Thus, in this tale the vampiric blood disease is still associated with curses and supernatural rituals.

The overall effect of this popular series was to transform the vampire depicted in *Dracula* from the evil Other that had to be destroyed into a sympathetic creature who wished only to be human again and to have a normal life. Fans quickly embraced him and many identified with this version of the archetypal outsider, the prodigal son, the lonely misfit who desperately wanted to fit in. This was a nice guy with the unfortunate luck of having something bad in his blood that drove him to deeds he did not want to do. While the genetic and neurological sources of addictions had not yet been discovered, there appeared to be some kind of truth in this character that caused people to identify strongly with him. In addition, the series seemed attuned to subtle cultural shifts that in retrospect reveal Barnabas's struggles as the harbinger of change in the basic vampire tale.

The development of Barnabas not only prepared the way for a fuller exploration of the vampire's psyche, but it was a clear indication that our cultural response to the vampire was parallel to the way fundamental theories of reality were evolving. Before discussing the vampires of the 1970s, let's summarize those developments. Of course the latter occurred much earlier than shifts in our cultural images; it generally takes a while for mass culture to catch up to science and academics.

All matter is being created and destroyed—even what appears to be inorganic matter—and every subatomic particle, the basis of all existence, is part of an energy dynamic. Showing how physics abandoned one way of viewing reality to approach a more fluid view provides a parallel to the way concepts of the vampire flowed from the strict good-and-evil scenario of Stoker's time to a more ambiguous postmodern interpretation.

The following account offers only what is relevant in the history of physics to make sense of its effects on our popular-culture archetypes.

Thesis, Antithesis, Synthesis

While seeming to be solid, the world is actually made of vibrating molecules, atoms, and atomic subparticles, and showers of high energy continually bombard the earth's atmosphere. It's all a cosmic dance, which Fritjof Capra described in *The Tao of Physics* (1975) as similar to the Hindu dance of Shiva, a dance of eternal life. Gary Zukav wrote about this, too, in *The Dancing Wu Li Masters* (1979). They both describe how mysticism's awareness of fluid reality had much to teach the physicists of the Western world. Two decades later, in 1996, NASA astronaut Edward Mitchell, a doctor of aeronautics and author of *The Way of the Explorer,* joined them in this enterprise. After walking on the moon, he described a profound sense of connectedness that made him go beyond science to the mystical and paranormal, which complemented and extended his scientific training. Taken together, these three diverse thinkers offer a perspective on the way that our understanding of the world has changed. Reminding the reader of our notion of the scientist as someone who seeks to know essential reality, we can continue.

In short, Dracula could be understood in a context of absolutes: he was a supernatural creature that did not fit with the reality of the material world. But the vampire of today's narratives is a more morally ambiguous figure, an uneasy, unstable, and changing mix of both good and evil. There is nothing arbitrary or gratuitous about the way our understanding of vampirism and the compelling central figure of vampire fiction has evolved. Let's see how developments in physics over the past century help us to understand this.

Physics is the basis of the way reality gets perceived in everyday life, regardless of whether or not the perceiver has ever taken a physics course. Scientific ideas affect us. And since the foundations of scientific ideas have been shattered and rebuilt through the years as emerging anomalies change theories, that affects us, too. It's called a paradigm shift: many theories once believed to be true have been cast off and replaced by others that better explain the facts and observations. In other words, when a religious perspective prevailed as "truth," Dracula could be repelled with holy wafers and a crucifix. No more. In a postmodern world, where almost nothing is absolute, vampires hang out in cathedrals, wear crucifixes, and admire the beauty of a defunct religion. There's been a paradigm shift. We understand vampires differently, and our writers represent them differently, because we view the world differently.

Back to physics. Let's look first at how Bram Stoker understood the physical world. Classical physics in the nineteenth century, when *Dracula* was written, defined a world having solid material substance and uniform order. Things operated by physical laws and were predictable. That kind of thinking evolved from the ancient Greek cosmologists, who strove to discover the essential nature of things. To some, the one essential principle of reality was change, while to others it was permanence. Yet a few thinkers saw reality as mental rather than physical, and it wasn't long before reality was divided into two essences: mental and physical, or ideas and things. It was Aristotle who began to organize concepts about the physical world, and his approach to science long defined its methods in the Western world. The mental or spiritual perspective was relegated to the realm of religion, where it lost prestige with scientists, while science focused on what could be observed, measured, and categorized.

In the seventeenth century, French philosopher René Descartes decided that the world worked like a machine. Everything had a physical context. He then used geometry to relate time to space, and shortly thereafter Isaac Newton made this the foundation for his laws of motion. According to these laws, which dominated scientific thinking throughout the nineteenth century, mass was essentially passive and all physical events could be accurately measured and predicted. We had a representational map that laid things out, and with which we could make sense of a creature like a vampire (who didn't fit) and find a way to kill it.

That's how things developed in Western culture, but not so elsewhere. Thinkers in the East embraced the mental view that scientists had cast aside. For a while, Eastern mysticism was ignored, but that was to change—and that change would eventually affect the development of the vampire. Our monsters are based in our fears and our fears derive from our understanding of reality: if reality changes, so do our fears.

Mysticism says that the world is unified and interrelated. Practitioners seek immediate experience through disciplined meditation. For them, reality is internal, complex, and subjective. Because mystics want direct experience of reality unmediated by theoretical symbols, they dispense with the abstractions so fundamental to Western science. Instead, they rely on the use of metaphor and paradox to offer insights indirectly.

Absolute knowledge cannot be communicated in words, or "the Tao that can be expressed is not the eternal Tao." Einstein likewise said, "As far as the laws of mathematics refer to reality, they are not certain. As far as they are certain, they do not refer to reality."

So during the time when Dracula roamed London in search of new blood, we had two worldviews that seemed mutually exclusive. Yet things were to change in surprising ways, first among scientists and then in the culture at large. The vampire tale was in for a major shift when the insights from these diverse perspectives joined. Western science came to an impasse that meant scientists needed a new theory.

It was the discovery of the quantum universe that changed everything, and that universe was so small and so dynamic that it could not be observed directly. Trying to explain their insights, scientists looked to the language of mysticism. At the subatomic level, the parallels between quantum reality and mysticism were striking. For example, the behavior of light: in some contexts it acted like a wave, in others like a particle. Could it be both? Physicists had no concept for grasping this, so they dispensed with Western logic and embraced paradox. (This is important, too, for the notion of vampires being both living and dead.)

This kind of thinking is best understood in the Zen koan, which is a perplexing riddle with a unique solution. ("How can you not step on your shadow?" or "What is the sound of one hand clapping?") When logic provides no answer, the koan awakens consciousness to a nonverbal, nonrational reality that is closer to the relationships of unconfined dynamic energy than to a neat arrangement of building blocks.

Now Western science was freed from the box.

The new breed of scientists devised quantum theory, in which it was hypothesized that quanta, or energy packets, were the fundamental aspects of nature. Reality wasn't made of hard irresistible atoms that operated in deterministic ways. Rather, the building blocks of nature were beyond sensory perception and could only be known indirectly—just like koans. As Capra states, "I see science and mysticism as two complementary manifestations of the human mind; of its rational and intuitive faculties." Each has its own specialization, but they supplement each other in a dynamic interpenetration.

Before we apply this to vampires, let's summarize:

1. Scientific certainty has dissolved into notions of probability and approximation.

2. The "facts" of the universe are dynamic packages of unpredictable energy rather than solid particles.

3. During the twentieth century, the scientific method itself undermined the "truth" of science as it had been known up to that point.

The emerging idea is that reality has multiple dimensions and that different methods of approach come away with different ideas, although each has encountered the same basic reality. Physicists probe matter, mystics probe consciousness, and both develop patterns of organization not available to ordinary perception. Viewing them as aspects of the same reality allows for a fuller understanding.

The lesson for us as we look at the vampire tale is that if we try to define something in a manner that has no ability to shift and change, it won't correspond to our inner reality. In that case, a tale that belongs to the old reality will become obsolete. Only what's truly essential in the vampire to a core psychological archetype will remain intact across time, and the rest must either change to meet our specific needs or fall by the wayside.

Quantum Vampires?

So what does all of this physics and philosophy have to do with our notions about vampires? More than you might think.

The vampire story is about the rhythms of human existence, and our experience of reality flows into all of our endeavors. Because the vampire tale is a monster story that mirrors aspects of ourselves, watching how the vampire tale evolves opens a window into our shifting perceptions about what we experience as truth. I offer the argument that our comprehension of the world in which we find ourselves has influenced our myths and narratives, especially those that endure. Just as the early incarnation of the vampire held to a strict morality based in an idea that good and evil were separate and opposing forces, so do our contemporary creations show our willingness to see them as two sides of the same coin. The vampire is now more attuned to the mysticism of paradox. The vampire itself is a koan.

We may try to re-create old truths as we once saw them, but they lose force in an evolving society that has a new set of anxieties and a more informed perspective. Even as the mirror and crucifix no longer matter to vampires who discard a religious context, other aspects of the myth are developed that do matter. For example, a vampire today might be more repelled by an antivirus vaccine than by holy water.

Knowledge is always in process, and narratives that serve us must be so, too. Let's return now to the vampire tales of the 1980s, where the seeds are planted for much more dramatic leaps in the 1990s— even to the point of understanding the vampire as an element of the mystical.

Emerging Trends

Despite Barnabas's immense popularity into the early seventies, Stephen King retained the Draculean vampire when he wrote 'Salem's Lot (1975). It is about a vampire infestation in Jerusalem's Lot, a small town in Maine. The vampire in the book, Kurt Barlow, is animalistic and disgusting, akin to Max Schreck's portrayal of Count Orlock in Nosferatu. Barlow runs an antiques shop and preys on the town's residents, turning them into vampires with a desperate compulsion to suck blood. They do retain their human characteristics, but their personal shortcomings are now magnified. Like I Am Legend, the town's percentage of bloodsuckers multiplies until nearly everyone who lives there has been turned. King uses a child to show that it's not the symbols of faith that repel a vampire but the honesty of the heart. A stake to the heart rids the place of Barlow but fails to have the same effect it had in *Dracula*. His victims are still vampires.

In *Danse Macabre*, King discusses his ideas about writing *'Salem's Lot*. In part, he wanted to write a literary homage to Bram Stoker. " *'Salems Lot* was the ball," he says, "and *Dracula* was the wall I kept hitting it against." His novel was a product of different times, he realized, and an expression of different free-floating anxieties, although he believed that the recurrent rape scene depicted in vampire novels seemed always to be in fashion. He retained some of Stoker's ideas: the staking of a vampire, the drinking of the vampire's blood, the inability to touch the sacred Host, the vampire hunters who slowly realize what they're up against, and the ability of the vampire to command rats.

Nevertheless, King observed the way changing times influence horror fiction, with increased anxieties during periods of social stress . . . at least, to a point. Extreme stress shuts down the horror market, as if the collective human mind at times determines that it has had enough. Horror is useful for exercising certain emotions, but sometimes the mind needs to withdraw. Yet it can still be drawn out with the disguised version of sadomasochistic sex that vampire tales often utilize. Such sex involves fluid removal, oral pleasuring, and complete abandon to the one who commands. While King chose not to make much of this angle, he was not unaware of its force.

'Salem's Lot continued the trend since *Dracula* of creating animalistic vampires, and other authors such as Robert R. McCammon with *They Thirst* (1981) followed his lead. Yet they had a lesser impact on how the culture at large would perceive the vampire than did those authors who were drawn to the disguised sexual interplay that has always been a part of vampire fiction, and who fully exploited it.

With the expiration of *Dracula*'s copyright, the midseventies brought a new wave of vampire antiheroes. Fred Saberhagen presented

Dracula as a good guy in *The Dracula Tape* (1975) and Van Helsing as a bumbling oaf who knew less than he claimed. The Count indicates, for example, that it was Van Helsing's ignorance over blood types and transfusions that killed Lucy Westenra, not him. In a later novel, Dracula even teams up with Sherlock Holmes to solve a crime.

Yet it was a tale published in May 1976, less than a year after King's book, that was to make the greatest impact on the vampire concept, not just in the United States but worldwide. With the appearance of this novel, the vampire condition itself was to become morally neutral; it would soon be defined as good or bad according to what one did with it.

Anne Rice's *Interview with the Vampire* was a different kind of book. She wrote it in five weeks just over a year after the death of her five-year-old daughter from leukemia. Having lost her mother to alcoholism, she'd seen the vampiric effects of these diseases close up, and coupled with a rather lurid Catholic education and an upbringing in New Orleans, she was ready to create a vampire who expressed the depths of grief, loneliness, and guilt.

Like Rice, this vampire, Louis de Point du Lac, wants to find out the truth about God, and like Rice, he becomes utterly disillusioned with all the promises made by his religion. Searching for family, he helps his vampire progenitor, a French aristocrat named Lestat, to turn Claudia, a five-year-old orphan, into a vampire, and for sixty years they live uneasily together in New Orleans. Then all hell breaks loose as Louis and Claudia try to kill Lestat and flee to Europe in search of kindred souls. That doesn't exactly work out, either, and finally Louis comes to the conclusion that as a vampire, he's no closer to knowing truth than he was as a muddled mortal—yet now he must live with the pain of his condition for eternity. Another vampire, Armand, tells him that it's this very isolation that makes him the embodiment of his age.

As it turned out, the novel itself was the embodiment of an era filled with people searching for self-growth, companionship, and truth. Although Rice had written about vampires on a whim, seeking a way to express suffering through a distanced perspective, many people were experimenting with drugs, therapy groups, alternative forms of religion, and new identities. Louis's dilemma, existential angst, and heightened senses echoed a collective experience. At first this novel was an underground classic, just missing the bestseller list in hardcover but generating an enormous sale in paperback and movie rights (for a film that was made almost two decades later in 1994). Yet it didn't end there.

Louis meets up again with Lestat, crippled by his inability to cope with the modern world, and then tells his story to a reporter. To his mind, there's no ultimate meaning, but the reporter believes Louis has missed the point entirely. To be a vampire is the most heightened exotic experience a mortal could hope to achieve, and the reporter becomes infected with the need to find out more. The novel remains open-ended, available to continuing episodes.

However, Rice did not publish a sequel until 1985, and by that time her perspective had evolved. While her emphasis on the young and beautiful vampire contributed a great deal to the 1970s shift into a more romantic vampire genre, the force of that was not fully felt until the mid-eighties, when she endowed the vampires with far more powers than she had initially envisioned.

Even so, more attention was turning toward the humanized vampire, and a number of authors penned their own renditions. Chelsea Quinn Yarbro is credited with writing the most popular of the historical romances featuring a vampire, and her four-thousand-year-old protagonist, le Comte de Saint Germain, is a gentleman in search of a home. He travels through numerous historical settings, develops his magic, and pleases the ladies (although he's one of those vampires who can't get an erection). Yarbro's first Saint Germain novel, initially inspired by *Dracula,* was *Hotel Transylvania,* published in 1978. It was to be become an extended series.

In a speech presented at the 150th anniversary conference commemorating Bram Stoker's birth, Yarbro said, "I believe no vampire story written in English after 1920 is free of Stoker's influence, for that book and its theatrical and cinematic stepchildren have imbued the culture with icons and clichés to such an extent that whether or not a writer has actually taken the time to read Stoker's novel, he—or she—has his or her creative landscape littered with Dracular images that are inescapable."

When she herself turned to *Dracula* to try to analyze just how Stoker had so successfully made his novel compelling, she realized that a contemporary vampire novel would have to take a different approach. To her mind, Stoker had done the manipulative seducer as well as anyone could. Yarbro decided to develop her own character, albeit still supernatural, as a metaphor of humanity indifferent to the trappings of institutional religion. She wanted him to be involved with human experience. Vampire novels did not necessarily have to be about seducers and prey; they could depict vampires and other characters in emotional relationships.

Then she set her vampire milieu in Louis XV's Paris and did extensive research on the historical Comte de Saint Germain, an alchemist. She noted the vampiric facts about his life: he dressed in black and white, never ate or drank in public, claimed to have lived for many centuries, kept his nationality a mystery, had multiple aliases, and was wealthy, elegant, intelligent, and cultured. Yarbro managed to work his character across a dozen novels and to transform the parasitic nature of the vampire into more of a symbiotic involvement between predator and prey.

The Vampire Boom

In *Our Vampires, Ourselves*, Nina Auerbach attempts to analyze the vampire's rise and fall in the context of the American political climate. She makes a surprising observation when she states, "When Ronald Reagan's powerful persona took control of the American imagination in the 1980s, vampires began to die." It must be that her professed hatred for Republicans blinded her to the number of significant vampire novels and films that came out during that decade.

It began with Suzy McKee Charnas's *The Vampire Tapestry*, published in 1980 and featuring the vampire Edward Weyland. An ancient being who can hibernate between periods of awareness and forget whatever he has experienced in previous eras, he understands the need to adapt to whatever time in which he finds himself. In this novel, he teaches anthropology at a small educational institution, yet also pursues his needs in a predatory manner, getting blood from victims by pricking them with a needle extension hidden under his tongue. He even poses the question in class about how nature might design a vampire—an indication that Charnas gave a lot of thought to his biology.

In an essay, "Meditations in Red," Charnas wrote years after the fact that her original intention was to make *The Vampire Tapestry* an animal tale. She had seen the romanticizing element in recent vampire narratives and decided to resist that and develop a ruthless predator, "a true tiger in human form." She wanted no supernatural or sentimental trappings. She made her vampire intelligent and attractive so he could get close to his prey, but she also wanted him to remain simple in his animal needs.

Yet to her chagrin, romance inevitably crept in. He became the "transformable beast," conquered to some extent by love, while the humans around him demonstrated their own predatory natures. Vampire and human worlds interpenetrated, each showing its virtuous and parasitic ways. Charnas closed this essay by explaining that her story evolved in this way because our knowledge that love is stronger than fear "comes from the part of us that refuses to exclude the monstrosity but won't settle for it either." The monster is about ourselves and the monster tale will be affected and changed as we are affected and changed.

In response to a question about Weyland's origins, Charnas said, "I conceived of him as an ancient predator from the outset, being bored with the vampire as melancholy seducer trailing his aristocratic past and his soulful woes wherever he goes. The latter figure works very well indeed, which is why so much mileage has been got out of him, I don't deny that. But I am a restless sort of person, mentally, and easily bored; I just did not see the point of writing about a vampire unless I had a fresh slant. I liked the idea of a predator who was really a predator, not a seductive human being with an ultra-long history and some nasty habits. His 'human' qualities are part of his disguise, like markings on a giraffe, except for the emotional ones he begins to develop during the course of the book, and on which the resolution of the story ultimately hinges.

"Part of what I enjoyed was working with someone who is a blank slate to himself, as it were, each time out of the gate, so that he's essentially ignorant and at the same time is in the existential position of making himself up as he goes along.

"Weyland actually began in science of a sort: I'd been reading about efforts to synthesize blood and thought I might do a vampire tale connected with that, which immediately located my vampire in an academic setting—an adjunct to a teaching hospital or medical research institution where people would be working on such a project. His ancientness was influenced by the fact that I live in a part of America [New Mexico] where ancientness in various forms is on open display, in the stripped-down landscape in which layers of time are recorded, and in the ruins left by indigenous populations long gone.

"Once I saw that what interested me was not the idea of synthetic blood but the provocative idea of a creature with ancient roots evolving through time to keep pace with his evolving prey, I dropped the synthetic blood. So, thinking of him as an animal all along, I naturally did some consulting with people like doctors for the effects of an all-blood diet and a zoo vet in designing him. At the same time I was reading extensively in the traditional literature and came across the needle under the tongue in Polish vampire lore, so I can't claim to have originated that, only to have found it and recognized it as far superior to those laughable fangs."

Whitley Strieber's *The Hunger* (1981), George R. R. Martin's *Fevre Dream* (1982), and S. P. Somtow's *Vampire Junction* (1984) worked other changes on the vampire legends. Many of these authors of the eighties made vampires appealing, even in their aggressive drive, because eroticism became an increasingly stronger element. Forbidden desires emerged into the open.

In *The Hunger* (which was continued two decades later in *The Last Vampire*), Miriam Blaylock is an immortal alien associated with a powerful group called the Keepers, who "keep man as man keeps cattle." She couples with a long line of mortal partners and then must endure their inability to remain with her forever. While she makes them into vampires, after a certain amount of time—two or more centuries—they rapidly age. To try to avert this, Miriam engages the services of a female scientist, Sarah Roberts, an expert on aging whose work might hold the secret to a youthful immortality.

"I created Miriam as a member of an alternate species," Strieber explained, "because it seemed like an interesting thing to do. I had not read much modern vampire literature, with the exception of *Interview with the Vampire*. At the time that I wrote *The Wolfen* and *The Hunger*, I had no idea about close encounter experiences, but the creatures I created in them—the Wolfen with their brilliance and their dark, haunting eyes and Miriam Blaylock, tall, blond and appealing— seem to prefigure in some way the large-eyed gray aliens and the enigmatic tall blond humanoids that some years later became features of so many close encounter stories.

"Keeper anatomy is imaginary. I don't think that there is any scientific resource that suggests how a vampire might work. In any case, this is very incidental. It's how they look and act that counts for me. I want the anatomy to be believable enough to satisfy the reader and get the blood-eating process out of the way. My stories are not about bloodsucking, they're about the way our world is unfolding around us, and how we live our lives, just like other stories. The 'vampire' is a set of observations concerning the way one segment of the human population addresses the rest of us. Put Adolf Hitler in a blond wig and you have Miriam Blaylock."

In 1983, *The Hunger* was made into a classy film starring Catherine Deneuve and David Bowie that drew a lot of attention to the "new" vampire, and by 1985, Anne Rice's sequel, *The Vampire Lestat,* became a bestseller, followed three years later by *The Queen of the Damned.* In most novels, the existence of vampires was now taken for granted and the stories followed a different tack than that of the vampire hunter who figures out the mystery. That meant that authors felt free to explore the nuances of the vampire's own story, which included explanations for how they emerged, thrived on blood, and spent their time. The possibilities were limitless.

Lestat came on strong as a rock star and focus on vampire communities set the stage for the advent of vampire role-playing games. Lestat was now an author, intending to tell his own story and recasting Louis's tale to announce himself as a new vampire for a new age. In fact, he presented a new type of hero. He embraced his vampirism (or said he did), and as other authors further dissolved many of the vampire conventions, the vampire changed even more. This creature was now a sympathetic outsider in a culture where minority groups were vocalizing their concerns and making plenty of demands. He (and she) had a more diverse range of preternatural powers and felt everything with the amplitude of the Romantic poets. Thanks to vampires like Lestat, readers wanted to be vampires.

Throughout this decade, the vampire slowly became more cerebral, although bestial aggression still lingered. They acquired a spiritual dimension, like fallen angels who had once been in the presence of God and who therefore understood the celestial qualities of immortality. Rice viewed them as ancient deities. She saw vampires as creatures outside the human sphere who were nevertheless able to address it because they had once been human.

Yet there was a backlash to all of this as well, and some horror writers claimed that the vampire's impact had been watered down. F. Paul Wilson, author of *The Keep*, (1981) said, "I can't buy trying to romanticize that type of creature." Nancy Collins, creator of the edgy vampire Sonja Blue, felt that the vampire is "everything that is bad with humanity." In that tradition, the vampire was presented as nihilistic and brutal. Yet no one could change the fact that Rice's vampire universe was a huge success with readers and was influencing a new generation of writers.

Even as more attention went to the vampire's inwardness, female vampires were getting their due—at just the time when feminism was making a strong showing in the culture at large. No longer just "vamps," they were powerful creatures with real leadership positions. Rice made her vampire progenitor, Akasha, a commanding female, and then set a pair of female twins against this Egyptian queen, making them the heroines. Another forceful female in that series was Gabrielle, Lestat's mother, who proved to be emotionally better equipped than he was to endure immortality's inevitable isolation.

Then a number of female protagonists showed up in a series of short stories written for an anthology called *Vamps,* while in 1987 readers were treated to Nancy Collins's street-smart Sonja Blue in *Sunglasses After Dark.*

"In early twentieth-century America," said *Dracula* scholar David

Skal, "the female vampire icon was largely downgraded into the non-supernatural 'vamp'—arguably as powerful and influential a modern myth on its own terms as the undead, Draculesque male. After all, Theda Bara provided the basic template for the modern movie star—certainly the most mythic icon of modern times. This probably has to do with the much larger cultural, mythic, and anthropological questions of why representations of the devil are overwhelmingly male. The Dracula/vampire image has largely supplanted the traditional image of Old Scratch in popular iconography. On a primal level, male and female archetypes both have terrifying aspects, but males are generally more terrifying because they're bigger, stronger, make war, rape, pillage, and are capable of worse things than even the worst female archetypes."

Still, female vampires would continue to have more prominence.

Beyond the Books

By the end of the decade, *Psychology Today* ran a cover story on why vampires had been such a hot topic throughout the eighties, and several classic vampire movies appeared, *Near Dark* and *Lost Boys* among them. While plans were in the works to bring back *Dark Shadows* (which succeeded and then failed), *Nick Knight,* the 1989 movie, sparked a solid run as a television series about a cop who inadvertently becomes a vampire and who wants to set things right.

In fact, vampires were appearing everywhere. They showed up on cereal boxes as Count Chocula, in commercials for candy, mouthwash, and nail polish, on *Sesame Street* (Count Count), on greeting cards, and in cartoons. There was even a grammar book called *The Transitive Vampire.*

We also had the Vampire Information Exchange (VIE), the Vampire Penpal Network, and the Vampire Studies Society. Thousands of people became members of the Count Dracula Fan Club, run by Dr.

Jeanne Keyes Youngson, and the Unquiet Grave Press published interviews with "true" vampires.

Norine Dresser, a folklorist at UCLA also wrote a book at that time called *American Vampires* in which she documented vampire images in the media and described the effects on people who claimed to be vampires. She sent out a questionnaire, and out of 574 respondents, 27 percent admitted to a belief in vampires.

Dr. Stephen Kaplan operated the Vampire Research Center and claimed that he'd been tracking "real vampires" across the country. He hoped to get a government grant to finance the analysis of a ninety-nine-item questionnaire for a more official count. Kaplan claimed that there were some fifty or sixty true vampires around the country and five hundred worldwide.

It soon became clear that some individuals were deeply affected by the mythology to the point of filing their teeth permanently into razor-sharp weapons, sleeping in coffins, avoiding the sun, and dressing exclusively in black. A few of them formed small groups to exchange blood in secret. While only a handful of such practitioners made these claims, before long the subculture would burgeon beyond imagining.

Expanded Powers

By the end of the decade, the vampire had dropped many limitations imposed by superstition—but not all—and had acquired more powers than previous incarnations. At the very least, those powers were more clearly articulated and exploited. A list of vampire traits by the late 1980s, including both the old and the new, would include:

- superhuman strength
- ability to levitate and even to fly

- ability to project their voices to ear-shattering levels
- ability to speak in decibels too low for humans to hear
- ability to project an astral form
- ability to move with great speed and jump to great heights
- ability to read minds and experience clairvoyant phenomena
- ability to shut out the telepathy of other creatures
- ability to scale up walls that appear to offer no leverage
- ability to heal their wounds and the wounds of their prey
- ability to regrow hair that has been cut, but limited to its original length
- ability to mimic language and musical instruments
- ability to read with hyperspeed
- ability to see in the dark
- ability to hypnotize or scramble the thoughts of humans
- ability to move objects at will
- ability to feel and perceive more vividly than they did as mortals
- ability to command animals
- ability to shift their shape
- limited ability to endure the sun
- the weeping of blood tears

The notion that vampires cry blood tears was a new and unique development, but not one that made biological sense. Presumably vampires have other fluids inside their bodies or else their saliva would be blood as well. Why the ingestion of blood would produce blood tears any more than the ingestion of wine would make us weep red zinfandel is a mystery.

The same goes for hair that must return to its original state when cut. We see this in *The Vampire Lestat* when Gabrielle attempts to shear off her long hair—a sign of her femaleness, which she desires to shed. Try as she might to adopt a more practical style, her hair inevitably grows back. That tends to indicate that vampires return to the state their physical bodies were in when they died, and yet in many ways they don't. As corpses, they never cried blood tears, they had no psychic powers, and no fangs. Why the hair must behave in this fashion remains unexplained.

That they would have heightened abilities such as speed, strength, and sensory acuity appears to be part of the mythical pact with the devil, since those were traits that Dracula exhibited. Yet they may also be rooted in a transformation of mortal biology, as we've seen in the discussion of immortalized cells.

While some of the powers listed above will be discussed in the next chapter, let's examine one area that received emphasis in the eighties and that has since influenced the creation of vampires: psychic powers.

The idea that vampires might be able to exercise mind over matter and achieve feats beyond anything a mortal can accomplish would seem to be a logical development. Just as immortal cells might be created from cells that deteriorate with the loss of telomeres, so vampire abilities might come from dormant mortal abilities. While many self-proclaimed psychics insist that all humans have this ability, that claim has never been scientifically demonstrated, although it has been shown that some people with abilities to "know" things other mortals don't know have unusual neuronal activity in some areas of their brains.

Psi is a Greek designation that has been applied to paranormal phenomena. These would include:

- mental telepathy (transmitting information from one mind to another)

- thought projection

- ESP

- levitation

- the ability to move objects without touching them (telekinesis)

- the ability to "read" traces of personal history from an object (psychokinesis)

We have vampires that can do most or all of these things, and some of them can fly (without changing into bats). Can humans hope to make such achievements?

It seems that certain forces in nature would have to be harnessed in some way to make these abilities possible. It might work through electromagnetism or possibly through strong and weak forces that operate at the subatomic realm. We could speculate on this, but let's look at relevant work already in process.

In 1979, the Princeton Engineering Anomalies Research (PEAR) program was started at Princeton University in Princeton, New Jersey. Robert G. Jahn, dean of the School of Engineering and Applied Sciences, wanted to examine the possible interaction between human consciousness and the physical world. He set up sensitive mechanical, optical, acoustic, and fluid devices and tested subjects to see if they could truly affect these objects merely with their minds. That is, could they make statements about their intentions ("I'll make this pendulum move") and realize these intentions without recourse to any physical contact?

Jahn had sufficient (if moderate) success with hundreds of subjects over millions of trials, making it seem likely that only the consciousness of the human operator could have influenced the results, and his work has encouraged others. Numerous experiments have been run in other places, such as the Freiburg Anomalous Mind/Machine Interaction (FAMMI) group, with expertise in applied psychology, and the Giessen Anomalies Research Program (GARP), a psychophysiology research facility, both situated in Germany. The PEAR staff also coordinates a consortium of international scholars who want to better understand how consciousness affects various scientific arenas.

Basically, their work consists of observing anomalies within a functional scientific framework that includes consciousness as an active agent in the establishment of physical reality. Paired operators get better results, especially when they share an emotional bond, and the effects can be demonstrated even when the operators are thousands of miles from the lab and making their efforts hours before the operation of the devices.

According to information on the PEAR Web site, "despite the small scale of the observed consciousness-related anomalies, they could be functionally devastating to many types of contemporary information processing systems, especially those relying on random reference signals. Such concern could apply to aircraft cockpits and ICBM silos; to surgical facilities and trauma response equipment; to environmental and disaster control technology; or to any other technical scenarios where the emotions of human operators may intensify their interactions with the controlling devices and processes."

In other words, understanding how human consciousness affects sensitive instruments can help to better design the instruments for this type of information processing. The research also suggests the possibility of a new area of creativity in the realm of human/machine interaction. It seems that strong human emotions like joy, wonder, and enthusiasm have some affect on the physical environment, and a scientific study of subjective phenomena would have to broaden its methods and theories to accept these experiences into a rigorous framework.

An interesting aspect of this work is that groups of people in certain situations seem to affect the devices in a way that beats the odds. People in sacred gatherings, creative endeavors, and group rituals show more constantly anomalous readings than do people at academic gatherings or business meetings—the latter groups doing no better than chance. In fact, one group created a rather impressive "paranormal" event.

While the following incident has not been replicated, it was reported in 1972 and remains a significant occurrence in the paranormal world. A group of eight people in Canada who called themselves the Toronto New Horizons Research Foundation designed a ghost, which then proceeded to "cause" numerous paranormal events. They named the ghost Philip, gave him a tragic history as an English aristocrat, provided some "unfinished business," and listed his habits and preferences.

For some time nothing happened, so they stopped concentrating so hard and decided to just relax. That's when they got results: raps or "answers" on the table in response to specific questions, the "answers" being in perfect accord with the invented personality. Then the table began to move, and one time it even shot across the room. There were cool breezes and metal-bending incidents, and all of this was captured on video cameras. When one member told "Philip" that they had made him up, the activity ceased. Then the group resumed its "belief" in Phillip and he began to act out again.

Whatever it means, there's reason to believe that the human mind and emotions may affect occurrences in the physical world. In that case, if vampires lose all the cognitive baggage that clutters up mortal beliefs (possibly limiting their psychic abilities) and if they acquire exaggerated powers, it stands to reason that their psi abilities would be heightened as well. Once they grasp what they can do mentally, they can perfect it with practice.

True Vampires

Even while vampires were spreading from fiction and film into other venues, researchers were devising natural explanations for the origins of vampire folklore. Although anemia had been suggested in *Dracula* as a possible cause for Lucy Westenra's disturbing condition, Dr. Van Helsing dismissed this possibility. Some of the symptoms were akin to anemia, but not all of them—in particular the puncture wounds on her neck. Nevertheless, even today people try to associate vampirism with some physical disease.

A suggestion that received a great deal of attention was put forward by Dr. David Dolphin, a chemistry professor. He did a great disservice to many people handicapped with this disease when he delivered a paper to the American Association for the Advancement of Science suggesting that cases of vampirism from folklore might have been the manifestations of porphyria. He suggested that people with porphyria were desperately drinking fresh blood to try to alleviate their symptoms.

Porphyria, also known as King George III's disease, is an abnormality of the hemoglobin. In the sovereign's case, it showed up as abdominal pain, fever, and constipation. As he weakened, his urine turned dark red, alarming his royal physicians. He couldn't sleep, and he complained of headaches and convulsions. Then he inexplicably recovered. All seemed well until thirteen years later, when the disease finally forced him into a stupor.

Porphyria tends to be genetically transmitted. The absence of an enzyme sends part of the blood pigment hemoglobin to the urine rather than to the cells. Porphyrins accumulate to toxic levels and attack the nervous system. While seven separate enzyme-deficiency disorders fall under the name porphyria, the acute types are the most severe. Some include skin symptoms, such as thickening, darkening, and blistering in direct sunlight, which is why David Dolphin suggested that there were parallels between this blood disease and vampires. However, he based his ideas on the mythology of the movies rather than on actual folklore or even on the evidence of *Dracula*.

The most severe form of porphyria manifests in scarring and an increased growth of hair, along with infections that damage facial features and fingers. Treatment involves removing blood to diminish the body's content of iron, while other treatments inject heme.

An examination of the folklore quickly disproves the porphyria hypothesis. Reanimated corpses came out at night, but no one said that they blistered or ulcerated in the sun, that their fingers fell off, or that their hair thickened. While King George III was repeatedly subjected to leeches and bleeding, no one fed him blood as a remedy.

A look back at the eighties shows how popular the vampire became as a cultural image and how malleable it was. Experimentation with the vampire in fiction proved that Dracula need not be the king vampire after all. Barnabas, Lestat, Saint Germain, and the others heralded a new age that would inspire authors and filmmakers to add even more changes.

Before moving on to the nineties, when a few more vampire "essentials" would dissolve, let's return to a core aspect of the tale: the transformation. What does science have to show us?

THREE
Creating a Vampire

❈—✠—❈

As Dracula chooses and connects with a victim, he appears to create a telepathic bond. The vampire hunters learn from Mina Harker that they can track his movements by putting her into a trance—the same sort of reduced resistance she felt when the Count had approached her. In fact, successive vampire tales embraced the mesmerizing power of the vampire as one of its key abilities, and Van Helsing and Dr. Seward both affirm hypnosis as a means to dominate the human mind.

The Power of the Subconscious

In *Dracula,* it becomes clear that after Mina is bitten, she has a subliminal awareness of her attacker's whereabouts. Under hypnosis, she can describe what she sees and hears as if she were inside the monster. When he's on board a ship, enclosed in a coffin, she can see only darkness, but she hears the crew at work and the wind in the sails. Using her mind in the grip of a trance, the vampire hunters can track

Dracula and prepare themselves for him. They take Mina with them to help them locate the bloodsucker, but the closer she gets, the less susceptible she is to Van Helsing's clinical skill. Ironically, Dracula has also used this same mental connection to figure out what the hunters expect and has initially thwarted their plans. Yet it appears that he can shut the connection down at will.

Let's review how hypnosis works, beginning with what the medical doctors in this novel might have known about it in the 1890s. Van Helsing asks Dr. Seward if he believes in hypnotism and he responds that Charcot has proven it well enough to accept as a fact. He and Van Helsing are both "students of the brain," and both are intrigued with how the vampire affects it. Van Helsing thinks that a hypnotist as powerful as Charcot can influence the very soul of the subject, and that seems to be what Dracula is doing as well.

It was Franz Anton Mesmer late in the eighteenth century who first brought hypnosis to popular awareness, making great theatrical displays and unwarranted claims for its power, but the conservative medical establishment regarded "mesmerism" as quackery. However, those who avoided exaggerated claims and did careful work eventually earned guarded respect for the process.

John Braid coined the term *hypnosis* in 1843, in reference to Hypnos, the Greek god of sleep. British surgeon James Esdaile tried to use it to cure patients with mental disorders in Calcutta, with moderately successful results. He even managed to perform surgery on a patient under hypnosis. In Russia, Ivan Pavlov—who would become famous for the behavioral conditioning of animals—described it as progressive cortical inhibition.

Throughout the nineteenth century, as psychiatry became a medical specialization, practitioners followed two main schools of thought, some believing that psychiatric disorders had an organic cause, others that it had a mental cause. Among those who championed the somatic theories was Jean-Martin Charcot, head of the Salpetrière Hospital in Paris and the man credited with describing the benefits of hypnosis in medical terms.

Charcot was a leading neurologist during the 1870s and he made his hospital for insane women into the first postgraduate institution for teaching psychiatry. He believed that psychopathology was rooted in degenerative alterations in the brain, and that hypnosis was a physiological phenomenon that could have a positive healing effect on hysteria (thought at the time to be exclusively a female problem). Because hypnotism was so effective with this patient population, Charcot viewed the trance as a manifestation of hysteria. While the French Academy of Science had thrice rejected mesmerism, they accepted hypnotism as scientific and that act inspired more neurologists to explore its effects.

Then Charcot's student, Pierre Janet, redefined hysteria as a mental disorder related to fixed ideas and memory impairments, and he used hypnosis as a means of treatment. To him, hypnosis was a dissociated state in which part of consciousness split off from another part.

During the latter part of the 1880s, Charcot also influenced Sigmund Freud, who was a poor hypnotist and who later came to view the process as being provoked by suggestion, which developed an eroticized dependency of the subject on the analyst.

It was not until the 1920s that hypnosis was subjected to rigorous experimental methods.

The modern therapeutic use of hypnosis has been influenced by the notion that responses to hypnotic suggestion involve some capacity to access mental functions that are normally beyond the reach of conscious control. In other words, the person remembers and acts in ways that are different from what is normal for him. Hypnosis has been utilized as a tool to try to fill in gaps in memory, add detail to accounts, facilitate certain behaviors, and ensure recall accuracy. The most popular techniques involve inducing a trancelike meditative state for past-memory regression and memory enhancement, although research has shown that the inducement of a relaxed state is not actually necessary for hypnotic manifestations to occur. Someone can be completely alert and still be subject to hypnosis.

Nevertheless, in a typical scenario, as that seen in *Dracula,* the hypnotist exploits the subject's suggestibility in order to produce a relaxed mental state. The willing subject closes her eyes and becomes attentive and less prone to critical resistance that can block memory. Going into a trance purportedly allows the heightening of imagination, with the hope that things might be recalled that would otherwise remain inaccessible, or that certain behaviors such as breaking a habit might be induced.

Historically, hypnosis has been variously understood as:

- dissociation of consciousness

- role-playing

- enhanced suggestibility

- an altered state of consciousness

- regression in service of the ego

- neurological inhibition

- a unique electromagnetic-field phenomenon

- contact with alternate realms of existence

The way many theorists understand it to work is that hypnosis appears to bypass the subject's psychological defenses so as to allow repressed material to surface, which provides greater access to thought, feelings, and memories that are not accessible during normal consciousness.

Martin Riccardo, an expert on vampire literature and a behavioral hypnotist since 1977, has studied this phenomenon at length. He uses it to facilitate changes in attitudes and behaviors, and for a while he taught classes on the subject. However, he does not trust hypnosis used to elicit information, because the power of suggestion can influence the subject to create fantasies that can be misperceived as memories.

"One of the oldest terms used in the field of hypnosis is 'rapport' or 'hypnotic rapport,' " he said, "and it is still commonly used by hypnotists today. While there is no universally accepted definition of this term among hypnotists, it often refers to the mental bond or link between hypnotist and hypnotized subject, possibly even to the point of the two becoming 'one mind.' According to one theory, the hypnotist essentially takes the place of the critical thinking faculties of the subject, in a sense replacing the thinking 'voice' or 'narrator' of the subject's mind. For those open to paranormal theories, the mental and emotional rapport between hypnotist and subject could also involve a telepathic connection."

Riccardo goes on to discuss hypnosis used in *Dracula*. "Van Helsing states that hypnotism can go 'into the very soul of the patient.' Dracula clearly seems to have a telepathic hypnotic power over his victims and there are many indications that Dracula has a strong telepathic influence over Renfield. In chapter 11, when Lucy sees Dracula enter her room as a wolf, she says in her account, 'I tried to stir, but there was some spell upon me . . .' Likewise, when Dracula assaults Mina in chapter 21, she says, 'I was bewildered, and, strangely enough, I did not want to hinder him. I suppose it is a part of the horrible curse that such is, when his touch is on his victim.'

"In that same attack on Mina, Dracula himself blatantly proclaims the telepathic hypnotic control he can exercise when he says to Mina, 'When my brain says "Come!" to you, you shall cross land or sea to do my bidding; and to that end this!' At that point, he makes a cut in his chest and forces Mina to drink his blood. This act apparently cements the psychic bond between them. Of course, it results in Dracula's own undoing.

"An interesting sidebar is that Stoker knew George du Maurier, the author of *Trilby*. In that novel, which was published in 1894, the nefarious figure of Svengali uses his hypnotic control over a young woman named Trilby in order to transform her into a magnificent singer. It seems quite likely that the character of Dracula in Stoker's novel was strongly influenced by the fictional Svengali, but Dracula is even more powerful since he exerts a supernatural and telepathic mind control over his victims. Ironically, *Trilby* quickly became an overwhelming bestseller and a highly successful play, far more successful than *Dracula* was during Stoker's lifetime."

Riccardo points out that he does not believe in hypnosis as mind control or as inducing an altered state of consciousness. He thinks of it more as a tool to enhance suggestion.

Among the problems involved with the use of hypnosis are:

- the possibility that a "refreshed" memory is incomplete or inaccurate

- that a refreshed memory is based on some leading suggestion that affects the way the memory is retold

- that confabulation, or filling in the gaps with false material that supports the subject's self-interest, will occur

- that a posthypnotic suggestion will be retroactively integrated into the subject's memory so it becomes part of the original memory

- that "memory hardening"—which occurs when a false memory brought out through hypnosis seems so real that the subject develops false confidence in it—will occur

A persistent controversy and one that's relevant to Mina Harker's case is the use of hypnosis to facilitate psychic phenomena or experiences such as alien abduction. In those cases, the subject appears to "recall" things that defy accepted standards of plausibility. It's difficult to know what to make of them, particularly when the recalled material has a lasting and profound effect on the subject. Since it's been demonstrated that it's possible to provoke recall of things that did not occur and that recall is shaped by inner needs, it's difficult to affirm the veracity of bizarre material.

Under hypnosis, subjects have reportedly engaged in extrasensory perception, psychokinesis, and seeing and "channeling" apparitions. In fact, the history of spiritualism is filled with reports of supernatural phenomena provoked during trance states. Unconscious processes were often considered entwined with the paranormal, so it's no stretch for Van Helsing and his cohorts to believe that Dracula could be supernaturally connected to Mina and that both vampire and victim can share the same perceptions. However, the phenomenon of spontaneous hallucinations also occurs during hypnosis, and there's no known method for distinguishing them from actual external perceptions. Theorists believe that they arise from a chemical shift in the brain, possibly influenced by electromagnetic fields. Do the psychic phenomena stimulate the brain to produce the perceptions or are these apparent perceptions merely the result of the brain's ability to mimic them? The answer probably depends on one's belief system.

At any rate, Seward and Van Helsing can only operate on what was known in 1893, which was a combination of mesmerism, primitive neurological findings, and spiritualistic trances. As for the vampire's hypnotic skills with potential victims, we may want to examine a more biologically based effect.

The Victim's Brain

When Dracula draws Lucy outside to the cemetery in Whitby and bends over her reclining figure, his bite and feeding are sufficient to produce in her heavy breathing, a "little shudder," and a swoon—a clear hint that she's achieved sexual orgasm from contact with him.

In fact, many vampire tales follow this erotic tradition, sometimes with complex descriptions of draining the blood, and in other versions all the excitement occurs in the victim's transformation into a vampire. In any event, the vampire's bite appears to have some special ability to bring the target person into a high state of physical excitement. He's not injecting something into the person (not usually), so it must be that the vampire can activate something in the victim's body, and it could be more than just desire. Since the main organ involved in the heightened erotic state is the brain, let's try to figure out what must be happening inside the head of someone in the vampire's embrace.

Researchers have demonstrated that the brain contains its own pharmacy and can duplicate many of the effects of psychedelic drugs. For example, according to the *Journal of Neuroscience,* the presence of substances like alcohol, cocaine, and stimulants appears to increase the production of morphinelike endorphins in a region of the brain that affects addictions. Ingesting them triggers activity from the brain's own chemicals.

It took a long time for scientists to locate specific areas of the brain that acted as binding sites for substances that controlled pleasure and pain. In the 1970s Solomon Snyder and Candace Pert made the first real discoveries at Johns Hopkins University. They located the first opiate receptor, while other researchers soon found opiate binding in nervous tissue. That meant the body had to be producing a substance for those sites. A year later, they found it. In Aberdeen, Scotland, researchers named it enkephalin and noted that it was contained in a pituitary hormone that had pain-reducing properties. Other peptides were found in that hormone that had morphinelike properties, so they were called endorphins, which means "morphine within."

Yet more than just acting for pleasure or relief from pain, the brain can produce its own hallucinogens. Since many recent vampire stories make transformation into a vampire fairly psychedelic, let's examine how that experience might affect the brain. Fortunately, there's a little-known drug that works in a similar manner.

When Dr. Rick Strassman performed a series of experiments with N, N-dimethyltryptamine or DMT, he interpreted the results in his subjects as the key to understanding the euphoria of mystical experiences. DMT is a plant-derived chemical also made in the human brain that was first discovered in 1931 when a Canadian chemist synthesized it from tryptamine (from which both LSD and serotonin are derived). Then it was associated with the plants known to produce psychedelic effects, and in 1955, a researcher in Budapest injected some into his own body. He experienced tingling, elevation of blood pressure, visual hallucinations, and euphoria. Later researchers who followed his lead felt as if they were flying, and one woman observed the presence of beings that seemed like gods.

It wasn't long before DMT was found in the brains of mice and rats, and then it was isolated in human blood. Next, DMT was discovered in the human brain, making it the first endogenous human psychedelic, i.e., made by the body. Scientists thought that perhaps it played a role in psychosis. Eventually Strassman found that DMT was closely related to the neurotransmitter serotonin, which is involved in mood, perception, and thought. The serotonin receptors received this substance in a way that indicated the brain hungered for it. At first, it was broken down and utilized for normal brain functions, but when the concentration got too high, weird effects resulted.

From 1990 to 1995, Strassman conducted clinical research at the University of New Mexico's School of Medicine with sixty volunteers who agreed to go through trials of increasing strength with DMT. He kept exact records of what these subjects said under the influence and noted how they often reported visions and experiences that sounded like people who'd described alien encounters and near-death experiences.

In a book on his work, *DMT: The Spirit Molecule,* Strassman associates DMT with the pineal gland, taking his cue from the mystical traditions that pinpointed it as the seat of the soul. He theorized that it may facilitate spiritual transformations via profoundly expanded consciousness, as well as being involved in birth and death experiences. In that case, it could certainly be implicated in the vampiric embrace, in particular with a person taken through mortal death and the rebirth of becoming a vampire. It may be that the vampire's bite releases excess DMT into the brain in a way that imitates the ingestion of high doses of the substance, thus producing the transcendent state that feels as if one is leaving one's body, as well as the perceptual hallucinations.

Let's look more closely at how Strassman describes DMT's physiological function.

At first the experimental subjects drank a DMT-laced tea and smoked DMT, and they reported visions and a feeling that their consciousness was separating from their bodies. They also experienced the "presence" of entities, as if they'd entered into a new realm inhabited by another type of being different from themselves. Then they were given a more powerful form of DMT through intravenous injections. Their perceptions intensified. Some heard inner voices, some were confused, some elated. While on the drug, they behaved in ways they could not recall later, but they did remember the feeling of losing boundaries, which for some was like freedom and for others quite frightening. All of them were affected by the experience and most saw its potential for personal awareness and growth.

One finding from the experiments was that the context in which DMT was taken had a strong influence on the quality and type of experience the subject had. If they were hoping for a transcendent experience, that's where it tended to go. If they were afraid, then anxiety was pronounced. In the context of the vampiric embrace (if DMT is indeed involved), that translates into the positive influence of seduction over aggression. The gentle, attractive vampire lover makes for a more inviting anticipation of what may happen to the brain's release of DMT than the attacking monster, who frightens the victim and inspires defensiveness.

Also, Strassman believes that the drug may shift the brain's ability to become a spiritual receptor. While he views this in terms of the possibility of actual external stimulants (angels and aliens), it could also be that the brain becomes more adept in the processing of something known as memory fields. That is, some researchers have proposed that memories reside not in the physical apparatus of the brain but in quantum energy fields outside the body.

Among the reasons for thinking this is the fact that stimulating certain areas of the brain will produce vivid, three-dimensional memories, but stimulating the same area twice fails to evoke the same memory.

Neurologist Dr. Karl Pribram found that removing parts of the brains of people with epilepsy did not impair their memory, so he proposed in his "holographic theory" that memory was distributed throughout the brain.

Following him, biologist Paul Pietsch removed a salamander's brain and then put it back. The salamander returned to normal, even if the brain was replaced upside down or backward. Even if he minced it!

In the 1960s, psychologist and memory specialist Karl Lashley experimented with mice and discovered that they appeared to be able to "remember" the shortest pathway through a maze even with 90 percent of their brains removed. In another experiment, successive generations of rats ran the same maze with increasingly fewer mistakes. Each was raised in isolation from the others, and yet somehow members of the thirteenth generation acted as if they had experience with the maze that they didn't have. That's suggestive of an inherited memory, but years later, a group of rats with no biological connection to the earlier groups performed just as well as those that had learned the maze through trial and error. Some scientists theorize from these results that memory may be stored in nature not in the individual.

Dr. Melvin Morse, a pediatrician and expert on near-death expe-

riences in children, claims that as we experience trauma, the ability to
process memory intensifies. He attributes this to activation of the right
temporal lobe. He feels that memories can and actually do exist independent of brain functions. He bases his ideas on the work of
Princeton physicist John A. Wheeler, who suggests that the human
mind is woven into the energy fabric of the universe, and that means
that memories are stored all around us in the patterns of life. The
memory that seems to be in our brain may actually be coming into it
from a universal memory field. The right temporal lobe, the one which
some neurologists claim is the cell of mystical experience, appears to
act as a receiver and transmitter of memory-formed energies.

In the discipline known as neurotheology, scientists studying specific regions of the brain are exploring what they dub "the science of
belief." The questions regard how people in an "enlightened age" can
believe in such things as the appearance of the Virgin Mary, conversations with God, and the intervention of angels. The research even
addresses the urge to make myths and rituals, the nature of near-death
experiences, and the associations made between religion and orgasm.
Andrew Newberg, a professor of religious studies at the University of
Pennsylvania, an assistant professor in radiology in their division of
nuclear medicine, and coauthor of *Why God Won't Go Away*, has a
theory about this based on extensive brain research. There is, he
claims, a biological basis for spiritual hunger. It may be that the feelings can be reduced to a brain function or it may be that the higher
reality is real and we connect to it through these brain centers. Depending on one's point of view, either idea works.

What it comes down to is that the possibility of the existence of
God and other spiritual beings—even the devil—is not inconsistent
with science, as has long been believed by both camps.

Newberg teamed up with Eugene d'Aquili, an anthropologist who
had proposed this idea about the spiritual brain back in the 1970s.
Together they used brain-imaging technology to find out what goes
on inside the head during mystical states. Using subjects who engaged

in an intense prayer session or immersed themselves in the peak moments of Buddhist meditation, the researchers applied a SPECT, or single photon emission computed tomography scan, which uses radioactive dye to take "photographs" of the way blood flows through the brain. The subject would go through his or her usual course of meditation, reach a deep state, signal it with a string, and then allow the dye to be injected through an intravenous tube. The SPECT camera then recorded the radioactive emissions via the tracer dye that circulated through the brain, carried by the flow of blood. The tracer quickly locked into the brain cells and remained in place so as to get as accurate a map of the brain as possible, as close to the moment of peak experience as possible. The subjects later described the feelings and experiences they had in order to compare them against the patterns shown by the dye.

Looking over the resulting images of the dye's residue in the brain, the researchers noted something unusual about what they dubbed the orientation association area in the left parietal lobe, also referred to as the OAA. (The right lobe also has an OAA, but it was the left one that showed the anomaly.)

The OAA's chief function is to make a distinction between oneself and the external world so that one can get oriented in three-dimensional reality. That means that it processes information from the five senses, and a normal blood flow in that area indicates that the neurons are firing. The stronger the blood flow, the more activity in that area. In contrast, during states of deep meditation, the blood flow thinned out, depriving the OAA of information. That would give the subject the feeling of freedom from boundaries and limits. There is no distinct self, which in itself is a rather profound experience. It's the ego's version of weightlessness, as real to the brain as anything delivered by the senses, and some view it as the experience of merging with a higher, unlimited consciousness, aka the state of grace, nirvana, and God.

Other researches say that other areas of the brain must disengage for mystical awareness to occur:

- the frontal lobe, which monitors self-awareness

- the right temporal lobe, involved in our sense of time

- the amygdala, which monitors threats in the environment

As far as the brain is concerned, it seems that God is everywhere, and the brain is wired to connect, as long as the conditions are right.

At the University of California at San Diego, it's another story. Flashes of God seem to accompany epileptic experiences—which they had only to read Dostoevsky to learn about. He described that phenomenon in excruciating detail. In Canada, Michael Persinger, a neuroscience researcher, uses helmets fitted with magnets to apply an electromagnetic field to subjects' brains. Most of them report some type of mystical experience, both positive and negative. From these results, he states that religion is nothing more than a function of the brain mixed with a religious context.

More interesting is a neurologist who also practices Zen Buddhism. His name is James Austin, he wrote *Zen and the Brain*, and he's invested several years in developing his ability to meditate. He recalls the experience of a heightened awareness of soundless, empty space in which he felt a sense of utter bliss.

Yet while the brain may produce a euphoric experience that can be described as a connection to a God consciousness, it doesn't exactly produce a belief system that involves commitment and faith. Some people say it is merely "an instrument played by God" to give a rewarding experience to those who apply serious discipline to prayer and retreat. Indeed, they add, it was God who created the brain to allow divine access.

At any rate, what does this all mean for the victim's experience of the vampire? From Dracula to the 1990's role-playing game, *Vampire: the Masquerade*, from Saint Germain to Lestat, there's often a euphoric quality to the embrace that can be tantamount to spiritual transcendence. If there's an endogenous substance, a brain function, or a memory field that can be accessed by means of a heightened experience, then the scientific study of these things can reveal the secret to the vampire's magic. If that heightened experience provides a sense of deified figures around us, then it's not such a leap for the new generation of vampire lovers to regard them as ancient gods.

But we're not finished yet. DMT isn't the only drug that reminds us of fictional accounts of the vampiric transformation. One more must be mentioned, since during the 1990s it became the drug of choice in the vampire subculture.

The Touching Within

In contemporary vampire circles, the attempt to achieve the feeling of being a vampire is often induced by the drug called Ecstasy. This drug, too, works on the serotonin neurotransmitter, with the idea of mimicking the overpowering emotional exultation of mindbody rapture. The Greek word *ekstasis* means "throwing the mind out of its normal state" or "mental transport" and the drug purports to achieve this effect. The feeling reported by users is that one can reach to the sky or go into the underworld to achieve a transcendent state, wherein one might touch the edges of life or death. One thing for sure, you can stay up all night, just like a vampire.

Ecstasy is a synthetic, psychoactive drug, MDMA or 3,4-methylenedioxymethamphetamine. It belongs to a family of drugs known as entactogens, which literally means "a touching within." A German company, Merck Pharmaceuticals, first synthesized MDMA in 1912 as an appetite suppressant. Yet in its use among therapists during the 1970s, MDMA proved to be a gentle disinhibitor, allowing people to open up to one another and talk honestly. They felt more unified and their reported anxiety was at a minimum. MDMA was both stimulating and relaxing. Therapists called it "Adam," a reference to the state of primal ignorance of the need for psychological defenses that it purportedly induces, and they saw benefits in it for treating stress disorders, phobias, depression, addiction, and other fear-based issues.

Ecstasy is the street name, changed by an enterprising dealer who heard about the consciousness-enhancing qualities of the drug. It's also referred to as XTC, E, X, hug, and beans. It moved quietly into the recreational drug scene, yet in 1985 it had become sufficiently popular to be featured in *Time* and *Newsweek*. However, by June of that year, the DEA made it illegal.

Ecstasy is almost always swallowed as a tablet or capsule, but snorting has been reported in some places, as has direct intravenous injection and anal suppository use. A "normal" dose, or "hit," is around 100–125 mg. However, street MDMA tablets vary widely in strength, and they are generally cut with other drugs.

Ecstasy works by affecting one of the brain's key chemicals: it causes the release of serotonin, the neurotransmitter that helps to control mood, anxiety, sleep, aggression, memory, sexuality, and appetite. Lack of serotonin can contribute to depression and cognitive dulling, and may even affect areas of the brain responsible for thought and memory. Those who participate in the "macho ingestion syndrome," which means stacking doses to prove their toughness, are even more vulnerable to the negative effects—particularly with memory.

While serotonin is being released, the effect is a chemical high, but once the drug effect wears off, the serotonin has been depleted. That results in depression or mood swings.

Although chemically related to amphetamines and mescaline (a psychedelic), X causes only minor hallucinogenic alterations of consciousness, perception, movement, or coordination. Unlike psychedelics, information or insight discovered during usage is readily recalled. The person does not feel "stoned." Sensations are enhanced and the user experiences heightened feelings of empathy, emotional warmth, and self-acceptance.

Vampires, like Ecstasy, possess "entactogenic" qualities, luring their victims through a hypnotic "touching within." On the vampire scene, those who identify with the predator prowl in nightclubs and all-night "raves," preying upon those under the influence of Ecstasy-induced euphoria. They understand the similarity between what the drug produces and the vampire mythology. However, the use of Ecstasy has also influenced a shift in that mythology, which we'll deal with in chapter 7.

Now that we've discussed the heightened experience of the vampire's seduction and embrace, let's get right to the main act: what happens when a mortal becomes a vampire.

The Transformation

There appears to be no consensus about how a vampire gets made, either in folklore or fiction. Sometimes it's through a single bite or it stretches over a long period of time as the vampire feeds and the victim weakens. In the movie *Love at First Bite*, the third bite was the charm. In contemporary times, it's even been surmised that a vampire is made via some virus, through being possessed by a reincarnated spirit, or by the awakening of something latent in an individual's personality. For some, vampires are simply an alien breed, a parallel species, or they come from a parallel world.

In certain cultures, all it took to become a vampire was to die unbaptized, in a state of unrepentant sin, a suicide, or a family exile. Sometimes it was the result of something as simple as an encounter with an animal between death and burial, or a witch's curse.

To get a sense of the range of possibilities involving the most popular notions of a mortal becoming an immortal, here's a list:

1. A vampire is made through the bite of another vampire.

2. A vampire is made by draining a mortal of blood and giving him special blood from the progenerative vampire.

3. A vampire is made through some initiation process.

4. A vampire develops from contact with a specific virus.

5. A vampire is made through a supernatural curse.

6. A vampire develops from some unnatural or sinful quirk in a person's personality.

7. A vampire is made through spirit possession.

If we look at the first possibility, which is probably the one most entrenched in the cultural mind-set, we should examine the relationship between vampire and prey. This can be a random attack merely to feed, or more along the lines of a serial killer, in which for some specific reason a victim triggers the vampire's compulsion. Perhaps the vampire is in love.

In the first scenario, if the vampire bites someone, the victim will now become a vampire, and together they will populate the earth with increasingly more vampires, each one making another that will in turn make others each time they attack. While this scenario has a wealth of problems attached to it, notably that the earth would soon be choked with vampires, it does imbue the vampire with an interesting infectiousness and an inability to control its "procreative" powers. It's hungry, it feeds to survive, and it creates another like it that also competes with it for the food source. Not very adaptive.

In contrast, in scenarios two and three, there appears to be some degree of intentionality and choice on the part of the vampire. Among all the prey from which he might drink blood, he decides that certain humans ought to join him in his vampiric state. That means luring them into it, forcing them into it, or responding to their request—even plea—for it. Most recent vampire fiction in which we find a bloodsucker transforming mortals dramatizes this relationship. Some people are food, some are potential companions.

And then again, there are ways to become a vampire, apparently, which involve no contact with a vampire at all.

Dr. Jeanne Keyes Youngson, president of the long-running Count Dracula Fan Club headquartered in Manhattan (now known as the Vampire Empire), has received communications from many different people who claim to be vampires. One in particular stood out to her, and in 1985 she published a pamphlet, "How to Become a Vampire in Six Easy Lessons," written by this alleged vampire, Madeline X.

Youngson believes the question of this woman's actual vampirism is moot, since she appears to know what she's talking about. Admittedly, Madeline X gave it up when she fell in love with a mortal, and her subsequent offspring bore no signs of her blood-seeking nature.

In the pamphlet, she lists a number items and ingredients that one will need for the six-day procedure, and advises that none of the six days should fall on a Saturday. Among the items are eggs, vinegar, a black human hair, and an empty bottle. Then she spells out the preparations day by day. The entire ritual has to be kept secret, because the power of another person's awareness apparently can dissolve the magic.

At any rate, Madeline X advises us on how to handle the eggs, and then moves on to other ingredients, each with its own specific ritual. Chanting and clapping are part of the procedure, and apparently the end result must be pleasing to "the Master." If so, then on the seventh night, you will awaken as a vampire.

Since *Dracula* is our starting point, we'll examine Stoker's concept first. The Count attacks Lucy and Mina, and both are "infected" in such a way as to eventually transform them into creatures of the night. They're not just victims who feed the vampire and die; through them he has reproduced his kind. Even after the vampire is driven away from Mina, who has not yet died, Van Helsing knows that unless Dracula is destroyed before she dies, she will become a vampire. Dracula doesn't even have to kill her himself, which supports the idea that his bite starts an infection that works independent of him.

And yet we know that he has lived a fairly long life with an intense bloodlust, so does this mean that everyone he's taken has turned vampiric or is it possible that he can be selective about which victims become companions? Van Helsing seems to believe that he constantly "procreates," but this idea is based on folklore. We have no other source of information, except that Dracula's homeland appears not to be populated by vampires. The evidence seems to contradict Van Helsing's claims.

Other authors of vampire lore clearly define a more discriminating route.

In Rice's *Vampire Chronicles,* Lestat spies the drunken and depressed Louis de Pointe du Lac in New Orleans and decides to make him into a vampire. Lestat has certainly taken victims before this, and has even transformed a few into vampires—most notably his own mother. However, there's a process for doing it that one doesn't routinely perform with each and every victim. We see Rice's ideas about this when Lestat "makes" Louis.

First, there's a period of initiation. Louis has to prove himself by helping to kill a man and being in the presence of the corpse. Then he has to say that he does indeed want the "Dark Gift." Lestat helps him along by letting him know what it feel like to be at the very edge of death, and Louis decides that while he's been wishing for death during a mourning period for a deceased relative he in fact wants to live. Thus he encourages Lestat to go ahead and make him immortal.

What this means is that Lestat must drain him nearly to the point of death, just before the heart stops beating, and then give him the vampire's magical blood to drink. As it works on him, he goes through a physical dying process, losing his waste matter and feeling the pains of his bodily changes. Yet once the process is accomplished, which appears to take a few hours, he begins to experience the world differently. His senses are heightened to hallucinatory levels and his emotions intensified.

Returning to the idea of immortalized cells under the above scenario, it would seem that the vampire transfers some substance to the candidate vampire that goes to work on the replicative processes of the chromosomal telomeres. It could be something encoded in the vampire's own blood, or some special enzyme that enters the body's information processing system to put telomeric activity into effect. It could also be something in the DNA that scientists have yet to understand, but we'll get to that in a moment.

Given the complexity of blood and the functions of its different parts, it would appear that the white blood cells have some significance in the process of transformation. While some authors like Rice have it that the vampire candidate is drained nearly to the point of death, *some* blood still remains for the heart to keep beating. That means that it will contain red and white blood cells.

To review, white blood cells come in two varieties: phagocytes and lymphocytes. Phagocytes fight infection by destroying bacteria and lymphocytes assist the immune system by producing antibodies to bind antigens (foreign substances) and trigger the immune system to defend itself. The lymphocyte cells present three lines of defense. One patrols the blood stream looking for unfamiliar chemical signatures and sounding the alarm. The second group is programmed to target specific types of invaders, and the third group involves the learning cells. They offer an acquired immune response by reading the viral and bacterial pathogens and destroying their protective coatings with toxins.

For a vampire's blood to fill the mortal's circulatory system, whatever blood is left in the latter may try to fight and reject it. We have several options for bypassing the immune system:

1. The mortal's blood would simply be overwhelmed and crushed.

2. The vampire's blood contains a substance in a biochemical camouflage that disables the defensive lymphocytes at the same time as it harnesses them to create a new vampire.

3. The vampire pathogen shifts and changes too quickly for the mortal immune system to track and fight it.

However it happens, it's clear that something like a virus gets transplanted into the mortal to affect such things as her ability to tolerate the sun, her need for blood, her ability to fight off disease, and her longevity. If the process works like a virus, it goes like this: viral particles consist of a viral jacket wrapped around a strand of DNA or RNA, and this jacket has feelers that then bond to the outside of a cell. Once landed, it can inject its own DNA into the cell, where RNA polymerase interprets its commands and ribosomes create the enzymes it wants. These can create new protective jackets around replicated DNA and then burst from the cell to invade surrounding cells. So the vampire substance might be able to outdistance the mortal immune system, but might it also be able to disable some genetic process?

In 2001, researchers at the University of Missouri created cloned pigs that were engineered to lack a certain gene believed to be responsible for rejecting animal-organ transplants (xenotransplantation). The hope was that removing the gene from the equation would allow the immune system to accept the organ, and this removal was accomplished by introducing DNA that disrupted the gene. The cells that took up the DNA were injected into a surrogate pig mother who produced the clones, which were born without that gene. The next step will be to see whether or not this procedure actually assists in the acceptance of organs. That hasn't yet been done, but what's important for us is that scientists have engineered a way to manipulate the immune system. While there may be the threat of introducing a virus from the transplanted organs, that's not a threat to a vampire. So biology at least shows that it's possible to disable the immune system's rejection apparatus. While vampires aren't using precise genetic engineering, they might be injecting a type of DNA that invades the cells in a similar manner.

It's certainly clear that some kind of genetic process must occur to change a mortal body susceptible to damage and disease into one that not only remains healthy but can even heal itself—sometimes rapidly. It could be some form of genetic mutation set into motion by the vampire's blood.

Genes code for particular traits and direct the cell's life processes. A gene can contain as few as one thousand DNA base pairings or more than two million. Many traits are the result of the interaction of several genes. Cellular activities involve linking amino acids to construct proteins, and sometimes errors occur. Some mistakes can inactivate a protein and cause a mutation, which can also be caused by external forces like radiation or a toxic environment.

Gene mutations come in several forms, based on the pairing of nucleotide bases that compose the DNA sequences:

1. base substitution (the insertion of one subunit of a DNA strand when it should have been another)

2. base addition (adding one more than needed)

3. base deletion (removing one that should be there)

Lack of pigment for the skin is one such mutation, where a dramatic large-scale effect occurs from the change in a single gene. So a reproducing vampire might only affect certain genes to bring out the right traits for producing another vampire.

Yet mutations can also occur in the chromosomes, the result of something as basic as poor nutrition or the creation of free radicals through oxidation. Sometimes a segment weakens and breaks. It might then move to another chromosome or get repositioned on its own chromosome in the wrong way. It may just get lost somewhere in the cell. A set of chromosomes can also have something missing or something added, which happens during "nondisjuncture," or the improper separation of the chromosome during the process in which parent organisms each contribute half of their chromosomes to an offspring. The result can be a genetic defect caused by the wrong number of chromosomes ending up in the cells.

All of these conditions can affect what a person becomes. If the vampiric transformation involves genetic mutations or chromosomal rearrangements, then traits that define someone as a mortal can be engineered to redefine that person as a vampire. (Presumably, we could create a vampire this way in the lab, and thereby get a blend of Dracula and Frankenstein's monster.)

Genetic engineering involves transferring individual genes from one cell to another. In a process that results in what is known as recombinant DNA, the DNA is cut out of one cell and reestablished in a new host. The newly rooted DNA will direct its activity toward the production of a specific type of protein that will affect the cell. It can even produce a new species.

Researchers from different neurobiology centers have transplanted genes that affect innate behavior from one species into another—notably, they put developing neural tissue from a quail into a chicken embryo. When the chick developed and emerged from the egg, it had both quail and chicken neurons. Sometimes the researchers got a chicken that made noises like a quail, and other times the chick showed quaillike headbobbing. The chicks did this automatically, without exposure to quails. Yet when they grew up and mated, they produced normal chicken offspring, which suggested that something intrinsic to the tissue itself was critical to the behaviors.

The implanted cells also seemed to influence perception, as some of the "chick-ails" preferred the sound of a quail to that of a chicken. Scientists hypothesize that those transplanted cells sent signals to the forebrain to elicit the behavior. How such a transfer would influence more complex behaviors is still unknown (at least in the lab). The point is that certain behaviors coded in DNA can be transferred, and DNA foreign to a specific organism can be accepted by DNA from that organism that will affect how it develops.

Yet overt manipulation like this is not required for the body to inspire its own rearrangements and become something other than what it is. Sometimes it happens via what's called transposons or "selfish genes." They insert themselves into other chromosomes and thereby reorient the cellular process, causing mutation. Generally this happens on a small scale, but it could be these very genes that hold the key to the vampire transformation. To talk about them, we'll back up and describe what scientists have called "junk" DNA.

DNA that seems to have no role in coding for the regulation of life processes is junk DNA—and there's quite a large percentage of it in the body's cells. Scientists think it might be from inactivated viruses from past evolutionary history (also known as cryptic viruses). There's even evidence that genetic exchanges between these cryptic viruses and active viruses from outside the organism can help the active viruses to repair themselves. (That could be an aspect of the vampire's self-healing ability.) When an active virus mates with a cryptic virus, it can then evolve. So what goes on inside junk DNA can show us a whole new side of ourselves.

Selfish genes, or transposons, are part of this junk DNA. They replicate themselves faster than most other genes and they act only in their own best interests. They can be detrimental to the organism and are thus considered parasitic (vampiric), especially because they may obliterate their healthy counterparts on other chromosomes. Often they're activated under stressful or unusual conditions, which is a good description of the state of a person prior to being turned into a vampire. In fact, there's some evidence to suggest that as these transposons pile up, they may physically change the chromosome and produce a genetic anomaly.

Junk DNA mutates quickly, but it isn't considered to be functional. Yet what's not functional for a mortal may be just fine for an immortal. If selfish genes were to replicate and overpower an organism, they might turn the entire organism into something that behaves according to the dictates of the selfish gene—a vampire.

Now that we've seen how the biology of transformation may work, let's talk about some of its effects.

Magnified Senses

There's a long tradition in vampire fiction for transformed mortals to acquire extra powers, including heightened senses. Rather than go through these powers one by one, we'll examine what may happen with vision and olfaction, because the same principles would hold for the others.

Dracula, as well as other vampires, can see in the dark. The visual system uses almost one-fourth of the brain's cortex, connecting to receptors on the retina. Rods, which pick up levels of light, and cones, which detect colors, comprise the photoreceptor cells. Using the light-sensitive protein rhodopsin, rods help us to perceive motion and shades of black and white, so they make vision possible in situations with dim lighting. Yet to have great acuity with that kind of vision, we sacrifice something in our detection of colors. Only so many rods and cones can fit in the inner surface of the eye.

Vampires who can experience the world of color with greater clarity rely on three forms of opsins, the chemicals that bind to the cone cells for sensitivity to light of a specific wavelength. It might be that these chemicals are processed more efficiently in vampires, that they have a stronger effect on the receptors, or that they hit the optic nerve with more force, and that nerve connects to the occipital lobe in the brain. As mortals, we can see within a certain range of electromagnetic spectrum, but we have limitations. Vampires may have the means to broaden that range, verging into the infrared and ultraviolet areas. It's all a matter of degree of sensitivity of the receptors, and that's affected by genetic programming.

Vampires, like animals, appear to be better than mortals not only at seeing things but at sniffing things out. Those that can change into wolves and mingle with rats probably have a sharpened olfactory apparatus. Rats, for example, have almost the same level of ability for differentiating among odors that humans have for faces. In fact, understanding how the odor receptors work to encode smells that pass from nose to brain provides information for the biology of more complex behaviors.

It's thought that the sense of smell was the first to evolve and it's more closely associated with memory than are the other senses. The average person can recognize several thousand scents, drawn to the cilia of receptors in the nasal passages. Each area, called the epithelium, has about five million neurons. If its area were extended, the odor detection level would increase as well. On the other hand, biologists hypothesize that over the course of evolution, as humans came to rely more heavily on their eyes than their noses, up to 60 percent of our odor receptors have become nonfunctional. They're still there; we just don't use them. It could be that the vampire condition wakes up those receptors and allows the vampire to behave more efficiently as a predator. In a complex environment, the ability to process odors and select the one that leads to success favors the nose that knows.

As for learning new behaviors attendant upon an increase in sensory apparatus, scientists are discovering that the brain regenerates cells in the hippocampus region of the forebrain—a specific type of learning center associated with memory. Tracey Shores, a behavioral neuroscientist at Rutgers University and associate professor in its psychology department, says that in fact the hippocampus generates up to five thousand new cells every day, but most die a quick death. To see if a certain pattern of learning increased the life span of these cells, researchers used the Morris water maze. They trained rats to rely on spatial cues to find a platform in a pool of water. The rats learned with one part of the brain when the platform was kept above water where they could see it, but submerging it forced them to use the hippocampus. The result was that hippocampus-dependent learning increased the survival of the newly generated neurons. While the jury is out on exactly what this means, it does bode well for mortals becoming vampires who must rely on a new mode of orientation for learning. The brain's plasticity is essential for adaptation and survival.

Now that we have some idea about how a vampire is made and what the transformed mortal may experience, we'll take up the subject of psychology to see how the mythology of vampires has affected some people. There is such a thing as a vampire mental illness—a mutation of the personality, so to speak.

FOUR
Vampire Personality Disorder

✦━╋━✦

In an episode of *Kindred: The Masquerade,* a vampire named Stark-weather (based on a famous spree killer from the 1950s) goes on a rampage. He's locked up and studied by psychiatrists, and when he tells them he's a vampire, they diagnose him as schizophrenic. Since he's clearly a danger to others and possibly to himself, he remains under observation. However, since he's actually the "real thing," he kills the psychiatrist who comes to talk with him and then escapes, leaving behind a bloody signature, "Blood Brother," which only confirms the diagnosis.

While there's no category for this kind of behavior in the psychiatrist's code book, the *Diagnostic and Statistical Manual for Mental Disorders-IV,* as there is for narcissistic or antisocial personality disorder, there's certainly evidence that people walk among us who act like vampires. Something psychological drives them and frames their fantasy. They thrive on the resources of those they encounter, drain them until they're empty, sometimes even bite or kill them, and move on in search of the next source.

That's the nature of the vampire. From simple exploitation to out-right murder, those with what I call vampire personality disorder (VPD) deserve a psychiatric category all their own. Under this concept I include compulsive sexual killers excited by blood, diagnosed "clinical" vampires, and people who use the vampire image to act out some fantasy scenario in a way that harms others. I might even include psychological vampires, those people who encourage a codependent relationship merely for the purpose of "using up" another person to gratify themselves.

While there are many more cases than we can hope to cover here, we can examine the range of vampiric behaviors and see what the psychologists have to say.

Famous Vampire Killers

We know of several dozen sensational cases of men and women who committed crimes that involved drinking blood from a victim. Sometimes the offenders attacked by biting and sometimes they committed murder. A quick list of blood-obsessed historical figures includes

- Erzebet Bathory

- Gilles de Rais

- Vincenzo Verzeni

- Bela Kiss

- Martin Dumollard

- Fritz Haarman

- Peter Kürten

VAMPIRE PERSONALITY DISORDER   103

We'll save some of these cases for later chapters, but take a look at a few of them now.

Erzebet Bathory

She was a Hungarian countess born in 1560 and reputed to have bathed in the blood of virgins to restore her beauty. While that's the stuff of legend, there's evidence that she did harm and kill quite a number of people. Among vampire aficionados, she's considered one of the first known real-life vampires.

Apparently Erzebet experienced overwhelming seizures that produced a violent rage, but since she had the status of nobility, she got away with more than an ordinary person could have. She grew up, married, and managed the affairs of a castle, learning from her sadistic husband how to discipline the peasants who worked the land. For example, he taught her how to spread honey over a naked woman and leave her out for the bugs.

After her husband died in 1604, Erzebet moved to Vienna, yet his absence didn't gentle her in any way. In fact, she increased her arbitrary punishments and was soon beating the servant girls mercilessly. Eventually she started to butcher them, assisted by other women. She might stick pins into sensitive body parts, cut off a girl's fingers, or break the bones of her face. In the winter, women were dragged outside, doused in water, and left to freeze to death. When Erzebet was ill, she supposedly even had girls brought to her bed so that she could bite off their noses or pieces of their flesh.

She might have continued unabated had she not turned her blood thirst against young noblewomen. After she killed one in 1609 and tried to disguise the murder as a suicide, the authorities investigated.

They arrested Erzebet the following year and tried her in two separate trials. In the second one, a register found in her home was introduced as evidence; it indicated that she'd had as many as 650 victims. Each name was entered in her handwriting. She was imprisoned in a small room in her own castle, where she died three years

later. After her death, the rumors that she'd actually bathed in the
blood of her young victims ran rampant.

Historian Raymond McNally, author of *Dracula Was a Woman*, made a
case that Bram Stoker was influenced by accounts of the life of Bathory
while writing *Dracula*; he also argued that Stoker's vampire seems to grow
younger after taking the blood of young women.

While it's difficult to know what motivated Erzebet, other killers
since her time have been easier to study. Some are simply excited by
the sight or taste of blood, others are deluded about their need for it,
and still others have been so influenced by their identification with the
vampire that they act like one.

Bela Kiss

This man's nefarious activities started with his wife's infidelity. In
Czinkota, Hungary, Bela Kiss married a pretty woman fifteen years
younger than he. She took up with a neighbor, and in 1912 both of
them disappeared. Then around Budapest other women turned up
missing, and when Kiss was drafted into the army in 1914, he, too,
disappeared, supposedly after receiving a fatal wound. Apparently
he'd bought a number of metal drums in which to store gas, and army
officers confiscated seven of them. The drums seem to be full, so the
officer, opened them only to find in each the alcohol-preserved corpse
of a naked woman. Not only had the victims been strangled, but they
also had wounds on their necks and had been drained of blood. A
search was begun and seventeen more barrels (other reports give the
number variously as between nineteen and twenty-four) were found,
including those containing Kiss's wife and her boyfriend. Since authorities believed Kiss was dead, they closed the case.

A vampiric turn of events occurred when they heard from the nurse who supposedly had attended to the wounded Kiss at the battlefront. Her description of the dying young soldier named Kiss failed to match the appearance of the man thought to have committed the murders. Then reports of Kiss surfaced in Budapest. Each time the police checked out the rumors of a sighting, Kiss had vanished. He was never caught.

Psychological Assessments

Throughout the ages, attacks on people have been attributed to supernatural creatures like werewolves and vampires, but during the mid-1880s, a German neurologist named Richard von Krafft-Ebing noted the sexual presentation of the attacks, observing that they were compulsive and often aimed at a victim in a way that suggested lust or anger. His book *Psychopathia Sexualis*, published in 1886, describes a violent eroticism triggered by blood or corpses in many of the cases. Some of the most brutal acts were done postmortem.

It seems that some individuals can get excited only at the sight of fresh blood. In 1827 a moody twenty-four-year-old vine dresser named Leger murdered a twelve-year-old girl in the woods. He admitted that he also drank her blood, mutilated her genitals, tore out and ate part of her heart, and buried her remains. He talked about this with no show of emotion or remorse, and when he was sentenced to death, he seemed just as indifferent.

There was also the case of the man who cut his arm for his wife to suck on before sex because it aroused her so strongly. Another man dissected his victims and got so caught up in the gore that he trembled with the desire to wallow in it and consume it.

"A great number of so-called lust murders," said Krafft-Ebing, "depend upon combined sexual hyperesthesia and parasthesia. As a result of this perverse coloring of the feelings, further acts of bestiality with the corpse may result." He also pointed out that "anomalies of the sexual functions are especially seen among civilized races," and it's a generally accepted fact among experts on serial sex crimes that most of the truly perverse acts are committed by white males. For some, the normal sexual stimulants simply fail to work and they seek out, and then get addicted to, more bizarre forms of eroticism.

In Krafft-Ebing's time, doctors who dealt with such cases found no trace of any hereditary disease, epilepsy, or brain disorders. Many of the lust killers had mistreated animals and failed to hold jobs for very long.

By the time clinicians began to address the vampiric manifestation in their patients, interpretations had a decidedly psychoanalytic flavor, influenced by the popularity of Freudian thought. In a paper published in 1931 called "The Vampire," Ernest Jones, a famous disciple of Freud's, viewed the sucking and biting activities of the vampire fantasy as a regressive infantile manifestation. The person has fixated at the rather primitive oral stage of developmental maturity, during which most pleasure is centered around the mouth. The person harbors incestuous desires for his or her parent of the opposite sex and then feels guilt over those desires. He or she suppresses a certain degree of anger against that parent and may even have fantasies of assault and murder, either against the parent or by the parent against themselves.

In contrast, followers of Jung, one of Freud's students and an early apostate of orthodox psychoanalysis, might view vampire delusions and behavior as part of an archetypal pattern born of universal primal instincts. An archetype is a blueprint of basic human experience, based on our universally shared developmental and reproductive biology. Archetypes include the innocent child, the wise elder, the villain, and the young hero. Those who develop their needs through the vampire fantasy may be expressing their craving for either power or surrender. In fact, the fantasy may even be a manifestation of a deep spiritual thirst connected to what Jung called the archetypal Self—which some see as another way to understand our experience of God.

Jungian analyst Robert McCully of the Medical University of South

Carolina documented a case in the 1960s of auto-vampirism, where an adolescent boy drank his own blood. McCully described how this boy would puncture his carotid artery and force the blood to spurt in such a way as to catch it in his mouth and drink it, which proved to be highly erotic to him. Even as he cut and drank, he experienced sexual excitement and had an orgasm.

To comprehend this behavior, McCully researched vampire lore from ancient cultures and concluded that "some long forgotten archetype somehow got dislodged from the murky bottom of the past and emerged to take possession of a modern individual." The boy probably suffered from immature ego development, McCully said, and was compensating for it by acting in a way that got him closer to the kinds of acts people participate in when they wish to drop their emotional guard and became bound to larger forces. McCully speculated that the vampire image has been contained in "the psychic substance" of humanity since the dawn of history. On the positive side, the vampire's promise of renewal meant transformation; on the dark side, the predator survives at the expense of another.

McCully also interpreted the culture's interest in vampires as a tendency to "extravert" its collective shadow side. We project away from ourselves those aspects of being human that we wish to deny or eradicate. "The vampire is surely a vivid symbol for the sado-masochistic side of evil," he said.

Malingering the Vampire

Although true cases of human vampirism are rare, some criminals find in them a means to create a certain impression on a jury. Malingering is the term for faking a mental disorder by feigning the symptoms. One of the most famous cases of so-called vampirism, that of John George Haigh, was more than likely a fraud. It didn't work with the jury, but many authors today who pen books about vampires accept

Haigh's claims at face value and present him as a genuine example of aberrant vampire behavior. Having studied the case, I see him as no more a "vampire" than Kenneth Bianchi, one of the Hillside Stranglers in Los Angeles, who was a genuine case of multiple personality disorder.

Haigh was arrested in England in 1949 for the possible murder of a missing woman who lived in the hotel where he resided. She'd told friends that she was meeting him that day and she was never heard from again. Upon his arrest for suspicion of foul play, Haigh immediately asked about the local mental institution. That, in itself, was suspicious.

Rather quickly, he launched into a confession that involved killing six people in order to drink their blood. He said that he lured them into a storage area that he rented and then hit them over the head to kill them. Then he would cut open an artery in their throat and fill a cup with blood, which he proceeded to drink, claiming that it made him feel better. To be rid of the evidence, he would dissolve the corpse in large metal drums filled with acid. He later added the names of three more victims to his tally, none of which could be traced to real people.

Haigh insisted that he was not motivated by personal gain. Instead, he'd been plagued by nightmares of demons telling him to kill and of images of bloody crucifixes. "It was not their money but their blood that I was after," he stated, adding that he'd often licked his own bloody wounds to gain spiritual enlightenment. At some point, he'd simply realized that he needed to get fresh blood from others. It was all quite compulsive. He couldn't help himself.

Nevertheless, each time Haigh actually did kill someone and dissolved that person's body and personal effects, coincidentally he was also in debt. Each time he killed, he devised an elaborate scheme to acquire his victim's assets. There is no evidence that he acted under a compulsion, and the planning and care with which he committed and cleaned up his crimes fails to support a case for mental illness. In fact, twelve physicians examined him while he was in prison and only one thought he had an aberrant mental condition—egocentric paranoia. Even this doctor, working for the defense, did not think the blood dreams or claims of blood drinking were authentic. The rest of the doctors believed that he was malingering. In fact, his apparent lack of interest in sex further undermined the idea that he had any compulsion at all.

A detailed inspection of Haigh's personal history reveals that he had studied various forms of psychosis, so his claim to be a vampire in need of human blood was most likely the result of a wish to present the most shocking case he could think of. It was simply a way to avoid the death penalty. In fact, he was no stranger to faking things: when it had suited his purposes, he'd posed as a doctor, a lawyer, and an engineer. In this case, he posed as a psychotic person who drank blood.

But it didn't work. The jury convicted him, and as he awaited his execution in prison (where three more psychiatrists examined him), he showed no further compulsion to drink blood.

The Criminal Type

Nevertheless, there are cases of people who do feel so compelled. In San Francisco in 1998, Joshua Rudiger, twenty-two, claimed to be a two-thousand-year-old vampire and went about town slashing the necks of the homeless with a knife. He hurt three men and killed a woman sleeping in a doorway, and when the investigation of one of these murders led to his arrest, he insisted that he was driven by a need to drink human blood. In fact, the woman he killed did actually die from a severe loss of blood.

"Prey is prey," he reportedly told investigators. He also said that he was being punished for a crime he'd committed in another lifetime and had no choice but do what he was doing. It was his destiny.

Not surprisingly, Rudiger had a history of mental illness, having claimed at different times to be a vampire and a ninja warrior. Dr. Paul Good, a forensic psychiatrist, described Rudiger's background in court as strewn with disadvantages, and reported that when the accused was four, he was diagnosed as psychotic. Rudiger had been in several foster homes and psychiatric hospitals, where he was caught licking the chests of other patients. He told a therapist that he was going to go suck out the blood of the people around him. Released when he was eighteen, he started his attacks. In 1997, after shooting a friend with a bow and arrow, Rudiger was diagnosed with schizophrenia and bipolar disorder. The following year, he turned to murder.

Although his attorney entered a plea of not guilty by reason of insanity, Rudiger was found guilty of second-degree murder. Despite the attorney's insistence that he be sent to a psychiatric hospital for treatment, he got twenty-three years-to-life in prison.

Not long after this in the same city, Eric David Knight was arrested for biting a bus driver in the neck to suck his blood, telling police, "I need the cure."

Is there a difference between "criminal types" and someone who's genuinely mentally ill? For many years, those who attacked for blood were considered criminals with aberrant appetites, and even Bram Stoker raises this idea in *Dracula*. Van Helsing talks about Dracula as a born criminal, and Mina agrees. She cites the work of "Nordau and Lombroso" and then says that the Count has "an imperfectly formed mind." It is thus clear that by 1893, some prominent theories were circulating. Let's check on the state of the art to which these characters refer.

The science of man, or anthropology, had its roots in the early nineteenth century when scholars presented differing arguments about the origins of the different species of human beings. Researchers looked for evidence in the formation of bones and facial features, especially the cranium. Then Darwin came on the scene and his theories intensified the debate. In France, *bertillonage* or anthropometry, in which eleven separate measurements were taken of criminals who were arrested to build an informational data bank, became the rage. One purpose of this was to facilitate the identification of recidivists, but such data was soon supplanted by fingerprint techniques. Another purpose was to aid in the development of theories of criminality, or "inferior vs. superior" types.

European anthropologists compiled hundreds of measurements from skeletons and continued to apply what they learned to ideas about criminal types. The father of criminology, an Italian anthropologist named Cesare Lombroso, was convinced that certain types were born criminals—*l'uomo delinquente*—and these men could be identified by specific physical traits, such as a bulging brow, apelike nose, bushy eyebrows that met over the nose, large jaws, and disproportionately long arms. Those traits signaled a throwback to more primitive species and could be seen in a craving for evil (including drinking blood) and the desire to torture, mutilate, and kill. During the 1870s, he became quite famous for his theories, which appeared to be supported by evolutionary science, and it came to be the case that appearance alone could be a factor in convicting people of crimes. What a person looked like was also exploited to extend a prison term. Lombroso's ideas inspired widespread prejudices that victimized innocent people.

Prior to the publication of *Dracula*, Cesare Lombroso published *L'Uomo Delinquente* in 1876 (translated in French in 1895 as *L'homme Criminel*). His disciple was Max Nordau, who published an English translation called *Degeneration*, also in 1895. In his book, Lombroso elaborated on the idea of the degenerative personality, which soon became a preoccupation throughout Europe, with many good people worrying over their latent heritage.

Scholar Ernest Fontana points out that Stoker uses these ideas in *Dracula* when the Count tells Jonathan Harker that he is a descendent of the warlike Huns, and even of Attila himself. As a vampire, he is set apart from normal human beings, which is how the criminal was similarly conceived during the nineteenth century. Lombroso saw his criminal types as genetically predestined for criminality, having characteristics identical to the epileptic. In fact, Dracula resembles Lombroso's criminal in that he has a hooked aquiline nose, massive eyebrows, and pointed ears characteristic of apes. His sharp teeth come over his lips, with developed canines, and he shows an unusual agility, especially with his toes.

When Dracula selects his victims, he looks for those with whom he may share a primitive kinship—traits of which they themselves may be unaware. They must be capable of the same sort of savagery and attraction to a precivilized world as Dracula himself. Renfield is clearly of this type, but so are Dracula's women, including Mina and Lucy. Even their civilized ways cannot prevent their return to atavistic behaviors, because these are innate in their being. Even as Dracula is destroyed, his blood mingles with that of future generations through Mina's child. There's no escape from this primal force.

However, Lombroso's theories eventually fell out of favor. You couldn't tell a "criminal type" from physical appearance, and "criminal types" were often much more complex than the theory allowed, as were "civilized types." Yet it took us into the 1970s before handsome, intelligent killers like Ted Bundy shocked us into realizing that even the nicest person could harbor vicious traits. Even today, many lay people expect a criminal to look a certain way.

Rather than view the vampire as a criminal type, then, it is more instructive to narrow the category and examine the underlying mental illness. Thus we turn to the notion of "clinical vampirism."

The Clinical Vampire

It's not fair to say that all of those who identify with the vampire are mentally ill or have a personality disorder, and we'll see that more clearly when we look into the vampire scene of the 1990s. Yet there's no denying that some people who adopt a vampire persona use it as a license to manifest violence against others.

There's quite a difference between a diagnosed clinical vampire and someone with a violent sexual fetish who acts it out in a vampiric manner. The former is often delusional to some degree, as we saw with Rudiger, while the latter exercises some rational control. For the purpose of understanding VPD, we'll stick with cases that fit the former category.

Many psychiatrists and psychologists have written about vampiric symptoms. In an article on just what clinical vampirism means, psychiatrist Philip D. Jaffe and juvenile delinquency expert Frank DiCataldo first make a distinction between those who drink their own blood for self-gratification (as in McCully's case history) and those who crave the blood of others. They look over a range of papers to summarize the way psychiatry approaches these disturbed people. Too often psychiatric professionals simply group disorders that share generic vampire characteristics in a single category—and this article seems to be a case in point.

To be clear about what they mean by *clinical vampirism,* they offer a case. Although they disguise the name, it's not hard to figure out from other public reports that this is the disturbing case of James Riva.

Riva claimed to hear the voice of a vampire before he shot his grandmother four times in the spring of 1980. He then tried in vain to drink her blood from the wound in order to get eternal life. Finally, he set her corpse on fire. He claimed to have acted in self-defense because she was drinking his blood while he was asleep. He believed that everyone was a vampire and that he needed to do something to become like everyone else. The secret, he was told, was to kill someone and drink that person's blood. Afterward, the vampires would throw a party for him.

How he arrived at this delusion shows the progression of his mental illness, coupled with a helpless family and a medical system that did not have appropriate procedures to deal with him. His parents were perfectly ordinary, his father being an engineer and his mother a teacher. On the side, she taught astrology, which Riva interpreted as witchcraft. He claimed that she abused him, but his accounts of this varied sufficiently to put the claim in doubt.

At the age of five, Riva had pneumonia, and it was during his convalescence that he started drawing pictures of bloody needles and open wounds. He became enraged by something his father had done and rigged a mechanism intended to hit him in the head with a hammer. Riva's depictions of death soon became so graphic that a teacher notified his parents. It wasn't long before he became an avid fan of horror novels.

Fascinated with vampires since the age of thirteen, he drew pictures of violent acts and began to eat things possessing a bloodlike consistency. He killed animals, including a horse, to drink their blood. He also punched a friend in the nose and tried to spear another in order to procure blood from them, and claimed that he had attacked strangers to get it, but didn't want to kill anyone. He kept an ax by his bedroom door and once told a psychiatrist he was going to kill his father. He took to walking around mostly at night.

He appeared to his mother to be in the grip of a serious mental illness, so she would not allow him to live in their home. When he told a psychiatrist that he was hearing male voices warning him to watch out for vampires, he was diagnosed as a paranoid schizophrenic. Riva went through several hospitalizations but failed to recover—in fact, he obtained blood from other patients. He tried living with his family again, but they were terrified of him, so he moved in with his grandmother.

He decided that at night she was using an ice pick to get blood from him—although she was an invalid in a wheelchair. He also believed that she was poisoning his food. On the day that he killed her, he was convinced that he was going to die. He got a gun, painted the bullets gold, dressed in a suit, and confronted his grandmother. She begged him not to hurt her, but he shot her in the heart.

Despite a confusing courtroom battle between mental-health experts, the jury returned a verdict of second-degree murder, with a life term. From prison, Riva sent threatening letters to his mother, believing that she was responsible for his conviction. He showed every indication of extreme paranoia. He stopped drinking blood in prison, he said, because he couldn't get enough and he thought his body, used to human tissue consumption, was metabolizing his own tissues. When he tried to kill a guard, he was reassigned to a forensic hospital. He'd never wanted to kill anyone, he assured interviewers; he just wanted blood.

Jaffe and DiCataldo use this case to discuss vampirism as indicative of an unstable sense of self. They differentiate it from psychopathy, a personality disorder that allows for more organized behavior than Riva exhibited. Yet if the two conditions come together (become comorbid, as the psychiatrists like to say), then a truly dangerous individual is the result.

In fact, psychopaths actually exhibit behaviors that one could call vampiric. More subtle than drinking blood is the "vampire" who targets vulnerable people to drain their "resources"—everything from money to self-esteem to life itself. Such a person is a narcissistic psychopath. Many people think that psychopaths are always criminals, but in fact they're simply remorseless manipulators, some of whom choose to engage in criminal acts. They're also found in large systems like corporations or political parties and manipulate their way through the ranks. Sometimes they even become entrepreneurs or adventurers, because they love risk.

The most striking thing about a vampiric type of psychopath is that he feels no guilt over what he does. You can't appeal to his conscience. He just doesn't care. He takes what he needs and moves on to the next victim. What he wants is the excitement of getting something from someone else at the other person's expense. Research indicates that psychopaths process information differently than other people do. They appear to have an undercharged and hyperreactive autonomic nervous system. That means they're motivated to do things that will excite them. In other words, like vampires, they exploit people to feed off the energy the game arouses.

Among those traits that align them with the vampire are:

- superficial, agenda-motivated charm

- deceptive and manipulative behavior

- a view of their own needs as dominant

- a lack of empathy

- poor self-control

- involvement in multiple short-term relationships; promiscuity

- the appearance of an ordinary life that covers criminal behavior

- a low level or absence of feeling

While it seems that clinical vampirism is definable according to whatever theory the mental-health professional takes, there's one definition that has stability, and that one, interestingly, is based on a character in *Dracula*.

Renfield's Syndrome

Psychologist Richard Noll, author of *Vampires, Werewolves, and Demons,* says that the clinical cases of vampirism have things in common with fiction and folklore, and in fact these people go much further in terms of brutality than the vampire tales record. "Man's actual capacity for evil," he says in *Bizarre Diseases of the Mind,* "far outstrips any imaginary evils."

Noll is noted for his suggestion to rename clinical vampirism Renfield's syndrome. Contrary to some popular notions, Dracula's visit to England had nothing to do with Renfield's desire to drink blood. This lunatic was already a patient under Dr. Seward's care before Dracula arrived in that country. Seward had made many notes in his journal about Renfield's zoophagy, or desire to consume lives, starting with flies and working up to more complicated life-forms like cats.

Given his unstable frame of mind, Renfield becomes the person that Dracula exploits to gain entrée into the asylum. He gets Renfield to let him in and then commands him as a slave. Noll points out that this is consistent with a notion that the devil hones in on those suffering from delusions, as described in Johann Wier's *De Praestigiis Daemonum* from 1593. He believes that Stoker provided a human counterpart to the vampire, both of whom desire to absorb lives, and Noll names clinical vampirism after Renfield because clinical vampires are living humans.

To get right to it, people having the symptoms of this syndrome are primarily male, and they tend to endow blood with mystical qualities, as if it could somehow enhance their lives or empower them. Noll, a professor of clinical psychology, described the typical progression into this mental condition.

"Renfield's syndrome is a psychiatric syndrome and the character of Renfield lived out in his own life the same stages of development that clinical vampires manifest. The first stage involves some event that happens before puberty where the child is excited in a sexual way by blood injury or the ingestion of blood. At puberty it becomes fused with sexual fantasies, and typically the person with Renfield's syndrome begins with autovampirism. That is, they begin to drink their own blood and then move on to other living creatures. That's the zoophagous element that Dr. Seward talks about in *Dracula*. The typical progression in many cases is ingesting blood from other people. That's what we know from the few cases we have on record. It has fetishistic and compulsive components to it and it's more than likely that if you used the *DSM-IV* for diagnosis, you would classify it as one of the paraphilias.

"The novel was published in 1897, and at that time in both occultism and science, there was a great deal of belief in the idea of 'correspondences,' where two beings who shared some sort of essence would eventually find each other. That's an ancient scientific theory that goes back to the Greeks, and by the nineteenth century, it had become an occult belief. However, in biology, the theory of vitalism was to some degree a theory of correspondences. The term 'gene' wasn't coined until 1909, and Mendel published his famous work in 1900, so before we really knew the mechanisms of heredity, it was thought that some vital force was passed down in a way that like would attract like. There was also a theory of degeneracy that was based on the idea that degenerates would attract one another. It takes one to know one.

"I think Stoker used Renfield as a literary device because he needed not only a supernatural vampire, and therefore an immortal one, but also a mortal vampire. I think it makes the figure of Dracula less distant, absolute, and supernatural. I think Stoker understood that if he could show that within human beings the same psychological characteristics could be manifested as those found in the supernatural being, it would be more comprehensible to readers. Having a mortal vampire probably kicked off all sorts of feelings of recognition, and having Renfield die in the novel confirms that he's mortal."

In his book, Noll adds that blood will sometimes take on a mystical significance as a symbol of life and power. Ingesting it produces an experience of well-being. In short, Renfield's syndrome is a sexual compulsion in which blood drinking is a necessary component.

While many professionals, Noll among them, believe that clinical vampirism is predominantly a male phenomenon, there have certainly been cases of women who developed an erotic attraction to blood.

Often they didn't attack people, so they may not have come to the attention of doctors on psychiatric wards. Yet several women have talked freely to reporters about how they were treating a bruised knee or applying bandages to their own cuts when they grew excited over the act. After that, they sought out ways to lick a wound and imagined themselves partaking in a sacred ritual. The experience made them feel more alive.

The clinical vampirism that most concerns us involves violence. We've already seen historical cases of this mental instability, and one case that clearly fits Renfield's syndrome is that of the "Vampire of Sacramento."

Richard Trenton Chase was afraid of disintegrating. To prevent this from happening, he needed blood. During the late 1970s, Chase killed several people before the police arrested him. In his apartment, they discovered evidence that he was planning to kill again over forty more times. His criterion for entering a house, he later confessed, was simply being able to find an unlocked door, because into those homes that were locked he was not invited—just like a vampire.

He was preoccupied with any sign that something was wrong with him, and he once entered an emergency room looking for the person who had stolen his pulmonary artery. He also complained that bones were coming out through the back of his head, his stomach was backward, and his heart often stopped beating. His life grew increasingly disordered and he sank into hypochondria and drug abuse.

Chase soon began to kill and disembowel rabbits that he caught or bought, and eat their entrails raw. Sometimes he would put the intestines with the animal's blood into a blender, liquefy them, and drink this concoction in an alleged effort to keep his heart from shrinking. He once injected rabbit blood into his veins and got very ill. He believed this rabbit had ingested battery acid and that this seeped into his own stomach, but in fact he had a bad case of blood poisoning.

While incarcerated in a psychiatric facility, Chase bit the heads off birds (like Renfield) and was known to the hospital staff as Dracula. Once he was out on his own, he purchased or stole dogs and cats to drink their blood.

Eventually he was deemed no longer a danger and released. Although on antipsychotic medication, he remained unsupervised. One day, police officers found Chase's Ford Ranchero stuck in sand near Pyramid Lake in Nevada. Two rifles lay on the seat along with a pile of men's clothing. Blood smears on the vehicle's interior and a blood-filled white plastic bucket containing a liver made them not a little suspicious. When they spotted Chase through binoculars, he was nude, and blood was smeared all over his body. He saw the officers and ran, but they caught up with him and took him back to his pickup. He claimed that the blood was his. It had "seeped out" of him. The liver, it turned out, was from a cow.

Then he grew bolder.

He found the door at the Wallin home in Sacramento, California, unlocked. Entering, he encountered Teresa Wallin, twenty-two and three months pregnant. He raised his pistol and shot her twice. She fell and Chase then knelt over her prostrate body, firing another bullet into her head. Then he dragged her into the bedroom, retrieved a knife and empty yogurt container from the kitchen, and went to work on the body.

Hours later, Terry's husband, David, found her. She lay just inside the door, on her back, her clothing in disarray. Her left nipple was carved off, her torso cut open below the sternum, and her spleen and intestines pulled out. She'd been stabbed repeatedly in the lung, liver, diaphragm, and left breast. Her kidneys had been cut out, one was put back, and her pancreas was severed in two. In her mouth was dog feces.

On January 27, 1978, Chase killed Evelyn Miroth, a male friend who was visiting her, her six-year-old son, Jason, and her infant nephew. Chase drank Evelyn's blood and mutilated the baby's body in the bathroom. When he left the premises, he took it with him. Soon afterward he was arrested.

In prison, he told another inmate that he needed the blood to stop blood poisoning and that he'd grown tired of hunting for animals. He had never felt compelled to kill. He simply thought the blood would help him. At his trial, he was convicted of six counts of first-degree murder and sentenced to be executed. However, the day after Christmas 1980, he swallowed an overdose of antidepressants and died in his cell.

A New Development

Instability and mental illness appear to influence the manner in which such offenders violate another person for blood. In Renfield's syndrome, a blood-linked event becomes associated with sexual excitement, and then delusions intensify a belief in one's imagined need. Some people with psychological disorders get involved in the role-playing world of the vampire scene and seem unable to draw the line between reality and fantasy.

In early 2002, a German couple was tried for killing a friend seven months earlier in what appeared to be a satanic vampire ritual. Manuela Ruda, twenty-three, and her husband Daniel, twenty-six, stabbed Frank Haagen sixty-six times, drank his blood, and left his decomposing body next to the oak coffin in which Manuela liked to sleep. She claimed that she'd gotten a taste for vampirism in Britain and had delivered her soul to Satan, who then had ordered the "sacrifice."

In court, she described how she'd had her teeth fashioned into fangs and how she and others had gotten together in cemeteries to drink blood. She met her husband after he placed an ad in a music magazine that said, "Pitch black vampire seeks princess of darkness who hates everything and everyone." They did commit the crime, they admitted, but they were not responsible. They were merely Satan's instruments and had to "make sure the victim suffered well."

A psychiatrist testified to their mental illness and the judge sentenced Daniel to fifteen years and Manuela to thirteen years in a psychiatric institute.

While Manuela claimed that her involvement in the vampire subculture was a key factor in her service to Satan, it must be pointed out that the vast majority of participants are not killers and would not condone what the Rudas did. Nor do they feel some allegiance with Satan. The vampire games and social scenes do not make a person mentally ill. Rather the person who enters the scene with problems may use the pretext of predatory compulsion to justify acts of violence. When the fantasy provides names, ideas, and actions, such people allow themselves to go to extremes, as clearly occurred in the following two cases:

On Thanksgiving Day in 1996, Roderick Ferrell, sixteen, from Murray, Kentucky, led a pack of kids to Eustis, Florida, where he killed the elderly parents of a former girlfriend, Heather Wendorf. In Kentucky, he'd gotten involved with a fantasy role-playing game called *Vampire: The Masquerade,* but he supposedly said it wasn't edgy enough for his taste, so he formed what he called the Vampire Clan. He wanted to "open the Gates of Hell," and he understood that to mean killing people in order to consume their souls.

Although he'd already tormented and killed animals, the Wendorfs were his first human victims. While Heather was away from the house getting ready to leave with him for New Orleans, he used a crowbar to bludgeon Richard Wendorf as he slept on the couch. Then Ferrell went after Wendorf's wife with a knife, killing her. One of the other clan members, Scott Anderson, stood by and watched all of this, even as Ferrell burned marks in the shape of a *V* for Vampire Clan on Wendorf's chest. Leaving the corpses behind, the boys stole the family SUV, picked up Heather and the rest of the clan (two girls), and drove to New Orleans.

Within a few days, they were arrested in Baton Rouge, Louisiana. Initially, Ferrell told reporters from the *Orlando Sentinel* that a rival vampire clan had done the killings. Then he claimed to have been treated by psychiatrists for multiple personality disorder and that he'd been part of a satanic cult run by his grandfather.

He said that he had no soul and was possessed, and in fact he told the arresting officers that his vampire nature made him too powerful for them to hold him for long.

Of course, he was wrong. As his attorneys prepared to make opening statements for his trial, Ferrell pleaded guilty and was given the death penalty.

Sean Richard Sellers acted on his own, but his bizarre habits were known to everyone. His classmates voted him as the person most likely to become a vampire, probably because he brought vials of blood to school for lunch and drink them in front of other students. He also carried the *Satanic Bible*. He, too, ended up on death row for murder, which he viewed at the time as a "sacrifice."

During adolescence, Sean spent hours performing private rituals in his bedroom, using his own blood to write notes to Satan. He started drinking and popping pills, and soon found like-minded friends. They met to drink one another's blood.

Eventually Sean decided to try murder. He summoned a powerful alter ego to give himself courage, and on September 8, 1985, he entered a convenience store and used a borrowed gun to shoot the clerk. Not long afterward, he dressed in a ritualistic manner and shot his mother and stepfather in the head as they slept. After he was arrested and charged with the murders, he said that dreams about blood had influenced him.

Heightened Experience

Some people seek out intense experiences just to stimulate themselves, and psychopaths in particular may be born with a need for greater stimulation than the average person. Psychotic or otherwise, some people need something to galvanize them out of a feeling of emotional deadness. The way that activities tend to escalate in such cases, says psychiatrist Robert Simon, author of *Bad Men Do What Good Men Dream,* indicates that the acts fulfill a need for stimulation. In fact, some killers report that they feel normal only after killing. Thus, they become addicted to their compulsive behavior. It was clear in the case of Chase that he was planning to increase his brutal behavior quite dramatically, and there is every indication that Manuela Ruda, too, would have killed again. She and her husband had, in fact, gone out and purchased a chain saw in anticipation of further orders from the Dark One. Ferrell as well seems to have acquired a feeling of grandiosity from his murders that may have inspired him to continue. Many people who practice a form of satanic vampirism report similarly grandiose feelings. As their dark sides take over, Simon points out, the quality of their personal lives spirals downward and self-care diminishes. They have to feed a need, and they clearly portray the pattern of a drug addict. Neurological research has shown that intermittent stimulation of the brain has the effect of altering brain excitability and can even produce seizures. The brain becomes increasingly more sensitive to the stimulation and more prone to poststimulation depression. It could be, he suggests, that some killers have this type of mood disorder. Where it takes them will be a function of their fantasies. Some will only fantasize about their victims, while others will adopt themselves a role and act out their murderous fantasies.

Psychologist Michael Apter offers a theory about arousal in *The Dangerous Edge: The Psychology of Excitement* that may help to explain how these things happen. Once something is labeled dangerous, like vampirism or satanism, it exerts a magical attraction. This causes arousal, which is pleasant and makes us feel more alive. However, too much arousal can make us anxious, so we develop what Apter calls "protective frames." That is, we mentally create a buffer around our experience that helps us feel safe; that way we can get excited without being overwhelmed. A protective frame might be a story that provides an aesthetic distance, such as the monster came in, attacked, I found a weapon, and I destroyed it. Because we can defeat it, we can enjoy the excitement the monster's threat engenders in us. Within the frame, we welcome risk; we're eager to go to the edge to experience the sense of exhilaration. We can actually play with danger.

Apter describes three types of frames:

1. The confidence frame is one in which you feel positive about your abilities, weapons, or defenses.

2. The safety zone frame is the place where you experience no sense of danger.

3. The detachment frame is a fantasy that keeps you out of any significant interaction with the unsafe environment.

Each provides a degree of removal from the threats of the real world. With the safety and confidence frames, the individual is in the real world. In detachment, one is merely observing. Either someone else is perceived to be in danger or the danger is perceived to be past or imaginary.

Now let's apply this to clinical vampirism or to the kind of violence that some vampire role-players have committed. The frame that these people use is pathological. They add sources of arousal to increase the excitement that actually endanger others, like creating an alter ego, and they then use the frame to protect themselves from the consequences. Rod Ferrell, for example, viewed himself as a powerful vampire. Even if he did end up in prison, as a vampire he couldn't die because he was immortal. For him, the vampire was a protective frame that gave him license to do what he did and made him feel that he was too powerful to be saddled with any consequences. Sean Sellers said that because his "other self" committed the murders, he wasn't really responsible.

Some people must involve others in their frame in order to get sufficiently aroused by the scenario, but then may put those others at risk. The frame allows the fantasy to be actualized without seeming to be harmful to the perpetrator. He still feels safe, despite potential repercussions in the real world. Generally the frame forms from a fantasy that has an erotic buzz, like the predatory vampire. Then it involves preparation, which engages the person more deeply in the role. The next step includes a victim—perhaps initially in fantasy, but eventually in reality. Most of the killers we've discussed thought about their vampiric acts before they committed them; most realized they were going to kill. Most found it exciting and each killed as a "creature" more powerful than the victims.

Sometimes the victim's distress adds stimulation and enhances the image of power. For those not utterly psychotic the danger of discovery endows the experience with an added erotic sheen. Both Chase and Ferrell avidly followed the news reports of what they had done. That they viewed themselves in vampiric frames made them feel not only justified—this is true of Ruda as well—but invulnerable. They used the frame to re-create their lives and organize their chaotic impulses. As vampires, it makes sense to kill as they did. Victims are expendable and even necessary. The "vampires" were safe within this frame and able to view their crimes with detachment.

These cases illustrate how a mental illness that evolves into aggression and violence may find a form for these acts within a predatory mythology like that surrounding the vampire. While everyone uses frames in some manner, in this case, the frame is pathological and harmful to others.

Within the fantasy, the vampire can get away with murder. It's an elusive, powerful, and hypnotic creature, ultimately immune to the human justice system. However, the science of crime-scene processing has grown vastly more sophisticated since Dracula's time, and even since Rice's vampires appeared. Let's apply current criminalistics to a vampire crime scene—a real one, not the clumsy killings of delusional or psychopathic vampire wannabes.

FIVE

Night Stalkers: Forensic Vampirology

Immediately following the success of the daytime program *Dark Shadows*, in the late 1960s, producer Dan Curtis devised a tale about Carl Kolchak, a reporter who learns that a vampire is stalking and killing people. The television movie, based on a novel called *The Kolchak Papers* by Jeff Rice, was aired early in 1972, starring Darren Mc-Gavin, and in 1974 it became a series. In the movie, Kolchak discovers that a vampire named Janos Skorzeny is killing women in Las Vegas, but the police don't believe him, so he must battle the monster himself. In the series, he learns about attacks in Los Angeles and must once again track the vampire. Had he known what contemporary law enforcement now knows about crime scenes, he might have managed to convince more of the right people.

Nick Knight, too, is a detective who investigates vampires, but since he is himself a vampire, he has a significant advantage. The movie *Nick Knight* aired in 1989 and starred Rick Springfield as a vampire who became a cop to make amends for his evil. A spin-off television series, *Forever Knight*, aired in 1992 and featured Knight as a detective on the Toronto homicide squad. Not surprisingly, he works the night shift.

Many contemporary vampires realize that crime-scene investigation has become more sophisticated and they know they must be more careful—especially if they want to control the human world without being discovered. When detective Frank Kohanek arrives at the scene of a homicide in the third episode of the television series *Kindred: The Embraced*, he finds a psychiatrist dead in a locked room where a man diagnosed with schizophrenia had been kept. The man had claimed to be a vampire and he'd managed to rip through restraints, kill the doctor, bend open a steel grate, and escape. He'd also left a Manson-like message; written on the wall in the dead man's blood are the words BLOOD BROTHER. The same tag is seen again at another crime scene, and Kohanek knows that one doesn't give oneself a tag unless one intends to continue practicing one's "art." He also hears about witnesses who saw the killer, and they said that another man with him opened a wound on his arm and healed it. So there were eyewitnesses, but the weird story about the wound seems to undermine the validity of the account—except to a cop who knows better.

While the psychiatrists see this as a case of clinical vampirism, Kohanek knows he's got an actual vampire on his hands, which means taking an entirely different approach than he might take with a psychotic human being. He has to be on the lookout for linked crime scenes so he can get sufficiently acquainted with this vampire to eventually outsmart him. (He does end up doing that, but only with the help of another vampire.)

Vampires these days tend to clean up their crime scenes and get rid of the body, or at least heal the puncture holes they made. Nevertheless, even blood that's not visible can still be detected. Let's check the current state of the art for crime-scene processing and imagine the response of investigators who come across a crime perpetrated by a vampire.

The Vampire Crime Scene

On an *X-Files* episode called "Bad Blood," a series of crimes leads to dual interpretations, but Agent Fox Mulder's version involves investigating cattle exsanguinations in Texas that are similar to what happened to a man in the same area. Two puncture marks were found on his neck, so Mulder sets about trying to trap the offender, whom he believes is a vampire. He does unmask the vampire, and stakes him, but a coroner removes the stake and the vampire goes at it again. That leads to a whole new strategy, but the end result remains ambiguous. It's not the first time that Mulder has been confronted with a vampire, so he's learned to interpret crime scenes in a way that remains open to such possibilities. As a detective, he's a breed apart, yet it's clear that he must use both the typical crime-scene reconstruction and knowledge of the supernatural to solve such crimes.

What might a detective do who's less versed in vampire lore than Mulder? Certainly he'd follow standard protocol for a scientific investigation.

After a vampire has come and gone, there are several possible scenarios for what the first officer at the scene might find:

1. evidence of a crime, such as blood spatter, but no victim

2. a living victim

3. one or more deceased victims

4. a victim disposal site other than the primary crime scene

5. evidence that links this crime scene to others in the general area

The first officer must protect the scene by determining its boundaries and taping it off. She's not to touch or move anything.

In the case of evidence without a victim, a detective will decide its priority for processing. If it's just some blood spatters, a missing person, a room in disarray, or a scream heard in the night, it might be less urgent than, say, a refrigerator in which vials of fresh human blood are discovered.

Some vampires, aware of criminal investigation techniques, may kill their victims but then dispose of them with great care. (This is similar to serial killers who study crime-scene manuals to avoid making obvious mistakes.) That means that only people acquainted with the victim will know that something has happened. Generally that means filing a missing-persons report with a local agency. An investigator will then try to find out where the person was last seen, with whom, and whether anyone witnessed anything suspicious.

If there's a victim and the victim is alive, the first officer at the scene must see that this person gets the appropriate care until the paramedics arrive. Generally, however, vampires either kill their prey or make them forget what's taken place. They're pretty good about not leaving witnesses. Yet perhaps we have a vampire who's mentally damaged in some way or just getting started and is ignorant about covering her tracks. Then a living victim is possible, and that person will probably be bleeding from some small wound. He or she may also have suffered a considerable loss of blood. This person will be transported to a hospital and a police officer will come for a statement.

If there's a deceased victim—probably exsanguinated—the first officer must leave the body as is. A crime-scene photographer will take photographs of its position from several different angles. When the coroner or medical examiner arrives, he will check the eyes and take the body temperature to help determine time of death. He may also look for obvious wounds. If there's an apparent loss of blood, he'll direct the criminalists to check for blood soaked into the ground or a rug. The coroner then bags the hands and wraps the body in a sterile sheet to preserve all evidence clinging to the body, yet keeping its position intact as much as possible, and puts it into a body bag. He then gives the order for transport to a morgue for an autopsy.

The crime-scene personnel arrive to perform a number of functions:

- dust the place or area for prints

- look for anything that appears foreign to the scene

- look for pattern evidence like tire tracks

- collect trace evidence like hair, soil, or fiber

- examine serological or biological fluid evidence

- take photographs, make a videotape, take measurements, and draw the scene with notations on where evidence was found

- look for a weapon

Once the evidence is gathered, it's transported to the crime lab. Blood evidence must be collected and preserved in a specific manner in order to avoid degrading and contamination. If there's a bite wound, swabs will be taken from the skin around the wound to test for DNA found in saliva. The immediate task is to deliver the evidence and crime-scene notes to the detectives, who will need it for crime-scene reconstruction. They will try to figure out what happened when, and the way physical evidence is left at the scene aids in getting an accurate picture.

For a vampire attack, some aspects of crime-scene processing are more relevant than others.

If the crime scene is difficult to "read" or if it appears to be linked by some unique element to other unsolved homicides, then a profiler might be called in. That may mean using the FBI's criminal investigative analysis unit or a local forensic psychologist experienced with crime scenes and autopsy reports. While they can offer some idea on an offender's behavior from a single crime scene, the more behavioral clues they have, the better their assessment. Multiple crime scenes work best. Indeed, one of the most famous serial killers may actually have influenced the development of one of our more notable vampires.

Jack the Vampire?

Just two years before Bram Stoker began to write *Dracula,* a series of murders in London created a sensation. It's possible that Stoker was inspired by this man, who was known as Jack the Ripper, aka Red Jack.

According to Professor Elizabeth Miller, in *Dracula: Sense and Nonsense,* while the novel makes no obvious allusions to the Ripper murders, it's clear that Stoker was aware of them. Radu Florescu and Raymond McNally concur, discussing the notion in *The Essential Dracula* that an Eastern European was among the named suspects. In fact, says Miller, upon arrival in London, Dracula stored his boxes of earth in Whitechapel, where the five infamous murders had occurred. Stoker would certainly have known this and would be unlikely to have picked the place at random. Miller also notes that Dracula is ultimately dispatched with knives (not with a stake as many believe), and that a knife was Jack's weapon of choice.

"Of course Stoker had to know of the Jack the Ripper murders," Miller said. "And he specifically mentions Jack the Ripper in his own preface to the 1901 Icelandic edition of *Dracula.* Furthermore, his working notes for Dracula show that he was originally going to include among the list of characters a 'detective,' a role that then was subsumed in the character of Van Helsing."

Since crimes involving clinical vampirism center on bloodlust, and since our cultural myths surrounding the vampire may have their roots in Jack the Ripper's story, let's look at it in detail.

In 1888, in Whitechapel, a neighborhood in London's seedy East End populated by poor immigrants and desperate prostitutes, five women were murdered in the space of just over two months.

The first victim was Mary Ann (Polly) Nichols. On Friday, August 31, just after 1 A.M., Polly went out to earn some money. A friend saw her at 2:30 A.M., and an hour later, she was dead in the streets. Her skirt was pulled up to her waist, her legs were parted, and there was a severe cut into her abdomen and her throat made by a long-bladed knife. In fact, her head was nearly severed from her body.

Next was Annie Chapman, just over a week later, on September 8. Her dress was pulled up over her head, her stomach ripped open, and her intestines pulled out and draped over her left shoulder. Her legs were drawn up, knees bent as if posed, and spread outward. Her throat was cut, too, with a sharp surgical type of knife, and it looked as if the killer had tried to separate her neck bones. Several coins and an envelope had been arranged around her, and her bladder, half of her vagina, and her uterus had been cut out and taken away.

The writer of a note sent on September 25 to the Central News Agency, signed "Yours Truly, Jack the Ripper," claimed that he was "down on whores" and would continue to kill them. A tabloid journalist probably sent it, but the name stuck.

On September 30, two women were killed an hour apart. The ripper slashed the throat of Elizabeth Stride, forty-five, only a few minutes before she was found, and disemboweled Catherine Eddowes in another part of Whitechapel. Her throat was cut, and her intestines had been pulled out and placed over the right shoulder. Her uterus and one kidney were removed and taken, and her face was mutilated. Two upside-down Vs were cut into her cheeks, pointing toward the eyes, her eyelids were nicked, and the tip of her nose was cut off.

Then came a letter "from Hell," with half of a kidney that was afflicted with Bright's disease—a disorder from which Eddowes had suffered—

enclosed in it. The note's author indicated that he'd fried and eaten the other half.

October passed without incident, but then Mary Kelly, twenty-four, became the last victim. On November 8, she invited a man into her room. He pulled the sheet over her head and stabbed her through it. Then he slashed her throat and ripped open her lower torso, pulled out her intestines, and skinned her chest and legs. Blood was splattered all over the room. Her abdomen was emptied and its contents spread all over the bed and thrown around the room. Her heart, too, was removed and was missing, and flesh was cut from her legs and buttocks clear to the bone. Doctors estimated that his frenzy had gone on for around two hours. While officials awaited another note, Red Jack was never heard from again.

Many authors have linked this killer with vampires, but more interesting is the possibility that Stoker isolated from newspaper accounts the more lurid elements of the crimes and used them to create the alarming persona of the vampire. Like the Ripper, he moves in the night among the populace, seemingly invisible. His bloodlust drives him and he selects victims at random, strikes quickly, and manages to elude police. One officer, who was walking his beat in a state of heightened watchfulness, turned around and found the body of Eddowes where just moments before there had been nothing, The Ripper was like a vicious ghost that came, slashed, and left, in full awareness that the police could never get him. His abilities to commit these crimes without detection seemed uncanny.

Unfortunately, he has inspired others to try the same approach, and nowadays we have experts who know how to link crimes through behavioral analysis from clues at the crime scene. They're commonly known as profilers, although some would rather be called experts in criminal investigative analysis, with behavioral profiling as one area of concentration. Let's look at the profiler's work in some detail before we profile a vampire crime scene.

Profiling the Vampire

Probing for information prior to actually questioning a suspect involves looking at different types of data, including:

- whether a weapon was used, and what type
- evidence of more than one person involved
- the possibility that the victim was killed in one place and then transported to a separate dump site (both scenes are processed)
- the means of transporting the body
- the position in which the body was found and whether it was moved around at that scene
- the type and number of wounds inflicted
- minute details about the victim's known movements and habits (especially in terms of risks she took)
- offender risk factors—how much risk did he take to commit the crime?
- method used to control the victim
- evidence of staging the crime scene
- evidence of a ritual, signature, or removal of a "trophy"

The basic idea is to get as much information as possible about common patterns so as to develop a general description of the killer in terms of habits, possible employment, military history, educational level, marital status, and personality traits. A good psychological profile is an educated attempt to identify the type of person who committed a certain crime, based on the idea that we all tend to be slaves to our psychology and someone who makes killing a habit will inevitably leave a consistent trail of clues.

A criminal profile is most easily developed if the offender displays psychopathology, such as sadistic torture or postmortem mutilation. If the killer left a "signature"—a behavioral manifestation of a personality quirk—this helps to link crime scenes. If a pattern is detected, it may help to predict future possible attacks or likely encounter sites.

Generally, profilers rely on psychological clues about mental deficiency or criminal thought patterns. They also use actuarial data such as the age range into which offenders generally fall and how important an unstable family history is to criminality.

It's important to remember, despite New Age efforts to reform and refine the vampire, that vampires who kill their victims are serial killers (Lestat turns this around in *The Tale of the Body Thief* when he decides to prowl for serial killers to use as his own victims.) The essential vampire is the entity that transcends death to thrive off the living, generally resulting in the demise of his prey. The erotic power of the vampire lies in his ability to invite us close enough to fatally endanger us through his desire.

Although no trained profilers were around at the time of the Whitechapel murders, I asked former Supervisory Special Agent Gregg McCrary, who worked for ten years as an FBI profiler, to look over the details of a set of crime scenes attributed to a vampire. We have an advantage, a result of the killer's confession, in knowing beforehand that these murders are definitely linked, but I thought it would be interesting to see what a profiler with his own theory about "vampire attacks" might say.

I gave McCrary the following report, although I left out the actual location:

In the locked second-floor room of an inn at Köln-Mulheim in the Rhine River Valley, a ten-year-old girl was found murdered in bed. It was a summer day in 1913, and she was the daughter of the man who ran the inn. It appeared that she'd been disturbed while asleep, and there was evidence of a struggle and bruises on her neck. There were two small incisions on her throat, one shallow, about one to two millimeters deep, and the other nine centimeters in length, with some indication on the deeper cut that it had been made after several efforts, not with a single smooth stroke. A mat next to the bed had absorbed a large amount of blood, but there was little on the bedclothes. Bruising around the victim's genitals indicated forced digital penetration, but no semen was found. Her tongue was bitten through, and her body was pallid and without lividity. There was less blood in her body than there should have been. Found in the room was a handkerchief with the initials P.K., which matched those of the girl's father, but he claimed not to own the item.

A suspect, the girl's uncle, was arrested but freed as a result of lack of evidence. There were no other suspects and the murder went unsolved.

Sixteen years later, another young girl from that general area was found nude and stuffed under a hedge. She was eight. She had been stabbed thirteen times with a sharp object, including into the vagina and throat. The wounds appeared to have been made by scissors. Her blood had congealed in the head area, and her attacker had poured gasoline onto the body in an attempt to burn it. There were semen stains on her undergarments.

A week later, a forty-five-year-old mechanic was found dead next to a road, bleeding from twenty stab wounds, many of which had been to his temples. The police ruled out a common killer for the girls and the man, since they believed that the victims were too different.

Six months went by and then two girls were murdered at a local fairgrounds. The five-year-old was manually strangled and her throat was cut open. The fourteen-year-old was also strangled and then beheaded. Both were left lying a few feet apart near the footpath of a neighborhood vegetable garden.

Three weeks later, an adolescent was raped and battered to death with a hammer at night. Then, six weeks after that, a five-year-old child disappeared and a letter came to a local newspaper with a map indicating a factory area where the body could be found. She was there, strangled and stabbed thirty-six times. Her body was horribly mutilated. The map also indicated the location of another young woman who'd been missing for several months. She was left battered, stabbed, and hacked up in a local field.

Some of these crimes appeared to be linked, and the locals believed they had a vampire, because he was elusive, he operated at night, and the appearance of some of the neck and face wounds indicated that he was taking blood from his victims.

McCrary believes that the state in which some mutilated victims were found before people understood much about criminology may have helped to create werewolf and vampire myths. "Serial murder has probably been with us for as long as humanity has existed," he stated. "Yet there's a reluctance to admit that someone in our community would be capable of the kind of evil we see in brutal murders. Evil is so overpowering that we want to attribute it to some 'monster.' We don't want to know that a human is capable of such hideous violence. When the crime occurs at night, that helps to create the idea of mythical monsters that change during the night to do these things.

"Even today, we want to attribute such crimes to a transient killer who came through town. We don't want it to be someone in our community. It's better to think of someone who's not like us, because we can compartmentalize this. We're uncomfortable when these people turn out to be like you and me. We want bad guys to be totally bad and good people to be totally good. We see this reaction with child molesters. A dirty old man who molests a kid is one thing, but when it's the guy who's been a coach or schoolteacher for twenty years that everyone likes, we're uncomfortable. Communities really split in those cases: some will want to run him out of town and others will come to his defense. People don't want to believe that a good guy can be capable of terrible behavior. Yet they are. The reality is that many good people can have some terrible flaws."

When presented with the details of the series of crimes above, McCrary made quite accurate suggestions about the pathology and criminal history of the perpetrator. "We've got the initial homicide with the ten-year-old girl," he indicated, "which is indoors with no apparent forced entry. I'd wonder about how the victim's bedroom was locked and whether it was bolted from inside. If it was merely locked with a key, it would be easy for someone to lock it after leaving.

"When we time-line these crimes, we see a sixteen-year hiatus where apparently nothing happens and then we have this whole cluster within about a year. That starts with an eight-year-old female found outside, where he stabs her a few times and makes some attempt at concealment. Then you have a male, so that's different victimology, but he was stabbed twenty times, so that's of interest for similarities between those crime scenes. Then you have two young girls murdered together, and then an adolescent girl raped and battered to death. Then six weeks later, a five-year-old disappears and you have letters to the newspaper, with maps to the body. So we have a whole cluster of activity, which is more than we might find with a traditional serial murderer. The fact that he would write letters and send maps means he clearly wanted the bodies to be found, but the question is why.

"The other victims were found quickly. They were outdoor homicides and easily discovered, so he might have been frustrated that these last ones weren't being found and he felt a need to show the way. It could be that he wanted it to show up in the news or become more grist for discussion in the town. You can think of different motivations, but it's typical with serial murderers that they're powerless guys who are now in charge. David Berkowitz, the Son of Sam killer, for example, was in charge of New York City and he was thriving on it. He liked having everyone's attention.

"If I were investigating this and thought the first crime was linked to the others, I'd want to find out if there was someone who'd left town for that long hiatus period and then came back. He might have been in prison, too. I might also decide that the first one wasn't related. It's unusual that someone would be dormant after the first killing and then have so much escalation all at once. And seldom do you wake up and do something like this. Usually there's an escalation or devolution process before a sexual homicide. You have some indication that there were lesser crimes that would have preceded even the first crime, so he'd have a criminal history. I'd look into that.

"Then with the first killing, the mat next to the bed had absorbed a large amount of blood but there's little on the bedclothes. I'd be interested in seeing how they measured the amount in the rug and determined that some was missing. Maybe we can account for it and maybe we can't. The other interesting thing is the cutting to the neck. It looked like there were several attempts to do that. I'd like to see the crime-scene photos, but if they're like hesitation marks that indicate he wasn't sure how to do this, then she was probably dead or unconscious at the time, because she wasn't moving. If she were moving, you'd expect to see more irregular lines.

"I had a case in Massachusetts in which there were about twenty superficial lacerations across the victim's throat, none of which went deep, but they were all parallel. My read on that one was that she was not moving at the time. You see hesitation marks in suicidal behavior where they realize it's going to hurt. Victims who are conscious know the same thing. It's unusual for victims to remain still when someone is trying to cut them.

"If there clearly was blood missing, the killer might have carried it away or drank it. This could be a case of what's known as clinical vampirism, where people try to replicate the mythology of the vampire. One cut was two millimeters deep and the other nine centimeters in length, so a deeper cut had been made after several efforts. Yet the mythical vampire didn't have that kind of hesitation. My sense from those myths is that fictional vampires know what they're going after. They sink their teeth in and drink deeply—none of this hesitation. This might also have been some type of staging, to make the homicide look like something else, especially if there are myths of vampirism already being passed around. But this one doesn't really look like the traditional clinical vampire case, either."

So the items we gain from McCrary's profiling assessment are:

- a means for checking out suspects with a specific history

- some ideas on specific motivations

This helps to devise a plan for how to trap a suspect, as well as how to question suspects who are brought in. While criminal profiling is generally done when the suspect is unknown, in this case, we do know who the killer was and we can now look at the details of this perpetrator from Germany during the 1920s and see how it all fits. These crimes—and more—were the work of the Monster of Düsseldorf, Peter Kürten.

A necrophile, rapist, and killer, Kürten targeted almost any vulnerable person. His mild manner charmed women and children alike. He got his start when a neighbor taught him how to torture animals, and he learned to stab them to death while he was raping them, which linked his lust to blood. Then, when he was nine, he perpetrated an "accident" that killed two of his friends. Throughout his life he was jailed for various crimes from theft to nonfatal strangulation, but he upped the stakes in 1929 when he attacked twenty-three separate people. One woman who survived being strangled into unconsciousness recalled her attacker whispering in her ear, "This is what love is about."

So clearly we have a guy with an escalating criminal history, including murders that were written off as accidents. Some of these acts were done in private and not discovered, but others were on record.

When arrested after a rape, Kürten immediately confessed to everything. He explained that he'd committed numerous assaults and thirteen murders, drinking the blood from many of his victims because he found blood to be sexually exciting. He'd once bitten the head off a swan, he stated, and ejaculated as he drank its blood. He claimed he was insane, that his life had been wholly devoted to depravity, and that his role model was none other than Jack the Ripper.

Referring back to the young girl murdered at the inn in 1913, Kürten told how he broke into the room, choked the girl until she passed out, and held her head as he cut her throat. He said that the blood had spurted in an arc over his head, which had excited him to orgasm. He drank some of the blood, used his fingers to molest the girl, and then dropped his handkerchief at the scene before leaving, locking the door behind him.

After this, he found another sleeping victim but was frightened away before he could act. Then he struck two people with hatchets, achieving sexual climax over the blood he had spilled. When he strangled several women without killing them, he was arrested and went to prison for eight years. When he got out, he got married and moved to a different town, but was then charged with an assault on two domestic servants. Then he moved back to Düsseldorf and began his frenzied series of assaults in 1928. He set fires and attempted to strangle four women, then stabbed a woman twenty-four times. She recovered, but the man he stabbed did not. He killed the eight-year-old child around the same time. All three of these victims had been stabbed in the temples. He said in his confession that sometimes he drank blood from throat wounds he made and sometimes from the temple. Once he drank so much that he became ill, and another time he licked the blood from the victim's hands. He also got a thrill out of fantasizing about effecting mass disasters.

The rest of his attacks continued unabated, some of the victims surviving, some dying. Inexplicably he allowed a woman he had raped to go free and she led police to where he lived. That's how he was stopped.

At his trial, defense psychiatrists declared him insane, but the jury ignored them. Just before his execution in 1931 for nine counts of murder, Kürten said that if he could hear his blood bubbling forth from his neck stump right after he was decapitated, he'd die a happy man. "That would be the pleasure to end all pleasures," he announced.

Criminalistics and the Vampire

While entire books have been devoted to crime-scene processing, we can narrow down the vampire crime to some key elements. It gets a little tricky because we don't know if vampires have semen, or if they shed DNA through the epithelial cells from their mouths into their saliva, so we can't be sure that a DNA analysis will yield results. Even if vampires do have DNA, it might be formed from junk DNA, as discussed previously, which could throw off the entire analysis. And even if a reading is available for their DNA, the vampire must be included in a DNA database. That is, a DNA sample must be matched against the DNA of an actual suspect—and vampires are elusive devils. (If they *are* in a database, it's likely they got into it as mortals, so the report about them would list them as deceased.)

Let's move into those procedures that could actually show results good enough for the courtroom, notably bite-mark impression and serology.

Bite Marks

During the autopsy of a fresh victim, bite marks will generally be found. (Some vampires can heal these marks and leave no obvious trace of their attack, and others may not take blood through biting. We can't even address the crime scene of a psychic vampire.) There's no doubt that fang punctures will need further examination, and the medical examiner will call in an expert.

Forensic odontologists are the experts to consult for matching a bite-mark impression on a victim to the tooth structure of a suspect— or at least deciding what kind of teeth impressions left the mark. It wouldn't be difficult for an odontologist to surmise that a vampire bite mark is very unusual, since fangs are involved.

A tooth mark is like a mark on a tool. Such marks can be matched via idiosyncratic elements. Generally the teeth that leave the strongest impressions are in the front, both top and bottom—but a vampire bite would lead with the fangs (or in the case of Weyland, the vampire with the needle in his mouth, with the pointy thing under his tongue). The bite might even be identified as coming from an animal. A swab would be taken, but we've just discussed the potential problems with vampire DNA, so that might not be a productive lead.

As the vampire drinks, it may be that his other teeth leave bruises, too, and in that case, a good bite-mark impression might be cast from victims, either living or dead. An important thing to remember about teeth is that they can chip, get worn down, or be reshaped in various ways. Those factors help to distinguish one set of bite marks from another. Also, assuming vampires retain the teeth they had as mortals, there are restorations, fillings, rotations, tooth loss, breakage, and injury that can make one set of teeth unlike anyone else's. Sometimes a bite mark has to be charted and examined from many angles; sometimes it can be identified from one tooth.

The American approach to charting teeth is called the universal system. A number is assigned to each of the thirty-two adult teeth, beginning with the upper-right third molar and ending with the lower-right third molar. Each tooth has five visible surfaces, and the composite information about each surface makes it possible to make grids. Each individual's grid is unique, and typically a dentist has this information on file.

There are from thirty to seventy-six factors to consider when making comparisons, including matching for striations, whorls, indentations, pitting, and abrasions, and often this is done through computerized photography. What experts seek are a sufficient number of points of similarity between the evidence and a suspect to be able to say with a reasonable degree of certainty that the suspect is the perpetrator. Yet it's still a matter of interpretation.

When a bite mark is located on a victim—not always the neck, either—a silicone form is made from it and photographs are taken. If a vampire is actually found and detained (a trick in itself), a cast can be made and then fit into the impression to see if there's a match. (If the fangs retract, then the vampire might easily prove that the marks fail to match him.

Wayne Boden was caught by the skin of his teeth, but only after he'd killed several women in what some investigators thought was a vampirelike embrace.

A young schoolteacher, Norma Vaillancourt, was found murdered in 1968 in her apartment in Montreal, Canada. She'd been strangled, raped, and bitten many times all over her breasts. However, there was no sign of a struggle, and she even looked peaceful, as if she'd enjoyed whatever had happened. The crime was sadistic, but among the victim's many boyfriends, there were no good suspects. Whoever had done this, police believed that she'd wanted to be with him.

The next day, another victim was found in that town in the same condition, and the bite marks were matched, which linked the cases.

In 1969, Marielle Archambault told coworkers that she'd become entranced by a man she'd recently met. She, too, turned up dead ... and similarly bitten. However, she had put up a fight.

There were two more victims before the offender was stopped in 1971. The police arrested him and an odontologist got an impression of his teeth to match to the wounds on each of the victims.

Obviously caught, Boden finally admitted that he had indeed killed these women while having rough sex. He would strangle them and then become frenzied with the need to feast on their breasts.

Unfortunately, fictional vampires are generally difficult to catch, and even if they were to be caught and tried for a crime, the defense attorney could point out the following:

- A bite might penetrate the skin, but often only leaves bruising—and sometimes the blood marks of a bruise are mistaken for the impression of a tooth.

- Skin gets distorted when bitten or the teeth can slide during the act of biting.

Still, if the canines did penetrate and were not instantly healed (as in some vampire lore), it's likely the odontologist for the prosecution could make a good case.

In making a match, forensic odontologists study the physical characteristics of both the bite-mark wound and the suspect's teeth, including such things as the shape and musculature of the mouth, the distance between certain teeth, misaligned teeth, wide spaces, missing teeth, and unique dentistry. Patterns can indicate a "suck mark," which suggests a bite made slowly, or bruising that shows defensive movements.

It can also be determined from bleeding beneath the skin whether the victim was alive or dead at the time the bite was made (which would not be an issue with vampires, since they don't attack corpses).

Ted Bundy, a notorious serial killer during the 1970s, aligned himself with the vampire image, sometimes biting his victims. In fact, it was a bite mark that brought him down.

He began killing young women in the Pacific Northwest, and then moved on to Colorado and Utah. He was arrested in Utah and extradicted to Colorado, but escaped and fled to Tallahassee, Florida.

On the night of January 15, 1978, he attacked Lisa Levy and Martha Bowman in their sorority house at Florida State University. Less than a month later he abducted twelve-year-old Kimberly Leach, raped her, strangled her, and left her in the woods.

Yet he'd been clumsy. He'd bitten Lisa Levy on the left buttock, not once but twice.

He was arrested, discovered to be the fugitive killer, and tried in Florida, with the bite mark as a key piece of evidence. The impression was clean enough to make a match to a dental impression of Bundy's teeth.

Once Bundy had been sentenced to death three times for the three brutal murders, he began to talk. He eventually confessed to thirty murders in six separate states, dating back to 1973. Like a vampire, he killed to fill up his emptiness—figurative or existential, in his case. He said that he viewed his victims as objects that he possessed. They were there for his use, and he attacked in whatever way was necessary to subdue them—including biting. He said that during these encounters some malignant portion of his personality took over, craving satisfaction in a way that couldn't be denied.

Serological Analysis

Back to the actual crime scene, there are two areas of blood investigations: blood typing and blood-spatter pattern analysis. If the vampire bites into an artery, for example, she could produce a spray of blood. Presumably the more gentle vampires have acquired the art of catching the flow and leaving no trace, but there are some inexperienced or psychotic types who might lack finesse. They might chew, pierce, or tear in such a way that blood will be found on sheets, bedclothes, walls, or floors. Possibly even on ceilings. That can mean calling in a specific type of crime-scene expert, but even the most experienced rarely encounter a criminal like Germany's "Hanover Vampire." To better understand the work of the scientists concerned with blood evidence, let's look at the case.

Fritz Haarmann was institutionalized during the late nineteenth century for mental instability, but he escaped. Eventually he became a homeless vagrant and landed in jail numerous times for theft and fraud. Then he learned to butcher meat, but his growing interest was in molesting young boys. Seeking waifs in the train station, he offered them a place to stay in his home. Often they would simply vanish. In 1924, the police investigated the disappearance of one boy and caught Haarmann assaulting him. They arrested Haarmann, but what they did not realize was that he had the head of another missing young man right there in the room. They also didn't realize that he'd been committing crimes of this kind for several years.

In 1919, when Haarmann was forty, he met Hans Grans, a handsome prostitute, and together they trapped and killed an estimated fifty young men. After finding skulls and a sackful of bones in the Leine Canal in 1924, the police suspected Haarmann. They searched his rooms and found clothing that wasn't his. They also saw what they believed to be human bloodstains on the walls. They again arrested Haarmann and he confessed.

They soon learned about his predatory method of attack. He had Grans lure hungry young men—whom Haarmann called "game"—to his home and then fed them until they were sleepy. Then he would grab them, force himself on them, and as he had intercourse he chewed through their throat until the head was practically severed from the body. As he tasted their blood, he achieved orgasm. Afterward, he cut the flesh from their bodies, consumed some of it, and sold the rest in the market as butchered meat. Bones, skulls, and leftover parts he dumped into the canal.

Haarmann was executed by beheading, a fate he relished.

Should a case like this occur today, serology experts would arrive armed with chemicals for performing "presumptive" blood tests to check the blood spray on the walls and match blood to the victims. This technology was made possible by the discovery of blood types and blood enzymes (see chapter 1).

When a darkish substance is found at a crime scene, it must first be determined to be blood. There are several tests—presumptive tests used strictly for screening—that will differentiate between blood and other substances, but if other chemicals are present at the scene to which the test chemicals are sensitive, the tests may be vulnerable to corruption. For that reason, these tests are done with great care. A positive result from any of them is an indication to go ahead and use another test to confirm.

1. A powerful light is moved across every surface of a crime scene to check for traces not readily visible.

2. If blood is suspected, a chemical called luminol is sprayed across the scene; luminol reacts to blood by making it luminescent. The room has to be darkened to show the faint bluish glow. This test works even with old blood or diluted stains, and can illuminate smear marks where blood has been wiped away. However, luminol can destroy the blood's properties, so its use is limited.

3. The Kastle-Meyer Color Test uses phenolphthalein and hydrogen peroxide on a piece of filter paper. When blood is present, it turns pink.

4. Sometimes microcrystalline tests are also performed. Specific chemicals are added to the blood to make it form crystals with hemoglobin derivatives.

5. To distinguish animal from human blood, as we've already noted, investigators use the precipitin test

6. After the above tests have been performed, analysts can determine blood type with an ABO test, and then work on the source's gender. To get a more thorough enzyme/protein profile, they use a blood-soaked piece of cotton placed in gelatin on a slide and submitted to electric current; this is called electrophoresis.

Blood at a crime scene can offer further clues when the way it lands on a surface is analyzed. The various types of bloodstains indicate how the blood was projected from the body. People who perform such analyses practice a subspecialty known as blood-pattern analysis, or BPA, which plays an important role in the reconstruction of many crime scenes. These professionals examine the type of injuries inflicted if a body is present; determine the order in which the wounds were received; make distinctions among different types of blood present; determine the type of weapon that caused the injuries; determine whether the victim was in motion when the injury was inflicted; determine whether the victim was moved after the injury was inflicted; and measure how far the blood drops fell before hitting the surface where they were found.

Blood-spatter patterns can be traced back to their converging point by considering such factors as the surface on which the blood fell, the angle at which it hit, its resulting shape, and the distance it traveled. Choosing several stains and using basic trigonometric functions enables the experts to do a three-dimensional re-creation of the event. The shape of a blood drop can reveal a lot.

No matter what kind of analysis is used on the blood at a crime scene, care is taken to handle it properly to prevent putrefaction. Photos and notes are taken before any blood is lifted, and samples are protected from heat, moisture, or bacterial contamination.

Putting It Together

One of the most important aspects of evidence analysis is crime-scene reconstruction. Because there are many different types of crime scenes—even with vampires—accurate reconstruction requires experienced investigators. They have to put together a coherent picture from what witnesses say, evidence processing (which can take months because of all the lab procedures), autopsy reports, and suspect lists—and do all of this as fast as they can. Those who have been at it a long time say that it's important to keep an open mind, because the initial read of a crime scene is often deceptive. We might suspect the same to be true of a vampire scene. Despite the pervasive folklore, few investigators would jump to the conclusion that loss of blood and a bite mark add up to a vampire. Even if they're versed in clinical vampirism, they would still allow the evidence to unfold before drawing such a strong conclusion. The steps they would follow include:

- observe everything

- attend to anything out of place

- document everything

- come up with a flexible hypothesis

- test it against emerging test results and new evidence

- try to walk through the way the action seems to have happened at the scene to see if the evidence confirms the hypothesis

■ brainstorm with other investigators and check one another's logic

Once it's clear that the crime was indeed committed by a vampire—the victim returns to life and attacks others, the bite-mark impression matches a suspect and he's found in a coffin by day, the victim's blood type or DNA matches a stain on the vampire's clothing—then the next step is to decide what to do about it. Those vampires that can change into bats or mist have an advantage, in that they can't be held in most prisons for very long. Yet even vampires who can't change shape find ways to elude capture.

However, there exists a different kind of investigator than the ones we've been talking about, and for him or her, hunting and killing vampires is a way of life. This person recognizes the vampire crime scene for what it is and does not have to await the results of lab tests to know what needs to be done. Such an investigator is on a mission.

SIX

Body Count

✦—✝—✦

Investigators who are skilled at reading a vampire crime scene often have something more to gain than solving a crime. In *Dracula,* the vampire hunters strive to save Mina from the eternal curse and England from an army of vampires. In other tales, their concern may be to save themselves. Some hunters just have a personal vendetta, and generally they have some extraordinary assistance.

Let's look first at the group of men who track down Dracula.

The Vampire Hunters

Elizabeth Miller pointed out that Stoker had given some thought to using a detective in this novel but subsumed that persona into Van Helsing. Nevertheless, he kept the essential feel of detective fiction.

"The novel does have the familiar conventions of the newly emerging detective novel," Miller said. "It has mystery, investigation discovery, pursuit and destruction, and even the 'snitch' in the person of Renfield. But the vampire hunters are a sad collection of detectives. For someone who is obsessed with gathering data about Renfield— seemingly a trait of his empirical bent—Dr. Seward is dreadfully slow to interpret the clues that connect Renfield's behavior to Dracula. He does not even notice the marks on Lucy's throat until Van Helsing points them out to him. His lame explanation for Lucy's death is that she was bitten by a bat.

"Van Helsing is even more of a puzzle. He doesn't even follow his own rules! Over and over, he proclaims the way to destroy Dracula by using a wooden stake. Yet when the time comes, he raises no objection when Harker and Seward do it with knives.

"If there is a detective among the group, it is Mina. At least she has a more methodical mind: she sorts out the train schedules, and uses deductive reasoning to set forth the possible route Dracula can take back home and the most likely one to follow. And she is right, even though initially, the big brave hunters wanted to exclude her from the hunt."

All but Van Helsing begin as skeptics, but upon seeing the effect of the strange rituals on Lucy Westenra, all become convinced about the existence of vampires. They're also aware that Mina is deteriorating the way Lucy did, so time is of the essence. This group consists of three of Lucy's suitors (Dr. John Seward, Lord Godalming, and Quincy Morris), Mina's husband, Jonathan, and Professor Van Helsing. They attempt to find Dracula in one of his many real-estate holdings around London but discover that he's managed to elude them. By putting Mina into a hypnotic trance, they can learn what the Count is experiencing, and that allows them to deduce that he's on board a ship. They figure out which one, learn that it's bound for Transylvania, and find a way to head him off at the pass, so to speak.

Since Mina is vulnerable but also their key source of information, they take her with them and Van Helsing protects her in a circle made with items blessed by an agent of God. As the box containing Dracula draws near, the hunters prepare themselves. They scatter the group of Gypsies hired to get Dracula home, open the coffin, and destroy him. He dissolves into dust.

Therein lies the formula:

- something amiss with a loved one (usually loss of blood and puncture marks)

- a brilliant or mystically intuitive mind reading the puzzling clues to determine the source

- confirmation of the vampire's presence—and of the detective's brilliance

- steps taken to protect the declining victim (if he or she is alive)

- a battle plan derived from knowledge of the vampire

- putting the plan into effect

- confronting and killing the vampire to free the victim

- giving the reader or spectator a sense of closure, a feeling that that good has triumphed and things are again normal

In the case of Dracula, the vampire hunters are mortal men, aided by a woman who is herself moving toward the state of vampirism. They have a psychic means for tracking the monster and might not have been successful without it. That added element appears to be key to the success of the hunt—there's always something a little extra.

Archetypal as they are, this team wasn't the first in fiction to go after vampires. There was a vampire hunter, Baron Vondenberg, in Le Fanu's

Carmilla, who correctly interpreted the victim's symptoms and stormed the tomb to put an end to the vampire's seduction of a teenage girl.

Still, Van Helsing does appear to represent the epitome of the vampire hunter: an older man experienced in both science and the occult who knows what to do but who remains fairly secretive. He enlists the help of others, but as the detective, he clearly leads the way and they must look to him for guidance or risk making mistakes. He also can do things that the others cannot, such as preparing the rituals and inducing a hypnotic trance.

Even so, all the occult knowledge in the world might still leave the hunters with nothing more than a nice set of university lectures. They need a connection, and that's the key to success for vampire hunters. Mina's blood is mixed with the vampire's, so she cannot be considered altogether human. It is exactly this condition that makes her so valuable, and it is she who suggests that they find Dracula through her inner mind.

The Source

Since the vampire is a supernatural creature of no small power, and since not everyone who wants to be associated with vampires wants to be a victim, there's one other role that brings a person into the elevated realm of the vampire: the hunter/slayer.

A film version of the vampire hunter for modern times is *John Carpenter's Vampires* (based on John Steakley's novel *Vampire$*). It's one of the least interesting such novels from a scientific standpoint, since it relies on religious mythology and the power of the Vatican, but its formula, more or less, is "Van Helsing meets the Old West bounty hunter." The vampires arise out of the earth by night to seek their prey, and the novel's hero, Jack Crow, leads his group of hunters against them. They go up against Valek, a six-hundred-year-old vampire, with the mission to stop him before he discovers the ritual that will allow vampires to prowl by day. Most of the team gets killed, but Crow finally confronts the vampire with a priest and destroys him. He appears to have a way to find them and he certainly knows how to read a vampire crime scene—even when it's just a bloody mass murder.

The vampire hunter in contemporary tales is more typically either a cop or reporter, because they're trained to read clues from crime scenes, and what they find is a disturbingly different kind of pattern. A relentless vampire hunter is a key character in the 1996 television series *Kindred: The Embraced*. His name is Frank Kohanek and he's a police officer who has a major obsession with Julian Luna, a wealthy man with a mysterious past who appears to have financial control over the city of San Francisco. Frank believes that Luna runs the area gangster activities and he intends to find evidence to bring Luna down. What he doesn't realize at first but quickly discovers from his lover is that Luna is a powerful vampire prince and a very dangerous creature. To protect Frank, she offers her life in exchange for his, a deal Luna accepts. When Frank learns this, he's doubly determined to bring Luna down, no matter what it takes. Yet Luna has given his pledge, so in a strangely dangerous twist the vampire being hunted offers protection to the man who is hunting him.

Indeed, in an episode in which a renegade vampire named Stark-weather attempts to kill Frank by hanging, Luna shows up and saves him. In that same episode, Luna offers to join forces with Frank to track this vampire, since it is in both of their interests to destroy him. Thus, the vampire hunter and the vampire team up to become a kind of single predator with a vampire as their prey. While the vampire hunter has no special powers of his own, he reluctantly gains them from this dubious partnership.

The show was based on the role-playing gamer *Vampire: The Masquerade*. Created by Mark Rein-Hagen and published in 1991, it became a huge international hit. Begun as a tabletop card game, it soon evolved into live-action scenarios that involved players for hours—even days—at a time. Since it emphasized the art of storytelling, it offered a powerful way to exercise the imagination, and since it assigned characters to people based on personality types, it simultaneously offered easy access to an imaginary vampire realm.

The basic idea is that major events in human history are brought about by the manipulations of vampires who rule over seven clans. They're all descended from Caine, "the Third Mortal," who was cursed by God for murdering his brother, and they call themselves the Kindred. While they're condemned to repeat Caine's crime of murder, they also engage in numerous commercial enterprises. It's their "masquerade" as humans that protects them from detection. Their safety lies in staying close to humans so they can "know their enemy," and that's why they live among the mortal race. The seven clans strove for power and influence in various cities, but the Ventrue clan emerged as the executives. Each major city has its own hierarchy and those who are "embraced" into the Kindred (transformed via a blood transfusion into vampires) are expected to follow the Masquerade's rules.

To generate interest, the television show relied on the fact that a human with the resources of law enforcement at his disposal had discovered the secret of the Kindred and vowed to bring them down. He's one in a long line of mortals who develop the courage and zeal to eradicate the evil among us. When he researches the fiends, he discovers that after they've fed, they can actually walk in the sun (which may otherwise destroy the younger ones), but that if they're sufficiently damaged, such as being blown apart by bullets or cut up with a knife, they can die like humans; they can also be burned to death or beheaded. Among their gifts is the ability to experience a past era via psychometry and an ability to change into a wolf or predatory bird. They can also mingle their molecules with dirt, so if need be they can blend into the soil. When they need blood, their eyes change, becoming demonic. While they may fall in love with mortals and thus endanger their secrets, by vampire law the Kindred are the first priority. They can destroy their own.

In this case, a departure from the tradition in which the vampire hunter has supernatural powers, Frank's only real powers are those he acquires through his invisible protectors. Yet he feels no gratitude to them, even when they save his life. He simply adds to his knowledge through each encounter and maintains his determination to ultimately bring the vampires down. Their warning to him that Kindred are everywhere means nothing; Frank is driven by a moral imperative and by the need to avenge his dead lover.

Does he succeed? Unfortunately, the show was canceled before this question was answered, but given the power and charm of the lead vampire, it's doubtful that Frank would have killed him.

Often the vampire hunters in fiction and film are driven by some religious or moral motive that severely limits depth of character. In short, they're props, and Frank Kohanek is no exception. His character remains flat and one-dimensional. Even Van Helsing is a stereotyped scholar figure. He leads the vampire hunters against Dracula but does not himself pick up the knives that terminate the monster.

A real-life Van Helsing was Montague Summers, whose groundbreaking book, The Vampire in Europe, published in 1929, focused on the various accounts of vampirism on the European continent. He made a few visits to areas where people still believed in vampires and wrote about his experiences. Montague Summers is rather an enigmatic figure in vampire lore. He wrote several treatises on the supernatural, including The Vampire: His Kith and Kin (1928). He also wrote about werewolves, witches, and demonology. Both a scholar and an avid reader of occult fiction, he wrote at length on the motif of the vampire in various folklore traditions around the world and also believed that the vampire scourge in some places was quite real. It only required three conditions for existence: the vampire, the devil, and the permission of God. He even journeyed to some places in Eastern Europe where belief in vampires was most evident and compiled a detailed report of what he witnessed and heard.

Yet these scholars and hunters aren't distinctive in themselves. They only have specialized knowledge. More unique are the hunters who are endowed with heightened abilities, such as the one that could be hired in Bulgaria when a vampire appeared to be attacking the livestock. This person, called the *vampirdzhija,* had special perceptual powers that allowed him to locate vampires' graves and use the proper rituals to destroy them.

The *dhampir* was another vampire hunter who had extraordinary powers, but his derived from the vampire. Studying this figure will take us a long way to understanding the origin of such powers.

The Half-breed

In some folklore, a dhampir is a mortal child who results from the coupling of a vampire father and a human mother. (In Gypsy lore, it's a dead man returning from his grave as a vampire to have sexual relations with his widow.) While according to many (but not all) accounts, a vampire cannot biologically reproduce, there appear to be some unusual circumstances in which this can occur, such as when he's under an enchantment that might make him temporarily human (or when he drinks Spider-Man's radioactive blood, which Morbius did). Yet even as a human, he still carries his vampire nature, and some of that gets transferred to his offspring, although such children are mortal and don't require blood to survive. Nevertheless, they might develop the thirst for it. Often they fight this foreign nature by acquiring a mission—to track down and destroy vampires. Sometimes they hire themselves out for this purpose to make a living (and that could mean conning a village into paying them to fight off monsters only they themselves can see). They can pass on their powers to their male children, but they can't teach them. The ability is either present or it isn't.

It's also possible that the vampire has semen and that it's potent, as was the case in Poppy Z. Brite's *Lost Souls* (1992). Zillah, a vampire, mates with a mortal girl who dies giving birth to their offspring. That kid, named Nothing, follows the vampires to try to figure out his destiny, but he's not like the half-breeds that become fearless vampire hunters. In fact, when he finds his father, neither seems to know quite what to do with the other.

Vampire Hunter D, starring in a 1985 Japanese animated feature, is half-vampire, half-human. He's a warrior thought to be the offspring of a powerful vampire, a legacy that gives him a dark nature that lures him even as he strives to destroy vampires. Other movies feature such vampire hunters as well, notably *The Forsaken, Blade*, and *Blade II*.

In *The Forsaken*, vampirism begins as a curse that becomes a virus, with many parallels to the AIDS virus. It seems that in the past, eight French knights fell victim to this curse and then transmitted it. Some of those afflicted were hunted down and killed, but four survive into the present day. The vampire's bite infects the victims, slowly working on them as they themselves become vampires. However, they don't die right away, and as a result, those who become aware of what has happened to them can become vampire hunters. Thus, they're part vampire without being a dhampir, and they are able to detect a vampire because their own physical chemistry has changed. One such person finds a drug that slows the course of his illness; in this way, the bitten who take the drug can hunt down and destroy the source of their infection. Killing the knight who started the disease will free those who are still part human. However, the vampire must be killed on sacred soil; this story mixes science and religion, yet does provide a biological basis for the ability to hunt down a vampire. (It's sometimes the case that vampires hunt down other vampires, as Queen Akasha does in *Queen of the Damned*, but that's another story.)

More in keeping with the half-breed dhampir figure is Blade, an African-American vampire hunter who originated in a 1973 Marvel comic-book series, *The Tomb of Dracula*. However, he's not made a vampire by a vampire's seed but indirectly by his bite. The doctor who assists his mother during a difficult delivery is a vampire named Deacon Frost. He feeds on Blade's mother, which gives Blade immunity against vampire bites. However, Blade's mother dies, so others raise him. When he is nine, he saves the life of a vampire hunter, Jamal Afari, and they develop a strong relationship. Afari becomes Blade's mentor, teaching him the ways of a vampire hunter and helping him develop his skills with teakwood knives. Afari himself, however, encounters Dracula and becomes a vampire. Blade kills him and then seeks revenge against the vampires who have brought so much pain to his life. He acquires some friends who join his crusade but who are killed along the way. He joins with Quincy Harker, the son of Mina and Jonathan Harker, to track down Dracula. During this quest, he finds a vampire detective seeking revenge against the one who made him a vampire. Blade and the detective become a loosely allied team, and when their mission is accomplished, Blade goes on to fight other vampires. He eventually got a comic-book series of his own, as well as two films.

More recently, Whitley Strieber followed up on *The Hunger* with *The Last Vampire* (2001). Miriam Blaylock is still around and she has one last egg with which she can create an offspring. However, she needs the right lover. She soon learns that Paul Ward, an Interpol agent, is tracking her around the world, and he's relentless. He's made sure that entire lairs of vampires are exterminated, and he's particularly obsessed with the ever-elusive Miriam. She will be his prey. Yet when they come together, Miriam learns that he's more than human, which reminds her of the ancient attempts by Keepers to crossbreed with humans. Most of these offspring were destroyed, but one had a son. That's how Paul has gotten his special tracking powers.

So now we have three ways in which a vampire hunter acquires skills to track a vampire through his own chemistry: by direct parentage, by a delayed reaction to the initial attack, and by the vampire's power presumably moving via the blood through the placenta to an unborn infant. Let's look more closely at the first option, the blending of vampire and human genetics for reproduction.

Reproduction with Humans

At a cellular level, we're always reproducing, as each cell makes an identical copy of itself through mitosis. That's part of being a living organism, and regardless of whether we decide that vampires are essentially dead bodies or reanimated with some living spirit that infuses the cells, a half-breed with human parts is going to be biologically human. This will affect its abilities on every level, as well as its life span. So the vampire that passes on its nature to the offspring that has human biological makeup must be encoding the cells to carry its nature without either killing those cells or rendering them immortal.

But is a vampire's impregnating of a human female the same as a mortal's? This brings us back to the issue of which "juices" are left in the body upon transformation into a vampire. In some cases, vampires lose the ability to produce tears or sweat (recall those vampires who cried blood).

But does a vampire produce semen? The answer appears to be that some do and some do not.

If it's the case that some enchantment has made the vampire temporarily human, then there's no problem in comprehending his ability to reproduce. However, if a vampire passes on his blood thirst and his power to offspring, then something more is going on than two mortals copulating and conceiving a child. The vampire must have a means of transferring his or her genetic material into an offspring, and that involves a fertilized egg.

Sometimes during reproduction, chromosomes can fail to properly separate. That means genetic defects can occur. In Down's syndrome, for example, extra chromosomes pass from the parents into the zygote and create specific traits. It's possible that a vampire mating with a human can do something similar (if he has semen or the woman has an egg), passing a chromosome that codes for certain vampiric characteristics but fails to override certain human traits. (In some folklore traditions, it's worth noting, a vampire that returns from the grave to have sex with his wife produces a child with no bones.) If we're correct about junk DNA and selfish genes assisting the mortal in the transformation into a vampire, then whatever it is in the junk DNA that makes the transformation possible could also affect a vampire-fertilized egg. It may even be like the neural tissue transplant discussed in chapter 3 that carries innate behaviors with it into the brain of the fetus.

We may also consider that female vampires can become temporarily human by that same magic that works with males, conceive a child, and give birth. However, it's possible that the ability occurs during a temporary state—perhaps only a single night—and the return to a vampire state would not support a growing fetus. These issues, however, are not clear.

To return to the vampire father passing on some of his nature and skills to a mortal child, what forms might the genetic transmissions actually take?

The dhampir has certain specific skills. He or she can:

- sense a supernatural creature within a specified distance

- develop visions that provide guidance as well as intimacy with the vampire

- walk in sunlight

- eat as a human eats

- procreate and pass powers on to offspring

- control animals

- acquire extra strength in the pursuit of a single-minded goal

- achieve a mental edge that borders on psychosis

- destroy vampires

In a way, these half-breed vampire hunters resemble the witch find-ers of the Middle Ages. Both look for specific signs of their prey, are determined to expose them for what they are, are single-minded and passionate, and want to destroy vampires and thereby restore the moral order.

The Inquisition, the Catholic Church's means of eradicating heretics from its midst, started in the thirteenth century. During two centuries, witches were labeled heretics or devil worshipers, and thus began the epidemic of witch-hunts across Europe and England.

Witch judges or witch finders were men appointed (or self-appointed) to travel to places where the practice of witchcraft was suspected, find the culprit through specific signs, hold a trial, and apply the appropriate punitive measures. The *Malleus Maleficarum* (or *Witch Hammer*) was a comprehensive handbook that was used on prosecuting witches. Written by two Dominican inquisitors, it was published in Germany in 1486, and for the next two centuries it had a significant influence on what happened to the accused. Clerics were empowered by the pope to become witch finders because it was felt that secular courts weren't being sufficiently punitive. According to the Bible, witches were to be put to death. The *Malleus* is divided into three parts to indicate how the devil uses his followers to perpetrate harm against others, how witches cast spells, and what the legal procedures should be for interrogating and torturing suspected witches. Thanks to the traveling witch finders, thousands of innocent people were executed.

During that same period, Leo Allatius published the first scholarly book to examine the subject of vampires, and he took his cue from the *Malleus Malificarum* when he cited the same three conditions for the existence of vampires as for witches: a corpse, the devil, and God's permission for the devil to reanimate it. According to scholar J. Gordon Melton in *The Vampire Book*, that connection was the first that joined Satan with vampirism. That meant that the symbols of God, such as holy water and a crucifix, were useful in identifying a vampire, repelling it, and destroying it.

Once a vampire hunter manages to track a vampire, the next step is to destroy it.

Killing a Vampire

Robert Neville, the only person alive in *I Am Legend* who's not a vampire, finds out that sticking a wooden stake into the humans-turned-vampires during daylight hours, seems to destroy them. Since he doesn't buy the superstitions about this method, he researches it scientifically. It turns out that the virus that made people into vampires operates on an anaerobic system, but piercing the skin and leaving the stake in allows air to enter and disrupts the system. An anaerobic organism, like yeast cells or bacteria, gets energy not from using oxygen but from fermentation. It's not efficient and sometimes produces lactic acid, but it still yields energy. Neville introduces oxygen, which shifts the organism into an aerobic process. Thus, he destroys the bacterium that keeps the vampire alive—at least until it mutates.

Procedures in unenlightened countries where superstitions about vampires were rampant were not quite so precise. In fact, there were so many ways that one could become a vampire that prevention and destruction weren't always very clear-cut.

In such places, where there is some fear that a person might become a vampire after death, such as in the case of a suicide, a person born with a caul, or a person who has sickened slowly and died soon after the death of a relative, some precautions may be taken. As part of the burial, one tradition calls for stuffing the mouth and nose with garlic and another for turning the corpse facedown so that it cannot dig its way out. The gravedigger might also put sharpened stakes into the ground that could pierce the vampire as he tries to get to the surface.

Yet despite precautions, sometimes a vampire would still get out, and in such a case, it had to be caught and killed. There are a surprising variety of ways to accomplish this. Depending on which tradition one wishes to follow, vampires may be killed by:

- sun exposure

- simple beheading

- beheading, with garlic stuffed into the head

- cutting out and burning the heart

- burying the body on an island or tossing it into water

- a wooden (preferably hawthorn) stake through the heart

- cremation and scattering the ashes

- causing them to bleed to death

- a silver bullet (yes, that's also for a werewolf)

- burying a decapitated vampire at a crossroads and filling the coffin with poppy seeds. (This refers to the superstition that a vampire had to count every poppy seed, sometimes at the rate of one a year, before it could leave its coffin.)

- cutting the body open and washing it with boiling wine

- Excarnation—allowing scavengers to consume the soft parts

Many superstitions emphasize the use of a wooden stake to be hammered into a suspected vampire. Sometimes it's a particular type of wood, such as hawthorn or aspen, or the same type of wood as was used for Christ's cross. A ritual might accompany the act, but sometimes it was just a matter of pinning the corpse to the ground, and hammering the stake through the heart, into the naval, or between the shoulder blades. It had to be driven all the way through until the sharpened end went into the ground. One might also nail the back of the head to the coffin before placing it into the ground. More brutally, the corpse's vampiric afterlife could be curtailed by cutting the tendons behind its knees or mutilating its feet to keep it from walking around.

Since a head or heart can be surgically reattached, excarnation takes too long, a stake and garlic can be (and has been) removed, the sun and water aren't always potent, and poppy seeds can eventually all be counted, the most surefire method appears to be cremation.

In some tales, when a vampire was cut apart and burned, those who performed the ritual had to ensure that every tiny fragment of bone was consumed in the fire, because it was believed that a vampire could regenerate even from a sliver. (The alchemist Magnus tells his vampire child Lestat in *The Vampire Lestat* to be sure to scatter the ashes after the cremation, because to leave them intact risks reanimation.)

In one culture, during cremation, the living stood in the smoke because it was thought to offer them added protection.

So let's talk about cremation's requirements.

The average human body is 70 to 80 percent water, and while that percentage may decrease after the vampire transformation (as Saint Germain indicates), it's still likely to have a lot of moisture. That means that a cremation fire has to burn pretty hot. Otherwise, the flames will scorch the external parts and possibly leave enough of the body intact to permit reanimation. Unless the vampire hunter has a modern crematorium available, she'll have to pile up a lot of wood or gas-based fuel and make sure her fire has good air circulation. The fire has to burn hot for a considerable period of time to consume an entire body.

In *Death to Dust*, Kenneth V. Iserson describes the process of cremation in detail. He defines it as the application of intense heat to convert a body to its basic components through oxidation. That results in four to eight pounds of ash and bone fragments. Efficient cremation, he says, requires an initial temperature of around 1,100 degrees Fahrenheit; in a cremation chamber, this can rise to over 2,000 degrees. Some bodies emit black smoke when cremated; this can be reduced with the increase of air. Modern ovens can incinerate the average corpse in about half an hour, although some take longer, depending on body type and the kind of container used. Since 60 percent of bone is inorganic and therefore doesn't burn, some of it will become part of the cremains, which may then be pulverized.

While lower temperatures may also work, the process will take much longer, and the oven still has to be fairly hot.

Fated to Slay

Buffy the Vampire Slayer began its life as a full-length feature film in 1992. Gail Burnam read it in script form and proposed a television series, which it eventually became in 1997. As it developed, the show widened the moderate ambitions of the film. Buffy, sixteen, is a California girl, a high-school cheerleader whose superficial life of fashion and dates is disrupted when a "Watcher," a member of an international group based in London that has watched the slayers for centuries, approaches her and informs her of her heritage: she is a Chosen One, a vampire slayer. She shares with other young women in previous generations the ability to detect and kill vampires, thereby eradicating evil from the midst of unwitting mortals. She also learns that there is an ancient nemesis and enemy of her clan, Lothos, who will try to track and destroy her. Under the guidance of her mentor Watcher, she must develop both her offensive and defensive skills. She becomes a vampire-killing machine.

In the show's world, the vampires have many of the old gothic-literature vulnerabilities, such as the fear of holy items, burning in the sun, turning to ash when impaled by a wooden stake, and death by fire and decapitation. They need to be invited over a threshold, but they don't have to sleep in native soil. They can also be rendered harmless to humans through a scientific process, which means that their abilities are not altogether supernatural. The vampires in Buffy's world got their start when a demon mixed its blood with that of a human and left the latter possessed.

Returning to the days of Nosferatu, the vampires in *Buffy* are hideous when in the power of the bloodlust, which symbolizes their unmitigated evil. The show's creator, Joss Whedon, decided to give them batlike faces and keep them monstrous, and he devised his own rules for vampire life and death derived from the vampire movies and novels he most loved. This series spun off another one, *Angel*, about one of *Buffy*'s popular vampire characters, one who has a soul and therefore suffers over his evil condition like Barnabas Collins or Rice's Louis de Pointe du Lac. Yet alongside him there are plenty of monsters for the vampire slayers to take on.

Chris Golden is the awarding-winning, bestselling author of the young-adult *Body of Evidence* series, and in comic books he's worked with a range of characters, including the Crow and Blade. He's written novels and nonfiction books based on the *Buffy the Vampire Slayer* television series, including coauthoring *The Monster Book*, an official guide to the show's many monsters. He understands what modern-day vampire hunting is all about on a supernatural level, but realizes that the show is lacking in scientific explanations. "The way things are set up in the Buffy-verse," he explained, "is that the slayer is the chosen one and the only method that we're aware of for that is what's referred to as the Powers That Be. There's no reference to God actually existing, although that's also not refuted. The show just refers to the active elements in favor of 'good' and 'light' as the Powers That Be."

However, when the slayers are chosen, they get that extra power we talked about earlier: "The slayers are physically gifted. Their physical abilities have been enhanced and they can heal. As far as requirements for the slayer, it's always a teenage girl, but there's nothing specifically established that causes certain girls to be chosen. And while they have extra powers, they don't live very long."

Nancy Holder, too, has an enduring association with the series and has some ideas about why it's speaks so powerfully to contemporary audiences. A Bram Stoker Award winner for fiction, she has penned several official companion guides for *Buffy the Vampire Slayer;* her latest spin-off books include the *Unseen* trilogy and *The Angel Case-files.*

"One of the attractions to the show," she said, "is that there are a lot of layers. It started out as good and evil, and there was a vicious vampire that just had to be staked. Then things changed. Spike, an evil vampire who acquired his name because he rammed railroad spikes into people, was caught by a group called the Initiative. They were capturing vampires and demons and putting a chip into their heads that would prevent them from being violent toward humans. So Spike got one of these chips and now he's reluctantly joined the forces of good, so they couldn't just stake him. His character has been softened on purpose, which shows that the potential for complexity was always there. The show is forward thinking in terms of a coming-of-age tale. Buffy learns that good is not always good and bad is not always bad. The more she knows, the more murky it all is, and the more difficult.

"I think what makes the show popular is the fact that there's a true hero's journey. Buffy must be the slayer and she can't quit. She has to do it until she dies, so she's doomed to be the tragic hero. She will die in the service of her duty, and on any given day she doesn't know if that's the day she will die. She has real problems and makes real mistakes, so for all her supernatural milieu, she's extremely human. She's easy to identify with, she's strong, and she's brave. She's out there every night fighting against evil in ways that no one else can take care of. We get to watch a real person do noble and dangerous things. It's a perfect parallel to Joseph Campbell's idea in *The Hero with a Thousand Faces*. Campbell talked about the hero archetype being organic. It's built into our system and we respond to the universal structure of the tale. Storytellers who choose characters that resonate to the right energy will get an audience."

Archetypes are like masks worn by characters, and Campbell's outline of the hero's journey involves a person called to a mythically prodigious task who isn't too crazy about going. In other words, that person must grow and move toward his or her own higher self, but few go without resistance. The call is made, turned down, made again with the prodding of a mentor, and the hero then crosses the threshold. Now she's in a special realm, one she couldn't have experienced had she remained in her ordinary life. Along the way, she will encounter both allies and enemies, go through ordeals, and enter the innermost cave (otherwise known as the dark night of the soul or even physical death). Then she may cross another threshold and transform. She can take possession of her reward and return to the ordinary world with the treasure of her special vision or abilities, gained through difficulties and inner growth.

"Buffy has a mentor," Holder points out, "she crosses a threshold, enters the world of the supernatural, and fights the good fight. She has allies and enemies. She goes into the innermost cave, where she dies, and then she's resurrected and brings back something with her. It's the same pattern."

That gets us back to the way our mindbody operates. We've already suggested that the shifts and changes in the theories proposed by the most fundamental science, physics, affect how we think and perceive. We've seen how that science has come to echo ideas from Eastern mystical traditions to allow for paradoxical thinking and multiple realities. We've talked about the trickle-down effect into other modes of thinking and creating, and that brings us to the postmodern arena.

Buffy is one of the manifestations of the postmodern mind-set in popular entertainment, and vampire fiction, too, has been affected. More dramatic, however, has been the explosion of interest and participation in what's known as the vampire scene or subculture. From just a few isolated practitioners throughout the seventies and eighties, it grew into a population of thousands around the world. Although this was foreshadowed in the eighties, it was during the 1990s that we really got to see what the vampire could become. A great many people of all persuasions grabbed the vampire and claimed it as their own.

SEVEN

The Celestine Vampire

The postmodern vampire tale is a story that turns convention on its head and thumbs its nose at the notion that any human-invented explanation is definitive. It's about the flow of many shifting narratives, none of which is final. The television series *Buffy the Vampire Slayer* illustrates this philosophy. "In many ways it's reactionary," says *Buffy* tie-in author Chris Golden, "because in most mass entertainment the girl is usually the damsel in distress, especially in monster stories. Here the girl is not only the hero but also the boss."

Buffy's creator, Joss Whedon, took his cue from other novels and films, but then did his own thing. So did Mark Rein-Hagan and White Wolf, the company that developed the 1991 role-playing game *Vampire: The Masquerade*. What started as a card came much like *Dungeons & Dragons* inspired live-action scenarios (LARPs) around the world in which people who wanted to pretend they were vampires (or other monsters) could get together and act out those fantasies. There were rules, to be sure, but sometimes unofficial versions were spun off the original, so players could send their imaginations to the moon. At the same time, the popularity of chat rooms and other "meeting" grounds on the Internet turned role-playing into an art form. Some preferred a defined world such as Rice's *Vampire Chronicles,* while others made up their own rules.

Anything Goes

Vampires today do not have to avoid the sun, kill anyone, or even drink blood. They can have families, get a tan, and drink wine. Anyone who wants to devise a definition of the vampire condition has the authority to do so . . . and plenty of people have stepped forward to do just that.

We have sex vampires, energy vampires, emotional vampires, mortal vampires prone to illness, and vampires who've inherited their condition, or become that way by sorcery, reincarnation, or a virus. Vampires can eat food (including garlic), work on Wall Street, walk in daylight, steal souls, come from Mars, faint at the sight of blood, and put their makeup on in a mirror. One person says vampires around the world are one big family. Another insists the true vampire is a loner. Many view the vampire as compassionate, even empathic. Others insist on the sociopathic predator of nineteenth-century tales. Jana Marcus interviewed Anne Rice fans for *In the Shadow of the Vampire,* and even among those who accepted the reality of the novelist's world, there were many alternative interpretations. Just how many different vampires can there be? A man who emerged from a visionary near-death experience as a vampire claimed that there are over one hundred different types.

In science, it's the idea that once-thought-to-be unequivocal truths have proven to be indeterminate; in literature, it's that any given text offers itself to multiple interpretations; and in everyday life, black and white blends into many shades of gray; while values once thought stable are anything but.

Inevitably we feel the shifts and spins of our existential foundation, and even when we can't articulate precisely what it means, we manifest our resulting anxieties symbolically in our creations. Once conventional authority gets stripped away and centuries-old theories lose their reassuring validity, everyday life becomes situation-bound and art embraces the relative. Decades ago we "knew" what a vampire was; now no one can be told that her version of this creature fails to match the standard.

The vampire has evolved in many directions, moving in popular culture from a pure notion of evil to a conscience-bound but sexy seducer, even a hero. Many are attractive and romantic. While we still have a few brutally aggressive vampires lurking in the shadows, some novelists have portrayed their vampires as just plain nice.

"I think the answer to why the vampire has changed like this," says *Dracula* scholar Elizabeth Miller, "lies in the particular culture that has created the vampire. The vampire can be read as a projection of society's fears and anxieties. In Stoker's day, middle-class Victorians were anxious about, among other things, the displacement of religion by evolutionary theory, atavism, resentment about the immigration of foreigners, sexually aggressive women, and artistic decadence. All of these 'threats' are realized in the figure of Count Dracula. In spite of what the movies have done to the Count, there is no doubt in my mind that Stoker intended him to be the embodiment of evil.

"But if we view evil, at least in part, as a cultural construct, then we begin to look more sympathetically on the supposedly 'evil' character. This shift can be seen not only in interpretations of Count Dracula himself but also in the vampire figure in general. Furthermore, the general questioning of absolutes that characterizes post-modernism has led to a blurring of the boundaries between 'good' and 'evil'—giving the vampire a broader range of interpretations.

"Part of the evolution towards the ambivalent, even the sympathetic, can be explained by the fact that the vampire has become an apt metaphor for the 'Other.' Sort of a 'politically correct' vampire, if you wish. Lost in all of this romanticizing of the vampire is that the original vampire in folklore and in Stoker was anything but sympathetic. Embracing the 'new' vampire is done at a cost—the loss of much of the appeal of the original— the horrifying intensity of a confrontation with pure evil."

What has happened with these diverse interpretations, however, is that factions have formed. People who now identify themselves as vampires, rather than just spectators who enjoy vampire entertainment, have definite views on what a vampire is—and everyone else had better pay attention. Members of such groups say they're the "real ones," the only ones who know, and others are just pretenders. Another group disputes such claims and offers its own ideas. It's turned into a tedious game of so-called expertise, with contrived credentials and plenty of venom. Some want to take over and rule the entire vampire scene and others just want to be left alone. Whether vampirism is the result of a virus, a secret initiation, a blood disorder, or the more traditional vampiric transfusion is up for grabs, and there's no central authority to decide that matter. It appears chaotic, yet a glance over the vampire's evolution indicates three conceptual threads emerging that stamp the contemporary vampire culture with a unique pattern.

- The vampire is evil.

- The vampire has a romantic dark side.

- The vampire is a manifestation of alternate spirituality.

To give an example of how they merge, let's look at a typical vampire community in a large city, say New York or Los Angeles. Its members may meet at a club, which provides a place for like-minded people who identify with the dark figure of the night to gather, parade their fashions, and listen to music. Perhaps in secret rooms, they experiment with drugs or a blood exchange, or even some clandestine sexual ritual. Among them will be some who view this gathering as evidence that vampirism is a means of transcending mundane concerns and feel that they are special and set apart. They may even claim certain extraordinary powers and a perspective on life and death that elevates them above the common herd.

Others will be seeking a partner—for sex, love, subjugation, even marriage—and they view the dark secrecy of vampirism as a way of establishing and strengthening romantic bonds between kindred souls. To them, vampires are complex creatures that may suffer guilt over their urge to drink blood and treat others like "prey." Some among them will revel in the idea that they may be enslaved to a dominant entity who will treat them in ways beyond anything they imagine. It's the swoon, the feeling of rapture and surrender to a mysterious other that grips them. They may screen for "safe" partners or join a vampire "feeding circle" or "family," but they're looking for a spiritualized romance, an interrelationship of complementary hearts of darkness.

And yet even within this community there will those who have antisocial tendencies. As we've already noted, some people who are attracted to the vampire world see it as a license for violence. A few have killed and others have bragged about killing or told of plans to "sacrifice" someone. Attempts to dominate and control others are evident in rules and rituals that endow some people with "insider" status and shove others out. Such behavior has been characteristic of groups of humans since time began.

People have an instinctive fear of strangers, according to the anthropological studies cited by naturalist Lyall Watson in *Dark Nature*, and to feel protected, they devise a language that confers a certain status on their own tribe and turns outsiders into Others. One tribe of headhunters, for example, considers its members as the only human beings; members of all other tribes are merely what they eat.

This trend is true of contemporary vampire groups as well. Endowing themselves with the privilege of being a "vampyre," they look down with superior attitudes on others, considering them "mundanes." Obviously the word *mundane* has negative connotations, so to use this term is to convey the sense that what is done to those people is of little consequence. It's about being smug and dehumanizing.

There are even those who exploit their own. One young man who called himself simply "V" went about promoting his program of a community in which an elite core group would run the show through secret meetings and the rest would have to endure an initiation process to become members. Once in, they would be afforded protection, but they would have to use secret names, words, and signals to connect with other members. Under a benevolent guise, V endowed certain people with a high status, but in the meantime he used the resources of his group for his own benefit. He charged fees, which he pretended to spend on the club but actually pocketed. He stole ideas and presented them as his own; he promised wages for work done that he never paid—though he utilized the other members' talents and assured them that they were contributing to the community. V manipulated others for his gain and their loss.

So within the frame of a single social scene, we have many types of vampires mingling together, joined by an idea, though they may interpret that idea in vastly different ways.

Before going further into this world, let's return to fiction to see how it might have influenced some of these developments.

Psychic Vampires

The 1980s brought an abundance of vampire fiction and film, and late in the decade author Dan Simmons presented the massive *Carrion Comfort* (1989), which proved to be a huge success. It was about a group of vampires who compete in a game that involves producing death and destruction among humans. The players generate aggression and hatred in the human heart, and they feed off this energy. In fact, as the novel progresses, it becomes clear that many of the atrocious evils we've attributed to humans, such as the Holocaust and slavery, have been set in motion by these psychic vampires. They infect the minds of people they get close to and set off a chain of events that horrifies humans but delights the vampires. They get what they need and walk away without anyone being the wiser.

Carrion Comfort wasn't the first novel about energy vampires. In fact, that distinction goes to Charles W. Webber in 1853, with his *Spiritual Vampirism*. Arthur Conan Doyle likewise published a tale in 1894 about a vampiric creature associated with hypnosis. Three years later, at the same time as *Dracula* appeared, Florence Marryat published *The Blood of the Vampire*. A few more of similar themes followed in the early 1900s, and even the year after *Carrion Comfort* came out, Kim Newman offered another type of energy-depleting vampire in *Bad Dreams*. Colin Wilson's *Space Vampires* in 1976 were about life-sucking alien vampires.

Those people who embrace the vampire but do not wish to get involved in the practice of drawing or drinking blood take their inspiration from the idea that life energy can be taken from people. In fact, the earliest ideas about vampires had this "ethereal" quality, so some practitioners feel they're returning a more original form of vampirism.

One person, a "pranic vampire," explained her interest in the vampire's use of energy. "In the West," she said, "we've sacrificed the notion that everything possesses vital spirit in favor of living in a sanitized and controllable technological world. It is, however, a world without a soul. In such a world, where the natural exchange of energy between all living things is debunked as delusional and esoteric, of course vampirism is misunderstood. It has been marginalized into superstition and folklore."

To her, the fact that some people yield energy and others thrive on it is just part of the universal balance, a cycle of creation, destruction, and re-creation. The vampire may "feed," but may also transform that which is taken into something that blooms with abundance.

Life energy is known as chi or prana, and it's manifested everywhere. Those who can detach themselves from the material world can perceive it and appreciate its power. It takes a different kind of sense to "see" spiritual reality, and those who develop this faculty are often drawn to such Oriental disciplines as qui gong and feng shui. For them it's all about finding a way to make the energy flow in an integrated universe. Since energy vampires are not as connected to chi as humans are, they work to attune themselves to humans so as to exploit their vitality, which has already been transformed from the universal into something particular and corporeal in individual people. They digest and distribute the energy through their chakras.

While linking themselves with vampires, energy vampires dislike the image of the bloodsucker, yet they will often mingle with the latter in larger groups.

Handbook for Lost Souls

Another influential novel, published in 1992, was Poppy Z. Brite's *Lost-Souls*, set in the Goth subculture of New Orleans. Her vampires were mostly losers, not the beautiful immortals that populated many vampire realms from the eighties. She explored the alienated spirit and won a following among those who understood the outsider in this way.

Brite started writing *Lost Souls* when she was nineteen, living in Chapel Hill, North Carolina. She was fascinated with the fashions and death aesthetic of the Goth culture, of which she felt part. The vampire was one of its icons, and in her hands it became an image of erotic degeneration.

In *Lost Souls*, a vampire who is over four hundred years old tends bar in the French Quarter where a young mortal girl shows up the same night as three wandering vampires—who remind us of some of the more decadent rock bands of the era. One of them impregnates her and leaves her to the fate of mortals who couple with vampires: a violent bloody death while giving birth to a monster. The resulting creature is a vampire, but he appears to be mortal. This girl's child is named Nothing, and he is the archetype of the many "thin children in black" who call themselves Goths and who feel as if they truly are nothing—just society's cast-off trash.

"I very much fancied myself as one of them," Brite admitted. She would visit her father, who lived in New Orleans, and go hang out in the seedy French Quarter. The Goth kids were nice to her, introducing her to their tastes and taking her to their hangouts.

In the book, Nothing falls in love with a rock duo known as the Lost Souls, whose lead singer is Ghost, a sensitive young man who knows when evil is near and who feels the world's pain as his own. He wants to rescue Nothing, but Nothing joins his vampire father and learns the ways of his kind. The novel winds down in violence, gore, and despair.

To Brite, working with a familiar image like the vampire was a way for an author to show her unique take on things more clearly. What she thought about the vampire, she described in an introduction to her vampire anthology, *Love in Vein*: "The vampire is everything we love about sex and the night and the dark-dream side of ourselves:

adventure on the edge of pain, the thrill to be had from breaking taboos." The bizarre is something to be sought, explored, even surrendered to.

In fact, increasingly more people did just that. With the spread of role-playing games around the world and clubs devoting one night a week to the "vampyres," some of those who adopted a vampire identity portrayed themselves as the real thing. They lived it 24/7, they said; and they adopted clothing, names, and habits that would mark them as night creatures.

One club participant, who identified strongly with characters in this novel and who asked to remain anonymous, described a transforming encounter he had with someone who presented himself as a vampire.

It was when he bit me and licked away the blood that I first decided to become a vampire. Sexy, powerful, and mysteriously evil—he had everything I thought I ever wanted. So I asked him to show me and he did.

I watched him seduce people, all kinds of people, with his charming ways and sultry movements. I studied how he lured them in, how he trapped their vulnerable minds and coerced blood gifts from their weak bodies. It was so easy then . . . you know . . . to adapt the black art of seduction into my own personality. I became a vampire myself; and I created my secret self with great attention to details.

From the very start I could see it was going to be easy, enticing people to give me blood—particularly males. The young men seemed especially drawn to my appearance, sensing an intelligent product with a strong sense of purpose.

For me, being a vampire means fulfilling my needs through the willing sacrifice of others. I am offered blood, sex, and power over otherwise inert lives. Seeking respite from their own pathetic, aimless lives . . . victims prefer the distraction of pain, suffering, and bleeding.

You may wonder how one is so easily convinced to open a vein?

Well, its quite simple really, considering how often they do so to force something in. How much easier then to let a little of themselves drip out? They willingly submit themselves, twisting their own desires so that there is a mutual exchange. It's win-win.

As a vampire, my greatest power is intuition. I know, without words or actions, what a person wants . . . what a person needs. This power of intuition, combined with my adaptability, allows me to transform myself into whatever is necessary for the kill. I lock with the person's psyche, diagnose their deepest hunger, and become their provider and they my supplier.

Blood drinking is, for me, not the ultimate goal of being a vampire. It is necessary, and even desirable, but not essential for my survival. My life force is boosted when I drink and digest blood, but it is my ability to control the passion and desires of a person that nurtures my soul. Victims never see themselves as exploited in the relationship, but instead subvert their own identities in favor of becoming the possessed.

The ingestion of blood pleases me, it strengthens me, but it does not literally give me power. I am the master when I take their blood, the very life fluid of their existence, but my real power lies in owning control of their will. A person's will is more precious than their blood, the will being capable of summoning the heart, the emotions, and then . . . to any deed I desire.

You ask if I meet with others "like myself," and I answer you with: "There are no others like myself; I being the only one of my distinctive ability and power." Among vampires, I am unique, formidable, and solitary. I work alone. No one walks beside me. Deeds are best done alone.

Of course, being a vampire is a solitary experience. Life for all living things is solitary, being alone in one's mind always, but much more for vampires. Solitude, if properly understood, is the vampire's asset: vampires—good ones anyway—use natural states of being to accomplish their goals.

Human beings fear being alone, sensing it is the natural state of the human condition: we are born alone, we construct private worlds of thought alone, and we die alone—walking the final steps with no one at our side. Vampires are masters at using the solitary condition to their advantage, having probed the alchemy of oneness and discovered synergy.

I am strongest when I am alone, gathering energy from my own thoughts and internal forces. I am even stronger when I am in the presence of a sensitive seeker, one who searches for my kind. It is the seeker who finds me that brings spiritual awakening. I soar in the presence of one who desires to be taken as strongly as I desire to master.

This person refers to power and secrecy, yet another spoke about "healing" or "nurturing" vampires. This gets us into the New Age influence on the vampire culture, with its adoption of mystical practices and attitudes.

Dracula is to the postmodern vampire as Newtonian science is to quantum mechanics.

What once seemed solid in both physics and the vampire narrative turns out to be more fluid than we realized, and the two can somehow coexist as different perspectives on a similar phenomenon.

Even as these unique vampire novels got people's attention, authors like Chelsea Quinn Yarbro and Anne Rice continued their vampire histories. Rice had Lestat practice astral projection, become mortal again and realize he wanted to be a vampire, meet God and the devil, and finally get crushed by the evil he'd done. As beautiful and romantic as he was, and as much as he tried to circumvent his compulsion to kill, Lestat's behavior still indicated that Rice thought of the vampire as essentially evil. Lestat kills an older woman and knows that his nature is beyond his control. After visiting hell in *Memnoch the Devil,* he goes into a spiritual coma.

At this point Rice decided that the *Vampire Chronicles* were now over. But then she revived them in a new form by revisiting the characters in novels like *Pandora, Armand,* and *Blood and Gold.* Her fans, who were often writing their own fiction with her characters and who were role-playing those characters in cyberworld get-togethers, grabbed at all this new material. In New Orleans, where Rice lived, her fan club put on a "Coven Party" every Halloween. The powerful influence of fiction seen in those role-playing behaviors was striking, as was the amount of money spent by hundreds of people to costume themselves as one of Rice's characters.

Yet there were many who attended vampire gatherings who barely even read those novels and sought new images that answered their own needs. In the vampire subculture, we find many things: blood fetishism, sadomasochism, a fashion show, a music scene, a platform for creative expression, and escapism. Yet there can be something deeper, too. Some have carefully considered why they adopt the vampire as their symbol and can articulate what it means to them. From hunger for romance to what Foucault called the "limit experience," there's an underlying desire to use the vampire to feel more, see more, and *be* more than most ordinary people seemed to want. There's passion and transcendence. There's creativity and connection. There's even a rich sense of community.

It's ironic but true that many current participants in the vampire subculture are more akin to the vampire bat than was the original loner vampire. Such animals live mostly in caves in South and Central America. They sleep by day and emerge at night to seek a warm-blooded animal, sometimes human but usually a cow, to sink their razor-sharp teeth into and suck up blood with their grooved tongues. They're not there to kill, just to eat. Since blood digests easily and they don't take a lot, they need to drink often, but they don't always succeed in getting what they need. In that case, they return to the cave still hungry, and if they don't eat within three nights, they can die. So a group ethic takes over. If one bat comes in for the day fully sated and others are starving, the fat and sassy one regurgitates blood to feed the others. Thus they become donor and recipient, and if any takes but fails to return the favor, the others get aggressive. So even vampire bats can't be vampires in the sense of an entity selfishly thriving off others. It's a reciprocal arrangement meant to benefit all.

Vampire in Spirit

Darkness and mystery intensify experience. Darkness contains what we don't want to see, but if we take the time to look more closely, we may find something powerful. The vampire gives a name to that nameless part within us that feels connected to a larger source. Those who resonate to the image can explore more fully how it feels to be so connected. As one person put it, "The vampire is about the search for something genuine in an era when almost anything can be faked."

There's boldness in this impulse to contact subliminal lusts, and the imagined gains diminish the risks. Vampires seem to possess the secrets of both physical transformation and spiritual epiphany, and people long for both. It's not necessarily about defeating death, because these practitioners hardly ever claim to be immortal. Yet among them, vampires of legend are considered the gods of ancient times, the energy that empowers darkness by conforming to mythic patterns within us. Like the inferno that Dante passed through to find his way to God, they offer rebirth through descent. One man who has been part of this culture for years told me that people who connect with vampires are hungry for a sense of the divine—and they often find it. "It's a soul movement," he insisted. Fully present, vampires know the ultimate passion and invite us, if we dare, to partake.

"Modern man," said Swiss psychoanalyst Carl Jung, "must rediscover a deeper source of his own spiritual life. To do this, he is obligated to struggle with evil, to confront his own shadow, to integrate the devil."

Hespera, twenty-two, is the lead singer of Parisian Voodoo, a London-based rock band, and manager of VAD, or the British organization for vampires and donors. Attracted to the vampire, she became involved with a group that she calls pantheistic vampires.

I remember truly believing I was a vampire at the age of eight. I used to run around the playground at school in a black cloak and sleep with arms crossed in bed. It was all very funny and innocent, of course. I didn't drink blood or really understand vampirism, but I remember everyone thought it rather peculiar for an eight-year-old to behave like a vampire. In retrospect I suppose it had something to do with the BBC series *The Little Vampire* that was on television at the time. I was deeply impressed and viewed it religiously. Growing up, I realized very quickly that I am not a vampire, although somehow they always appeared entwined in my life. Then I became associated with the Vampires of Atilla through my own relations to the pantheistic scene. It seems only natural for me to donate blood and provide guidance. I am very proud of VAD, since we supply an alternative for mature, individual vampires who feel estranged from the otherwise mundane Gothic/fetish subculture.

To her mind, the British vampire scene differs from what she's heard and read about the American scene.

From my understanding of the American vampire scene, it is dominated by several alternative sectors: those who are heavily involved in the fetish scene and those belonging to covens and other occult-related clans. In Britain, you'll find an almost uncondensed division between

vampires and other alternative cultivations. Of course you'll find a British vampire who engages in the odd whipping or who practices wicca,
but most vamps in this country are not directly involved in the Gothic/
fetish scene.

Another observation I have had is that British vampires, by the very
nature of their culture and upbringing, are a lot more romantic and
visionary. I don't think they are as cynical and tough as American
vamps. I know the Americans may perceive us British as 'limey wimps,'
which is fair enough if you ask me, but if most American vampires find
scarification, S&M parties, and dodgy covens their ideal solution for
Saturday-night kicks, here you'll find vampires pursuing more subtle
and elegant means of entertainment that do not encompass violence or
hostility toward themselves or society. Whilst most vamps in the States
[appear to] enjoy living an alternative lifestyle aside the distempered
underground, I believe the majority of British vampires aspire to a
stately lifestyle among the elite of society and aristocracy. A little like
Lestat, wouldn't you say? Many vamps in the U.K. contribute to the
community and hold honorable professions, thus being beneficial and
productive to the very society they feed off, which is an interesting irony
in itself. One of my members in VAD is a pediatrician, another a former
parachuter in the Royal Air Force who fought for his country.

The bottom line is that while most American vampires seem to es-
trange themselves from the mainstream and resent it, blaming 'Uncle
Sam' for all their misfortunes and problems, British vampires are ex-
ceedingly proud of their heritage and choose not to alienate themselves
from society, even if they can't be honest about their true tendencies.
The British were never famous for their outspokenness anyway, so I
don't think a lot of them mind keeping their vampirism to themselves—
unlike the Americans, who like parading their intimate affairs.

Like many during the 1990s she feels there is no longer a stereotypical "real vampire," and in fact has encountered many people who

felt that the vampire has been poorly defined "and only *they* knew what it really is." Since the stereotypical vampire to which she refers grew out of mythology and fiction, it's not representative of those who participate in the vampire world. "Most people who have grown up on Hollywood's rendition," Hespera says, "and even fans of Anne Rice, would be surprised by what they find in the vampire subculture. It's not really what anyone expects who hasn't explored it."

Moving on to the combination of vampirism and pantheistic spirituality, she says that much of this realm is secret, but she can offer a basic idea from some of their writings. "*The Chronicles of Pan* are in fact the practice of pantheism, which is an ancient theology concerning the eschatological union between nature and the concept of god. One of the six orders is Atilla, and they are the assembly of vampires. The Chronicles of Pan have absolutely nothing to do with role playing games or New Age mythos. There are three sects of the Vampires of Atilla; one in New York, the other in Oregon, and the British bough is in Essex. They do not mingle with other vampire sects and they chose to alienate themselves altogether from the various vampire communities."

At the end of the decade, Dr. Jeanne Keyes Youngson sent out a survey to assess the situation of the vampire in our culture. In her abridged report on the results, she tabulated the data based on the 713 returned questionnaires out of the 933 distributed. One part was directed to those who considered themselves to be vampires and the other was for people simply interested in the vampire genre. A vast majority were Caucasian and one-third participated in the vampire lifestyle. There were more females than males in the mix. Of those who believed they were vampires, most kept it secret and most claimed to wear fangs and drink blood. Interestingly, few thought that they would have a longer life span than nonvampires. Three-fourths admitted to having been abused as children. Of their

favorite vampire movies, first on nearly every list was *Dracula*, starring
Bela Lugosi. Old vampires die hard.

The Deconstructed Vampire

Although they probably don't realize it, many members of the vampire
subculture confuse the notion of subjectivity with the more extreme
subjectivism. In other words, each person believes that his own experience is what defines the vampire rather than viewing the vampire
as a central image that each person can experience in an individual
way. It's the idea that if two different people feel the same breeze, and
one describes it as cool while the other says it's warm, then the air
itself is both cool and warm simultaneously. When meaning becomes
this arbitrary, how can we understand anything?

In the vampire world, when the claim is made that the vampire is
"X and only X," and there are competing and contradictory ideas of
what "X" is, it rapidly becomes clear that they can't all be right. If
someone says that true vampires are healers and someone else says
true vampires are destroyers, it seems obvious that they can't be both,
unless they're healing in order to later destroy or destroying and then
healing because they feel bad about destroying. But that's not what
people who speak about healing vampires mean. They see the vampire
as a sort of white witch.

We can say the same about many other traits now attributed to
vampires, from mental powers to longevity. So how did we get into
this morass of vampire typologies?

There's evidence throughout the vampire domain of the common
person's postmodern mind-set, which is not rigorously thought out
but which does embrace conceptual fluidity and the lack of closure.
To better understand this, let's get some background on the academic
understanding of postmodernism. It's here where the shake up in physics that yielded quantum and chaos theory has made an impact.

Postmodernism began as an academic term concerned with the arts but now describes broad-based shifts and changes in society at large. It's about examining the fundamentals of language and concepts in new ways and undermining past authorities. Formerly, it was believed that reality was just "out there" and language was devised to describe it. Now language is viewed as the tool that *creates* reality—something like the notion in physics that observers create reality relative to their position and frame of observation. We're immersed in language and we use it to maintain—or shift—our sense of self from one potential identity to another, any of which is equally viable. We produce our "self" in the act of describing ourselves, and we seek to be both fluid and grounded all at once. One "vampire," who works by day as a minister, calls this a "fluid fiction." He fully exploits it in his seemingly contradictory occupations.

The once-sacred search for absolutes and for the "true self" has yielded to a philosophy that says that absolutism is pointless and that if truth is to be found at all, it will require a radical break from former values. People have different kinds of identity-forming experiences, so the idea of a centered self is contrary to how our society currently functions. Our fragmented world fails to support a single consistent view of who we are. Rather, it supports a protean identity that is unafraid to shift and change.

However, if we believe that anything goes, we play a game without rules, so criteria are weakened and standards get lost. Postmodernists call this a good thing, and it can be. Chaos yields new life, and anything that becomes status quo and gets taken for granted usually needs a shake-up. Certainly Anne Rice's complex vampires were an improvement on the tired stereotypes of Count Dracula, and there will be new vampires that will improve on Rice's creations. But problems arise when that shake-up only disintegrates standards and offers no viable replacement: The trickle-down effect from rigorous philosophical speculations into the incoherence in popular culture promotes a widespread free-for-all. No one examines the ideas and assumptions; they just act on what feels okay.

Postmodernists react against the idea that there is fundamental order in our world that we can articulate with a single meaning. Coherence, they say, is only an illusion. All coherence derives from ideas that potentially conflict with one another, which of course makes no sense. It's a paradox.

To the postmodern mind, meaning can change with the underlying structures. There is no pure knowledge, no *essence* of something that we're trying to distill. In order to get meaning from a concept like "vampire," we need to uncover hidden assumptions in how it is presented, along with what has been left out of that presentation, and then decide whether we agree. Thus, we can't think of "vampire" in terms of what it "really means." Defining the essence is merely a culture-based habit of thought. It only traps us into believing in the illusion of static definitions. Our understanding of the word has been built up from certain origins, reinforced by certain cultural institutions such as fiction and film, and then taken for granted as fixed and stable. That it *is* fixed and stable, however, is a myth, a projection of our need for certainty.

Essentialists during the seventies and eighties claimed that the new vampire of those eras was going too far, watering the archetype down, defanging it. Those who wanted change said the old vampire had lost its edge and something more was needed to make the vampire interesting and relevant. Who was right?

For postmodernism, nothing is meaningful until we imbue it with meaning. What counts as the central function of any word or idea is where the meaning-giver stands in relation to it. There are no facts. There are only interpretations. Thus, we should constantly question the ground from which we form meaning and make judgments that remain ever open to new possibilities.

It's clear from the longevity of the vampire image that it has always been a metaphor with multiple meanings. There are many ways to appreciate it and even more ways to apply it. That has always been its strength and source of resilience.

Mark Spivey is a professional counselor, holding advanced degrees in theology and clinical social work. His training and more than fifteen years of field experience give him a unique psychospiritual perspective. He's studied the vampire subculture for several years and understands the urge to reinvent this figure for a new generation, especially for those who have long been silenced or left out.

"As individual freedom, privilege, and hope drain away from the landscape of postmodern life," he observes, "the shadow of the vampire steps into the light. In its timeless capacity to embody the human condition, the vampire is a poignant metaphor describing the psychosocial experience of the pariah—the outsider. The vampire is the Other that used to be human. The diseased, the mentally challenged, the homeless and hungry, people of color, people of different sexual orientation, and the working poor, to name a few . . . are all vampires in a way: the other who used to be human, the invisible who casts no reflection among us. Contemporary vampires look like us because they are us, each of us suffering ignominy on some level of our life experience."

So the vampire expresses many interests, but is there a point at which it can go too far? Can we even tell when that has occurred? Has the vampire a stable meaning at all anymore?

Perhaps a telling indication of how postmodern diversity has actually infected the vampire is the invasion of politics into vampire culture. More disturbing than the vampire's potential loss of elasticity is . . . yes, being politically correct. In many places, participants in vampire culture are required to conform to standards to "prove" themselves. Where once we expected the vampire to wear a tuxedo, have slicked-back black hair, and speak with a Hungarian accent, now it must conform to rules that say it should not do any of those things.

Yet it doesn't stop there. Not only are there things that a vampire ought not to do, because such acts play into passé ideas, but there are things a vampire *should* do in order to be embraced in the community. So much for the vampire as outsider.

And then there's the calculated recruitment of ethnic minorities to make vampire culture appear tolerant, and the diverse sexual and gender issues acted out as proof of vampiric "freedom." In some places, those who don't also practice some sort of fetish are supposedly not living out their full vampire potential and they're left behind as "fledglings" or wannabes. (It's not unlike the scene in *Interview with the Vampire* where Louis discovers a conformist coven in Paris, the members of which all dye their hair black because that's what vampires do.)

Even within "outsider culture," there are insiders and there are outsiders. Those who grab for firm ground in the midst of change try to force others to form a club and do the same. That's the shadow side of the postmodern approach. No matter how fluid we try to be, we still seek solid ground. Yet even that will somehow get punished, rolling us into a new dialectic of freedom and rules.

In a postmodern world based in created ideas, the life of the reader comes at the expense of the death of the author. In other words, there are more interpretations of an image than the image maker may intend. No one can say that a reader has misinterpreted. And the truth is, sometimes we do need a new vampire for a new age.

But how do we get a vampire with a grounded meaning in which we can all share in our individual ways? Not with subjective relativism. Thus far, at least, what we've gained with that is contradiction, incoherence, and infighting. Yet we won't get our grounding by returning to the illusory stability of a Dracula image any more than if we decided to cling to an outdated scientific model. We're too sophisticated for that, and there's no reason why such a malleable image can't be adjusted to new generations.

Black Is White Is Black

As the decade ended, the Sci-Fi Channel broadcast six episodes of a 1998 British vampire series called *Ultraviolet*. It was partly a show about criminal investigation and partly a show about the way the vampires ("leeches") feel as a species that just wants to keep its food supply intact. Homicide detective Michael Colefield's partner disappears and turns up again as a vampire, bringing Colefield in touch with a group of vampire hunters called "the Squad." Led by a priest supported by the Vatican, but also part of the government, they see themselves as fighting to destroy an insidious vampire network. Colefield joins them, but the more he learns, the more confusing things get.

In many ways, this series captures the contemporary concept of the equivocal vampire. Is it good? Is it bad? Do the powers of God have any effect or is the notion of a deity all just role-playing, too? And how does the technological world affect it? The program has a strong psychological undercurrent in that vampires can be defeated by traditional religious items, but only if they believe in the power of those items. Vampires are distinguishable from humans in that they don't show up on film, so the vampire hunters use a special monitor attached to their carbonite-firing guns to make sure that when they use those guns they have an actual vampire in their sights. If the person the hunters intend to annihilate fails to show up on the monitor, he or she is a vampire. They also use garlic teargas and ultraviolet alternative lighting that helps them to detect vampire bites that are difficult to see with the naked eye.

The vampires sleep in designer coffins, wear bulletproof vests, and use voice synthesizers to talk on the phone. They can't be seen in mirrors, so there are some traditional elements in the show, but the vampires also merge with the modern world and the show offers some new ideas about them—including a genetically crossbred human-vampire embryo not detectable by ultrasound equipment used for human fetuses.

The main point seems to be that it's never quite clear how to differentiate between the good guys and the bad guys—and that's the ultimate postmodern dilemma. The "heroes" have their dark side and their doubts, while the vampires defend themselves with obvious logic. (God says we must be destroyed because we're evil, but we're the only proof that God exists. If He doesn't, we're not evil.) Each perspective is represented within its own context, as well as from the enemy's point of view. Both are problematic *and* sympathetic.

The series was short-lived and as of this writing has not been re-made in an American version, so whatever else it might have explored is anyone's guess.

Yet even as we examine the blurred definitions of the vampire, it still has deep roots in tradition. According to Martin Riccardo, by the end of the twentieth century, over three hundred vampire films had been made and one-third of them were about Dracula. As much change as there has been in the vampire image, that initial archetype is still strong, and filmmakers of note such as Francis Ford Coppola and Wes Craven re-created Dracula tales for the 1990s.

So is there anything scientific we can say about this subculture, aside from showing how it follows the path of physics, from absolutes to chaos to patterns within the chaos? It seems to be a fact that complex systems—even mythological ones—are sensitive to change, and even a seemingly insignificant change can have a large-scale effect down the line. It's like a butterfly fluttering its delicate wings causing a wind-storm on some faraway part of the planet. As subtle changes have been introduced into the vampire tale, they've triggered complete up-heavals that will likely trigger a few more.

Nevertheless, even as some influences turned the vampire into a rock star, a hero, a deity, there were writers and filmmakers who kept the essence of evil intact—and it worked. Brian Lumley's multibook vampire series, starting with *Necroscope* in 1986, describes a race of all-out predatory "wamphyri" that hunt humans. They guide a soul's destiny in ways that can only be described as insidious, and like good psychopaths, they revel in this covert control.

In 2001, Willem Dafoe starred as Max Schreck (playing Count Or-lock) in the film *The Shadow of the Vampire*. The premise is that

Nosferatu director F. W. Murnau, played by John Malkovich, hires a real vampire to pretend to be an actor playing a vampire. There is nothing attractive about this predator, as he gobbles down a bird, attacks crewmembers, and lusts after an actress. Murnau has a difficult time keeping him under control. The atmosphere is dark, the monster's movements utterly creepy, and there is nothing much to redeem him, aside from his desire to get his part right.

While for some the vampire has become a means for self-expression and spiritual exploration, there are others who still appreciate its nefarious character. That, too, deserves some attention. There's still something to be said about the vampire's dark side.

EIGHT

Demonic Shamans and the Science of Evil

In the year 2000, lawmakers in Wisconsin considered a bill to outlaw the practice of vampirism. The bill was written to try to stop people who take advantage of kids who want to get close to a vampire. A case in point featured Phillip K. Buck, "the Sheboygan County Vampire," who invited teenagers into his home and then encouraged them to cut themselves with razors. Since there was no law against this, no one could stop him. However, someone reported him for engaging in illegal acts with minors, such as using alcohol. After his arrest in 1998, authorities learned that Buck had told the kids they would experience great pleasure from cutting themselves. Apparently he managed to persuade at least a dozen children to do as he advised.

✛

Elizabeth Miller is quite correct in her perception that the shifting concept of the vampire has diminished the force of our confrontation with evil. In fact, author Andrew Delbanco claims in his 1995 book, *The Death of Satan*, that Americans have lost a vocabulary for evil altogether. He discusses how we have become more tolerant of the many forms of evil in our midst and our explanations for it have never been weaker. We defuse it, humanize it, and too readily excuse it. This is certainly evident in our contemporary recycling of the notion of being a vampire.

Yet perhaps the vampire has taken a form that we don't recognize because we're looking at the wrong images. As I said in the foreword, perhaps the vampire can be best defined in terms of us rather than him/it—that is, in terms of our dread of being invaded and having our resources sucked away, rather than conceiving of the vampire as a creature that behaves in a certain defined manner. In that case, perhaps we can probe the realm of evil to rediscover *that* vampire. From the black arts to neuropsychology, the beating heart of darkness yields no end of images and theories. Despite all the changes, the vampire is clearly still adept in the arts of diablerie.

Savage Magic

Dracula appears to have been skilled in the occult arts. Van Helsing tells what he knows of Dracula's family history, saying that the Draculas were "a great and noble race, though now and again were scions who were held by their coevals to have had dealings with the Evil One." He also points out that vampires can use necromancy, which involves commanding the dead to give up information otherwise unavailable to the mortal mind. In such rites, the dead person arrives as a spectral being, forced by the skill and science of the necromancer to obey. This meeting generally takes place in a cemetery or tomb where the corpse is present. Necromancy assumes not only that the soul survives the body, but also that disembodied spirits of the dead possess superior knowledge.

Some form of necromancy was practiced in every nation of antiquity, sometimes for evil, sometimes for good. The rituals often involved sacrifices, which usually meant killing animals but might also involve children. The bodies were opened to "read" the message of the entrails. Necromancers who could make accurate predictions were held in high esteem. In later years, Christians were told that demons imitated the spirits of the dead and were not to be trusted (although the original word for demon came from the Greek word *daimon,* which referred to a spirit that made a liaison possible between mortals and the gods). Eventually necromancy was viewed as a path the devil took as he entered a human soul.

During medieval times, those who wished to invoke the spirits of the dead drew circles near or around a sarcophagus and spoke the dead person's name to call him forth. If he did not appear, the corpse was exhumed for examination. One way or another, the dead were going to give it up.

Some practitioners used a "necromantic bell," inscribed with symbols for seven planets and the name Tetragrammaton. Around the bell were carved the names of the planetary spirits that would assist in the sorcery. It was placed in the center of a recently dug grave and left for seven days to absorb the character of the deceased. The appropriate time for doing a ritual was within a year after the death, as that was how long a person, it was believed, hovered around his body.

So vampires, as the Undead, apparently have a better grip on how to command these spirits, presumably because they've passed through death in ways that mortals have not. (Sadly, in Stoker's novel we never actually see Dracula conjuring up a spirit or exhuming a body, which would have been fascinating.)

The notion of the vampire as a sort of shaman, or initiator into mystical experience, was in vogue in our culture throughout the 1990s. Before addressing it specifically, let's look at the general idea of a shaman.

The word comes either from the Manchu *saman,* which means "a raving man," or from the Tungus language, translated as "one who is excited, moved, raised." Siberian explorers considered shamanism to be savage magic that could control the physical forces of nature. Many societies viewed shamans as specialists in the spiritual realm, even emissaries from the gods, because of their ability to enter an agitated state that helped them move into what seemed like a different reality. In general, shamans seek enhanced visions and attempt to harness metaphysical energy. In a way, they could be considered "ghost whisperers," luring and taming the spirits for their personal use.

A shaman, in short, is someone who enters into altered states of consciousness for the purpose of healing, enlightenment, self-awareness, and gaining knowledge about other realities. Shamans may claim to interact with invisible spirits or to have auditory or visual hallucinations. Because they're, so to speak, spiritually centered rather than mentally ill, and because they possess the ability to transcend ordinary experiential limitations, they can venture further into supernatural experience than ordinary people, and then return at will. That's why in many places, shamanism is set apart as a calling and the shaman given special status. Their job is to take the risks of experiencing extreme spiritual states, witnessing the available revelations, and then returning to enlighten or heal members of their community.

Often they practice at night to reduce the distractions of ordinary reality. Sometimes they gain their powers from near-death experiences, from pharmacological substances, or by surviving a terrible illness. A shaman may even inherit the spirit of a predecessor shaman within his family who has died. They often learn of their calling from quirks of consciousness, such as disembodied voices, visions, encounters with the dead, or some thought disturbance. They must then undergo rigorous training in order to learn to control their altered states—or else they themselves may get mastered by the spirits and go mad.

The shaman's vision quest often involves an out-of-body experience, such as astral projection or soul dissociation. He might achieve this in a supine state, through extreme physical exertion such as dancing or rhythmic drumming, by ingesting drugs, through sensory deprivation, by chanting, or by climbing to some height—whatever it takes to disengage the normal thinking processes to allow access to other realms. A shaman may also allow spirits to possess his body or the bodies of animals in order to make their secrets known. In some places, shamans even have sexual relations with the spirits. Some have only to prove themselves with feats of magic, while others must be initiated. Sometimes wandering ghosts instigate the initiation, at other times a tribal elder does.

Initiation involves learning the ways of a mentor, which involves special languages, rituals, and experiences. A novice might descend to an underworld or seek to engage with the divine. These realms are generally connected and the initiates can learn through visualization and spiritual surrender to go from one to another.

There are traditions as well that view the shaman as aligned with the forces of darkness. In Tibet, shamanism is considered a demonic and degenerate form of Buddhism, while the Mongols believed that surrender to these frightening wizards ensured a form of protection. Within a community that views nature as inhabited by spirits and fairies, the shaman that can control them serves a practical purpose. He can deactivate the bad spirits and shield whomever he chooses. He is a guardian against malignant forces and can prophesy, cure disease, help others to attain their desires, and perhaps even delay death.

The Alchemical Ingredient

In chapter 23 of *Dracula*, Van Helsing mentions that in mortal life, Dracula had been an alchemist, so we can add this skill to his vampiric abilities.

Alchemy, which originated in ancient Egypt and integrated religion, psychology, and chemistry, was a mystical, pseudoscientific approach to universal healing and "soul refinement." This occurred through the symbolism of chemical substances as they were understood during the Middle Ages. The more narrow vision of Western alchemy derives from Greek rationalism, nature religions, Egyptian chemical technology, and astrology. For Egyptians, rituals mattered because they ensured the right kind of life after death, and that meant preserving the corpse. The body had to be transformed. Mummification was a way of bathing the corpse in "god-liquid," and it all had to be done according to the right alignment of the constellations—the moment favored by magic.

By ascertaining the right inner moment and involving all the right formulas, alchemists strove to produce a "philosophers' stone." This substance would transform base metals into gold and break down the limitations of the soul in order to unify it with the infinite. They could thereby attain a full understanding of the mind's spiritual power to transform matter and learn the secrets of the universe grounded in the self. The rituals of alchemy thus symbolized the elevation of human consciousness toward the end of both material and spiritual wealth. Alchemists' activities were known as the Great Work.

While natural science translated reality through its physical components, alchemy traveled an inner route. Alchemists were scientists of a different sort and just as disciplined as scientists about finding the key to the universe.

An alchemist might busy himself—usually in secret—crushing, heating, and dissolving substances in a laboratory and making careful calculations. He might also keep a careful record—a journal—of changes observed within himself. This might be done through dream analysis, shifting moods, creative flashes, and even physical changes.

The first phase of alchemy was the *nigredo,* or the black phase. The alchemist surrendered to the inner darkness of repressed aspects of himself in order to learn and develop better awareness. He might also attempt to break complex physical substances down into their most primitive and base forms.

Second, during the *albedo* (white) phase, the alchemist attempted to purify both himself and the physical materials with which he was working.

Then came a yellow phase, known as the *citrinitas,* and then the last phase, the *rubedo,* characterized by the color red. Just as the sun rises in redness, so came ultimate enlightenment, personal rebirth, and the emergence of the Philosophers' Stone.

To move through these phases, the alchemist had to transcend ordinary imagination and achieve true creative vision. This came through meditation and even hallucinations, or vivid daydreams of dialogues with invisible entities. Thus it is clear that alchemists were a type of shaman.

Add the Vampire

By viewing the vampire as a shaman, aficionados understand that the vampire's reality is an altered, transcendent reality. He may be a healer, an educator, a seer, a destroyer, or a magician. Since vampires often remain with those whom they bring into their world, they serve as guides and mentors, teaching the wisdom they have gained and offering a more complex experience than mortals generally have access to. The vampire point of view on mortal life offers a completely different understanding of the human condition. Once insiders, they are now outsiders who recall being human but who see so much more than they once did.

Interview with the Vampire was influenced by *The Teachings of Don Juan: A Yaqui Way of Knowledge* by Carlos Castaneda, published in 1968. This book was presented as a nonfiction account (though intensely disputed as such) about an anthropology student who met don Juan Matus, a Yaqui Indian and shamanic guide, at a bus station in Nogalez, Arizona, in 1960. Castaneda was researching medicinal plants used by Indians in the southwestern U.S., and as he got to know don Juan and learned that he was a sorcerer, he eventually became his apprentice. By taking peyote and magic mushrooms, he learned about "nonordinary reality" and gained mental clarity and spiritual power. It seems that don Juan came from a line of Mexican seers, twenty-seven generations long, and when he met Castaneda, he perceived the right energy alignments in him for shamanism. Their relationship continued for a dozen years, as Castaneda learned to release himself from the prison of his academic ideas. At this point don Juan completed his destiny and evaporated into infinity.

Rice reported being enthralled by the relationship between the teacher and student in this account, and used the vampire experience to describe an alternate path to the enlightenment so many young people in the 1970s were seeking.

So vampires have become a source of enlightenment and alternative spirituality. Their effect on the mortal brain, which at the very least invokes an erotic swoon and possibly even leads to the experience of boundlessness and union with the gods, proves their worth as guides into an unknown realm and as psychological magicians. That alone gives them a desirable aura. Yet is it for our good or theirs? Might they be giving us the ecstasy in order to more easily manipulate us toward evil?

It could be that cognitive dissonance supplies an element to this as well. When we're ambivalent about our options, and the options seem fairly equal, we tend to diminish the negative qualities of the option we choose. So if we see the vampire as evil yet human, we can transform the "evil" part into something psychological, like having a compulsion, and thereby develop more sympathy. Once this is done, it's not so hard to drop "evil" and reframe the vampire as a species like us who just kills to eat. The vampire is a lion or a wolf. We tend to forget that some vampires that we deify were once human and knew moral rules, and they are now defying those rules to take what they want for themselves.

That's not so far from the definition of a psychopath, some of whom we wouldn't hesitate to view as evil. Let's look at a few and remind ourselves about what evil actually is.

Manifestations of Evil

1. During the sixteenth century, people in the French countryside believed that serial killers of a particularly vicious variety were werewolves, i.e., men transformed by Satan into ravenous beasts. There was even a protocol for the investigation, arrest, and punishment of a werewolf.

   Gilles Garnier lived in the woods in the Franche-Comté region of France. He apparently believed that he could become such a beast and he began to stalk prey—local children. One day in 1572, he strangled a ten-year-old girl. Removing her clothes, he bit into the fleshy areas of her thighs. He ate a few of the pieces he ripped off and took some home for his wife to cook. Then he turned that same carnivorous attention on a boy. Within a six-week period, he attacked two other children but was run off before he could eat them.

   The authorities arrested him for "crimes of lycanthropy" and burned him alive.

2. In the summer of 1984, the "Night Stalker" began his vicious spree in Los Angeles. Richard Ramirez, who identified with the devil and loved the song "Night Prowler," murdered a seventy-nine-year-old woman in her home. He slashed her throat and stabbed her several times.

   Then he continued to rape and kill people, usually entering their homes to attack. In one place, he carved out a woman's eyes and took them away with him. Then in May 1985, he bludgeoned two elderly sisters, scrawling a pentagram on the body of the one who died.

Over a span of several weeks, he murdered single women and couples, and even beat up a young boy. One victim survived to provide an image for the newspapers, and some citizens who spotted Ramirez held him for the police.

He was ultimately charged with thirteen murders (though he claimed he'd committed twenty). Mugging for reporters, he flashed a pentagram that he drew on his hand. He was sentenced to death, and he's now on California's death row, where he reputedly instructs correspondents in how to worship the devil.

3. Jeffrey Dahmer was arrested in July 1991 in Milwaukee, Wisconsin, after a near victim of his ran down the street with handcuffs on and told police that he'd almost been murdered. He led them back to Dahmer's apartment; the powerful smell that hit the police when they went inside told them they'd stumbled upon a hellhole. Looking around, they found decomposing human heads, intestines, hearts, and kidneys. Snapshots showed mutilated bodies, and the discovery of chloroform, electric saws, a barrel of acid, complete skeletons, and formaldehyde told the rest of the story. In the days that followed, forensic workers found the remains of eleven different men. Dahmer confessed to murdering them, along with six more, and he quickly became the world's most notorious ghoul.

He got his start when he was eighteen. He brought a hitchhiker home, killed him, and dismembered him—a procedure that he found sexually exciting. He'd done it just to keep the guy around.

While he made plans to get more bodies by digging up

graves, it proved easier just to lure men to his apartment and drug them. In an effort to create zombie slaves, he drilled holes into the heads of his unconscious victims and injected acid or boiling water. Usually this killed them. Dahmer also tried to cut off the faces of his victims and keep masks, but was unable to preserve them correctly. While he was careless at times, so were the police, so he managed to get away with murder a number of times until he was finally stopped.

4. In 1973, twenty-eight bodies were dug up from the crawl space in John Wayne Gacy's Des Plaines, Illinois, home after Gacy became a suspect in the case of a missing boy. He later admitted to dumping five more, including the missing boy, into a nearby river. Gacy claimed that most of them had tried to con him or otherwise harm him, so he'd acted in self-defense. However, when a survivor described his ordeal in Gacy's home, it became clear that the man was a predatory killer. He'd find young men, offer them a job or money, and trick them into slipping on a pair of handcuffs. Then he sexually brutalized them until they died. To get rid of them, he buried them beneath his home.

While he claimed he was insane, he couldn't make a case, and the jury convicted him and sentenced him to die.

Former FBI Supervisory Special Agent Robert Ressler interviewed both Dahmer and Gacy in prison. He served as a profiler on the FBI's newly developed Behavioral Science Unit for sixteen years and became the first program manager for the Violent Criminal Apprehension Program. After he retired, he authored *Whoever Fights Monsters, Justice Is Served,* and *I Have Lived in the Monster.* Asked to consider his encounters with some of the most brutal psychopaths of modern times, he says that there's a distinct feeling one gets in the presence of someone who's truly evil.

"There's murder and then there's murder. There's murder that I think the average person can see as not justified but understandable. For example, a guy might rob a bank and kill a guard. He just wants to get away. Or two guys fight in a bar and a knife comes out. There are all sorts of homicides along those lines.

"But when you get pure unadulterated repetitive homicide with no particular motive in mind, and nothing that would make it understandable as a gain, you have something above and beyond rational motivation. You just have evil incentive and evil tendencies. I've had the feeling in interviews with these killers that there's something beyond what we can comprehend. With someone like Gacy or Dahmer, you're dealing on a different plane of understanding.

"What's different is that there's no rational motivation and when they're stalking people looking for a victim, capturing them, and locking them up—some of them were kept for days and weeks—the emotion is gone. It's a coolheaded decision. It's very methodical. There's no rage and the goal is just to get the victim and use the victim in various ways and then eliminate them."

The Problem of Evil

It's likely that evil dates back to the beginning of humankind. It might even be innate—so much a part of us that we'll never fully understand or eradicate it. Experts approach it variously as a manifestation of:

- insurmountable social ills
- a dysfunctional psychological development or personality disorder
- the lack of good role models
- an imbalance in biochemistry

- the result of miswired neurology

- a mix of too many human and environmental factors to calculate

- a failure of free will

Nauralist Lyall Watson looks at what we call acts of evil as part
of the fabric of nature—an argument that many a vampire has used
about "the savage garden." In *Dark Nature,* he argues that the behavior we see in serial killers and sadists reflects certain natural principles. It's not that these people are monsters set apart from ordinary
people, it's that they manifest something in the system gone awry. In
other words, at best nature is tentatively balanced, yet its equilibrium
is vulnerable to challenges. To work in a harmonious way, things must
occur in the right measure, because even too much of something we
consider good (rain, for example) can cause havoc (a devastating
flood).

Watson says that evil is actually commonplace, not uniquely manifested in an oddball. It's also not confined to the human species. He
himself has observed predatory animal behavior—even cruelty—and
the killing of offspring. If we understand evil as overstepping bounds
or going beyond due measure, it's really defined as whatever destroys
the integrity of the whole.

Living systems are dynamic; they tend to run down, grow disor-
ganized, and eventually disintegrate altogether. That spells death for
the system. With any system attempting to remain whole, capricious
forces enter in. That's threatening but inevitable. It's part of the force
that helps to redefine the system for growth, yet may still be viewed
as evil from within the system. In organic evolution, integrity must
coexist with capriciousness. Some things contribute to the order and
cohesion of life and some things fragment it. Nothing remains static.

Watson goes on to point out that evil can be equated with a pathogen that enters or exploits some aspect of the system, disturbing it

and knocking it off balance. Such disturbance can transform something considered benign and good, such as the drive to reproduce, into something malign—the drive to rape.

This happens when a "good" thing is shifted out of the context where it worked, when something disrupts the system, and when elements of the system fail to relate in a coherent manner. Once we understand this about nature, we can view evil as a simple force within a system that disrupts that which is defined within the system as good or healthy. (In that case, vampires can view *us* as evil within *their* system, as the leeches viewed the Squad on *Ultraviolet*.)

Dr. Stanton E. Samenow, an authority on the criminal personality, puts this idea in a psychological context by saying that the criminal's way of thinking is different from that of responsible people, because he follows "errors of logic" derived from a pattern of behavior that begins in childhood. His thinking appears to work within *his* scheme, but not within the greater social context. Criminals *choose* crime by rejecting society and preferring the role of a victimizer. They're in control of their own actions, but they assign blame to others, which prevents them from gaining insight about their intentions. They devalue people and exploit others to get what they want for themselves. Erroneously, they view committing a crime as a way to stave off emptiness, but the excitement doesn't last long, so they repeat it rather than try something else. Because they think poorly, they fail to learn, and what they do harmfully disrupts the lives of normal people. Hence, they're evil.

Along these lines, psychiatrist Carl Goldberg calls evil the manifestation of a deformed personality. The "devil" represents those people who have "transformed themselves into beings capable of extreme brutality and atrocity." They develop evil behavior for a variety of reasons that follow within a sequence:

- shame and humiliation during childhood

- impaired self-esteem

- self-protection through contempt for others

- rationalizing and justifying their actions against others

- loss of empathy

- treating others without respect

- learning to enjoy the infliction of cruelty

- lack of self-awareness

- magical thinking (I can make anything happen)

Going through these steps allows someone to gradually develop the ability to be cruel toward others and to feel no remorse. In other words, the injection of shame, callousness, and cruel habits (pathogens) into the personality system disrupts its healthy development and sends it down a darker path.

Where does it all begin? How do we understand what causes evil so that we can figure out why we apply the idea (or not) to the vampire?

The Roots of Evil

Dr. Jonathan Pincus, chief of neurology at the Veterans Administration Hospital in Washington, D.C., and author of *Base Instincts*, believes that violence is the result of variations on a trio of factors: brain damage, abuse, and mental illness—notably paranoid thoughts. He agrees with Dorothy Otnow Lewis, author of *Guilty by Reason of Insanity*, that brain damage and abuse are key, and he goes through the details of many criminals' lives and behaviors to prove it.

However, most other researchers think this theory is too simple. The three factors seem to apply to impulsive offenders but not to many people who coldly plan and execute a murder or another form of cruelty. There's nothing in the case histories of the two well-heeled geniuses, Leopold and Loeb—who kidnapped and killed a young boy in Chicago in 1924 just to see if they could prove their cleverness—that suggests brain damage or abuse. Even mental illness is questionable, aside from antisocial personality disorder. Yet their terrible act and lack of remorse are considered by many experts to be among the hallmarks of evil.

And what of the "Angel of Death," Josef Mengele? One of Hitler's trusted henchmen, he ran Auschwitz, the Nazi death camp that was part of the Nazis' mass slaughter of over six million Europeans, mostly Jews. As part of his job, he supervised over 400,000 deaths and performed atrocious experiments on children. He, along with many others, was permitted to perform his evil deeds by an entire culture.

Fred Katz, sociologist and author of *Ordinary People and Extraordinary Evil*, says that it's the ordinary person who commits most evil in the world. Try as we might to identify special traits that set evil people apart as "monsters," there are none. We use the vampire as a means to do this, but we're just shielding ourselves from the truth.

Defining evil as "behavior that deliberately deprives innocent people of their humanity, from small scale assaults on their dignity to outright murder," Katz focuses on how people get beguiled by evil in a way the makes them see it in a different light—one that permits them to manifest it. Hitler may have devised a wicked plan, but many ordinary people zealously carried it out.

The reason is that evil was made acceptable through the frameworks of nationalism and the service of a vision. They perpetrated large-scale evil in steps so incremental that they failed to see the big picture. Within such a culture, some evil acts were actually rewarded. Operating a crematorium, for example, served the national vision and made the operator heroic. It was an act of "higher" good.

While the sociology of evil may explain evil by a community, some people commit atrocities regardless—and sometimes because—of society's rules to the contrary. So it's not just the cultural influences and it's not just brain injury and abuse. In fact, several new theories view evil as a complicated manifestation of individuality.

There are people who say that symbols like the vampire just offer us a way to experience what we really want to do. They're our anti-heroes. They're clever, manipulative, suave, and powerful, embodying all the traits we want to have and doing what we wish we could do. In that case, since they're us, they're not evil. They're just an extension of our natural impulses. We all want to be as dominating and exploitive as they are.

According to therapist Robin Karr-Morse and her assistant, Meredith S. Wiley, in their book, *Ghosts from the Nursery*, our perception of violence and our capacity to act out develop within the first two years of our lives, starting at the point of conception. In other words, how we will respond to images like the vampire are set by those early factors, and it appears that there are too many to easily calculate. That is, no one can put a finger on evil's central source.

Asking the same questions is Debra Niehoff, a neuroscientist who read through the research from the past twenty years before she wrote *The Biology of Violence*. Specifically, she asks whether genetics or the environment causes the aggressive kind of violence that so disturbs us. Her conclusion: it's both. In her opinion, each factor modifies the other in such a way that the manner of processing a given situation is unique to each individual, as is his or her choice to become cruel or violent.

The way this works is that the brain keeps track of our experiences through chemical codes. When we have an interaction with a new person, we approach it with a neurochemical profile that is influenced by attitudes that we've developed over the years about whether or not the world is safe and whether we can trust our instincts in reading a stranger.

However we feel about these things primes us to set off certain emotional reactions, and the chemistry of those feelings is translated into our responses. "Then that person reacts to us, and our emotional response to their reaction also changes our brain chemistry a little bit. So after every interaction, we update our neurochemical profile of the world."

So how we learn to process things will affect our response to cultural images like the vampire: we may respond more strongly to its darker attributes, and thus prefer authors who write about aggression and exploitation, or we may prefer to have the vampire rewritten as a romantic hero. (It's interesting that despite Anne Rice's strong statements about her vampires' awareness that they're evil, many of her fans ignore that aspect and view them as romantic lovers or cultural heroes.)

Just from this glimpse at the many theories available to explain evil acts, we can see that none of the most recent offerings appears to cover all cases. While certain research supports theories about brain disorders, environmental stimulants, and poor role models, it appears that the development of an evil person is a unique combination of events—as is our own response to evil.

So how does this discussion relate to the fictional development of vampires?

While we can apply the many theories of violence to people, it's not as easy to apply them to creatures of the night, even though in many contexts the vampire once was human. (It's of no use telling a member of an alternate species that he's evil, sick, or morally wrong since he operates under an entirely different framework—as the counselor in *The Vampire Tapestry* discovered during her dialogue with Weyland.) Brain damage, parental abuse, a Nazi social order, and some damaged genes have little relevance to vampires.

But not really. Part of the vampire's power derives from his surrounding aura, which means the way a victim will perceive him. If our understanding of vampires is informed by discussions about evil and the many questions and contradictions that highlight evil's mystery, then the vampire takes on a more powerful allure. While the whole notion of evil might be irrelevant to them—except to those who were heavily influenced by religion as mortals—it's still relevant to those of us who want to comprehend their dubious appeal. Rice said of her *Tale of the Body Thief* that its inherent evil is that its hero, Lestat himself, is evil and yet he gets to continue killing. "Life is filled with those bargains with the devil," she said. Yet Lestat still insists that evil should not be befriended. He invites people to eradicate it—including his kind. (Of course, when he meets the devil he learns that God is the cause of all evil in the world—unless the devil is a liar.)

Yet for many vampires in recent fiction and film, evil is neither here nor there; they just do what they do because they're vampires. Julian Luna in *Kindred: The Embraced* tries to convey this to his mortal lover, but the language of their respective moral frameworks degenerates into mere word games.

And that brings us to another point about evil.

Despite the influence of a lack of self-awareness on such evil acts as violence, torture, and cruelty, it does seem that many repeat offenders come to realize what they're doing. One way to deal with this and keep going is to adopt a persona of evil, the way Ramirez did. Another is to deny that you're responsible, and still another approach is to change your frame so you can view what you're doing in a different way than society views it. If your victims are "prey," your predatory acts "the hunt," and your means of depriving another person of life "the embrace," it's easier to be a vampire. Sometimes it just comes down to language.

In 1942, the chief of the Third Reich's security services, Reinhard Heydrich, invited fifteen of the highest-ranking technocrats to lunch at Wannsee to discuss "the Final Solution." There was need for greater "efficiency" in "the Jewish emigration." Heydrich wrote notes about the meeting in neutral language, but once decoded, the gist was clear: these men were there to approve the use of death camps, gas chambers, and crematoriums. The "solution" was to utilize more "work camps," where people would die from "natural causes."

Speaking with one another in *Amtssprache*—office talk—all of those present acted as if they were merely part of a large machine, with no one personally responsible for turning the "on" switch. The suggestion was to send many more Jews "east"—to the concentration camps. There the able-bodied men would be forced into a program known as *Vernichtung durch Arbeit*, or "extermination via work." Heydrich proposed "liquidation" and offered a prepared report on how many people they could expect to "remove" in a specified amount of time.

Later, during his trial, Adolf Eichmann, who had prepared Heydrich's speech that day, was questioned about the Wannsee Conference. When asked whether it was difficult for him to participate in sending so many people to their deaths, he responded, "To tell you the truth, it was easy. Our language made it easy."

So despite all the reframing that authors, scriptwriters, gamers, and club leaders have done, those vampires that kill mortals to sustain themselves are still evil in our eyes—no matter how much we may want to identify with them or be loved by them.

The truth is, we like vampire novels because they're edgy; they portray a dangerous creature that brings to the tale a certain amount of friction and suspense—and not the suspense involved in romantic novels of waiting to see if he'll find his true love or save his home from destruction. The vampire is fascinating the way a seductive psychopath is fascinating: it's the ease with which he commits his acts against humanity, his daring, his mystery, and his passionate longing in the service of his own need that keep us turning the page.

Larger Than Death

When a vampire is charming, clever, successful, convincing, and dangerous, he becomes a magnet to which people gravitate. This is a good description of Dracula. He came to England with the idea of commanding an army of vampires. He told his mortal victims that they would obey him. His need was fulfilled at their expense and yet he never flinched from satisfying it. He became the center of everyone's attention, whether they admired him, hated him, feared him, or desired him. He was clearly a powerful figure. That kind of power, built on its own drive for stimulation, heightens the experience of those who get close to it. And then they, too, want more.

Many people who read *Dracula* noticed that the Count was the central figure, though he was rarely on the page. They felt a desire to experience that power for themselves. So when Barnabas Collins provided TV viewers with an idea of the vampire's interior world, and then Louis and Lestat added layers of guilt, denial, and desire, we were allowed inside the seat of power. We could feel what it was like to be a vampire.

After that, readers and other authors created their own vampire worlds. After all, there's so much potential. The vampire is a shapeshifter, mind reader, and mind bender, a life sucker, an emotional manipulator, a refined savage, and a creature of extended skills and abilities.

When we look for the full experience of a truly enticing vampire, we might follow the path taken by Douglas Clegg's character, Jane Boone, in a short story called "White Chapel" in Poppy Z. Brite's *Love in Vein* anthology. Jane hears rumors about a legendary savage residing in India who utterly delights his human victims even as he skins them alive. Horrified by this vile behavior, Jane is nevertheless fascinated. Her curiosity becomes an obsession that drives her toward a very seductive destruction. To her, the savage seems an artist of great skill. He's larger than life, larger than death. She seeks transcendence, despite what it may cost, so she's willing to make her body into a temple for the barbarously refined whims of this dark god. She's willing to go to the very edge to experience the ultimate fervor.

What lies at the heart of the vampire's danger is a form of eroticism that will not be denied. Sensual, sexual, and penetrating, the vampire tale is all about dominance and submission, no matter what form the vampire takes. Whether he entices us for evil or good, it's all about his ability to inspire us to surrender.

And that brings us to the center, although we've saved it till nearly the end. Just what is it about vampires and carnal desire?

NINE

Everything You Ever Wanted to Know About Vampire Sex but Were Afraid to Ask

+─I─+

There are those who claim that the scene in *Dracula* in which a quartet of "brave men" who enter the tomb to put the stake to victim-turned-vampire Lucy Westenra are in fact participating in a symbolic gang bang, and it's true that the four are rather excited about penetrating her with their wooden sticks. Elizabeth Miller calls it the Great Phallic Moment, and these words are close to the mark. Much of *Dracula* seems influenced by the need to glorify the "good" (i.e., unsexual) woman and demonize the sexualized female. It seems that the Count awakens in these women an erotic hunger that confuses and entices them but also enrages (and terrifies) their men. (It appears to be okay with Jonathan Harker that he be orally raped by the female vampires in Castle Dracula but not okay that Mina gets intimate with the master vampire—unless we count Jonathan's presence at her ravishment as consensual voyeurism.)

We can only imagine what marriage must have been like for Mina after her encounter with Dracula. How does a wimp like Jonathan measure up to one who inspires the dangerous desire of the Count?

One suspects she maintained a secret fantasy life, recalling her face pressed against Dracula's chest.

The symbolism of *Dracula* has been endlessly analyzed, from the stake as a phallic symbol of male domination, to theories of sex and class, to interpretations of the mother figure. All that sucking suggests an infantile state, and the repressed male sexual imagination of Victorian times (and Stoker's as well) gets a good working over. While sexual freedom is definitely part of the vampire's charm, the desire for it gets thoroughly punished.

Although Stoker didn't know much about Slavic folklore, his ideas about the vampire's erotic nature seem inspired by tales from several different areas. Gyspy folklore, says vampire scholar J. Gordon Melton, described a sexualized vampire, which was possibly based on the discovery of corpses with erections (a not uncommon occurrence). Gypsies believed that vampires left the grave at night to have sex with their spouses, who generally withered under the relentless activity. Russians and Malaysians also mythologized beautiful young people who as vampires lured villagers to their demise.

Almost all vampire fiction deals with a sexual aspect, either covertly or overtly, and the more exotic erotica can be found in narratives since the 1980s, when a surge of feminism, gay rights, and experimental pornography influenced the vampire's milieu. Whether a vampire can actually have sex is a controversial issue, but the theory of vampire impotence is definitely getting the stake.

The Kamasutra for Vampires

Male and female vampires are both sexualized creatures, but there's a tradition that male vampires have a certain erectile dysfunction that prevents them from having conventional sexual relations. This might be because their need for oral gratification is so much stronger than their need for genital gratification. It might also be that the way erections work in humans won't translate into the vampire body. Some people who create vampires think that since the erection is dependent on the penis becoming engorged with blood, the vampire ought to have no trouble with this, and what with all his sensuality and eroticism, he might in fact suffer from unwanted erections. Others say that since he's dead, he has problems with blood circulation. Yet some male vampires do indeed have sex. Some even procreate.

So the range of possibilities is:

- strictly oral contact, with the bite providing the erotic flourish
- an erection for genital intercourse but no semen, or semen but no sperm
- an erection with semen and potent sperm, similar to the human male

While only a few authors actually mention semen, those encounters that produce offspring must involve it. Poppy Z. Brite's vampires can have children with mortals, and dhampirs are the result of such a union. So to get to an egg in the female reproductive system for such fertilization, the otherwise spongy penis must first engorge with blood for an erection. Aside from in vitro fertilization, there's just no other way to do it. Let's see how this works.

During intercourse, smooth muscles contract to propel sperm through a tube called the vas deferens to mix it with a secretion from the prostate gland and seminal vesicles so that the sperm can swim in a watery mix called semen. A potent male vampire, then, must have several mechanisms working in order to produce a child. Engorgement of the penis is only part of the story. A lot more is going on behind the scenes, so to speak.

Yet let's say a vampire can participate in genital intercourse but without reproductive potential. In that case, the production of sperm and semen is unnecessary. He only needs to worry about the veno-constriction mechanism. The aroused male brain sends nerve impulses to blood vessels in his penis that instruct the arterioles to dilate and the venules to constrict. That makes blood flow into the penis, where it stays until orgasm, when the semen is projected through the urethra to be deposited in a female (or other places). Once the muscle contracts in the epididymus, venoconstriction ceases. If there's no semen to propel, the vampire may still have a "dry" orgasm like that of some eunuchs, or he may have mental control over how long he can keep an erection (as human males sometimes do).

Other physiological mechanisms that help things along include:

- The hypothalamus secretes a hormone into the blood.

- The anterior pituitary gland releases two hormones that stimulate the production of sex hormones in both genders.

- Nerve impulses from the brain dilate peripheral blood vessels.

- The Cowper's glands secrete lubricating fluid.

At any rate, that's for male vampires. We can't say the same for female vampires, and in fact, they're often presented as ravenous succubae that take more than just blood from their male victims. There's some suggestion in *Dracula* that the woman in Castle Dracula intended to perform oral sex with Jonathan Harker, although he declines to offer a description.

Female vampires should have no trouble having sex, particularly with another female. It may be the case that the greater and lesser vestibular glands that empty into the exterior labial folds for lubrication might dysfunction in a body that has died, but there are plenty of lubricants on the market to duplicate that effect. Females depend on the same brain mechanisms as males to secrete hormones and assist with arousal, and no one has indicated that a vampire's brain loses its functions during the transformation, so we can assume that eroticism is alive and well in most once-human vampires.

So in keeping with the many positions shown in the *Kamasutra*, let's take a look at some of the more popular vampire erotics.

In the nineteenth-century novella named for her, Carmilla comes into a family and gradually seduces the nineteen-year-old daughter, Laura. David Skal says that this is the first literary combination of the Undead with same-sex love. To get Laura's attention, Carmilla uses pretty sentiments, handholding, touching, and sensual kisses, and after offering an overwhelming degree of attention, she finally wins the girl's affection. At night, she goes into Laura's bedroom as a dark catlike creature to take the girl's blood, leaving her with bad dreams, a sharp little pain, and a small mark.

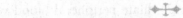

Chelsea Quinn Yarbro's St. Germain is four thousand years old, so he can be excused for being physically impotent. He makes up for it, as we can tell from the reactions of females, by invoking sexual ecstasy with his bite. It's the contact that provides the intimacy, and he even falls in love. However, in his cosmos two vampires cannot couple, so making a lover immortal solves nothing. Erotic intimacy for St. Germain is relatively short-lived, despite his long-expertise. Nevertheless, the greatest satisfaction comes for the vampire when he pleases his lover before himself.

Suzy McKee Charnas's *The Vampire Tapestry*, published in 1980, makes the vampire a breed apart from humans; he's not only potent but possibly fertile as well (he doesn't really know). Yet his sex drive is weak compared with that of a human male, and while he awakens with an erection as human men often do, he'd rather take care of this himself than engage in sexual intercourse. He tells a female therapist that he's interested in satisfying only one appetite, his thirst for human blood, and if he really must have sex as a means for getting it, he will. He tends to prey on gay males, since they're the most accessible, but he's also picked up women. He says that he's the only one of his kind that he knows, he had no parents that he recalls, and vampires don't reproduce by male and female mating. They may not reproduce at all, since his victims don't become vampires. It could be that he's merely a lone immortal.

"It just seemed to me," Charnas said, "that a vampire who could have sex with people had a lot more potential, fictionally, than one who couldn't. On the other hand, I had no interest whatever in yet another vampire society, full of hierarchy and decadent detail, and his being at the top of the food chain indicated a scarcity of competition, so I made him a species of one."

Since he does have a penis but sees no real function for it, he explains it as "detailed biological mimicry, a form of protective coloration." In other words, he needs it to move freely among his prey without arousing suspicion. To him, actually engaging in sex with humans would be like humans copulating with sheep. He's physically capable of it but not driven to do it except for the sake of appearances.

Nevertheless, he does indeed end up in bed with a female, is concerned about the possibility of pregnancy, and manages to satisfy both her and himself. Thus, while not being human, this vampire can engage in what amounts to human sexual activity.

While there's plenty of homoeroticism in Rice's vampire universe, with same-gender vampires partnering up, she claims that since vampires are outside human cultural boundaries, they can defy all gender restrictions and participate in a full range of desires. (Perhaps the closest she actually gets to offering same-gender sex is Armand's voyeurism as Daniel has intercourse with women. We can assume that if he *could* make love to Daniel, he would—and also with Marius.) However, as Lestat examines his nude body in a mirror in *The Queen of the Damned*, he specifically says that the male sex organ is useless. Even as vampire bodies harden with age, apparently that part just hardens in its limp state. (Otherwise those vampires might have some trouble getting around.)

Yet one erotic encounter in particular deserves attention. In Rice's novels, Akasha is the first vampire, the Queen of the Damned, and within her resides the vampire's full power. She can kill other vampires with a blast of fire and force any to do her will. She selects Lestat as her "brat prince," and when he realizes whom he's with, he grows hot for her. She apparently feels the same, so they engage in a vampiric embrace—sucking blood from each other simultaneously until they form an eternal flow, which Lestat claims is a pleasure unlike any he has ever known.

In *Interview with the Vampire*, Louis tells Claudia that sex is "a pale shadow of killing," strongly suggesting that sucking blood is more intense than the human orgasm. He himself doesn't know how any mortal can survive the profound intimacy involved in a vampire's bite. Lestat has the same opinion. When he acquires a body that allows him to be mortal again, he evaluates sex as a localized feeling, unlike the totalizing sensation of vampire eroticism. He doesn't care for the odors or the stickiness of it all, or for the way it isolates the participants.

✛

Among the most tragic of sexual encounters for vampires is the one between Angel and Buffy on the series *Buffy the Vampire Slayer*. He's a vampire, she's a slayer, yet they fall in love. Eventually they have sex—a first for her. However, Angel is subject to a peculiar kind of curse that turns what should have been an intimate deepening of their love into the threshold to hell for him.

"In horror movies," said Christopher Golden, coauthor of *The Monster Book* and several *Buffy* companion guides, "it used to be that the girl who gave in and had sex with her boyfriend was the next to die. So there's an element of that. Angel had once been the scourge of Europe. He was one of the most horrible vampires that ever lived. Then he killed a Gypsy girl and was cursed by her family. They returned his soul to him so that he would feel the guilt and horror of everything he'd done to that point. But they also made sure that giving him back his soul would never be a gift. That way, if he ever reached a point where he felt perfect happiness as the result of having a soul, he'd lose it again. With [Buffy], he had bliss, so he lost his soul."

After consummating his love for Buffy in sex, he once again turns into a vicious vampire (which was later modified so he could have his own series).

＋—＋

In Poppy Z. Brite's *Lost Souls,* we get it all: the vampires can eat, drink, have sex, and procreate. A vampire named Christian owns a bar in the French Quarter. A thin adolescent girl dressed in black silk comes in to order a screwdriver. She tells him she's waiting for "the vampires." A trio of vampires soon enters the bar and she knows them immediately for what they are. Right in front of her, they open a gash in their skin and offer it to Christian, who drinks. She tries to do the same and gets rebuffed, but a vampire named Zillah takes her to a back room and has intercourse with her. She can even smell his sperm, and she gets pregnant.

However, having a vampire's child has a high price: one doesn't survive the experience. Brite provides a birthing scene, a rarity in popular vampire horror fiction. An intelligent, aware infant emerges, half-vampire and half-human, although he ultimately follows his darker legacy.

＋—＋

Whitley Strieber offers some very hot scenes between Miriam Blaylock and her partner, a man descended from experiments with crossbreeding between vampires (Keepers) and humans. Because he has some vampiric traits, he has the effect during sex of triggering the release of her last egg and impregnating her. He also has the effect of making her believe she at long last has found a lover who can keep up with her own hunger and longevity. Their coupling is similar to that of two humans, but with the added energy of Keeper physiology.

A female vampire who has sex with human males, drinks their blood until they pass out, yet does not kill them is Dierdre Griffin in Karen E. Taylor's *Vampire Legacy* series, of which *Blood Secrets* is the first. Dierdre has sex in the traditional human fashion and seeks romance, even falling in love. However, her counterpart, Vivienne Courbet in *The Vampire Vivienne*, is more bloodthirsty. A pleasure-seeker, she understands that while men are good for sex, they're also just food. Aside from the bites and the blood, these books read like typical romance tales that feature strong female characters who like sex.

The psychic vampires among participants in the vampire subculture have no trouble with conventional human sexual relations, because their skill is for taking life energy—sometimes by touch, sometimes just by getting close—and they don't necessarily die to become a vampire. They can have sex or not, as they please, because it is completely separate from the process of sucking up energy.

The Covert Becomes Overt

For a long time, the vampire as a creature of secrecy, sensuality, and shapeshifting has been a symbol of the transgressive sexuality of gay culture. Homoeroticism flavors much vampire fiction, including *Dracula,* and is openly addressed in some works. *Cristabel* (1816), by Samuel Taylor Coleridge, was the first English poem to include a vampire—and a lesbian vampire at that!—which inspired the writing of *Carmilla* in 1872.

The first gay male vampire appeared in Roman Polanski's movie *Fearless Vampire Hunters* in 1966, and another one showed up in *Dracula Sucks.* After that, both gay males and lesbians appeared in an endless variety of imaginative vampire films in the 1970s and vampire pornography throughout the 1980s.

Yet on the literary scene, they showed up only in short stories until Anne Rice's novels attracted a huge gay following. Then more authors tried out same-sex scenarios, although few gay characters starred in novel-length form. In an essay tracing the history of this endeavor, Trevor Holmes makes an observation on the purpose of vampire narrative: "the displacement of real social relations onto the fantastic in order to foreground the fault lines in what is taken as natural in any particular social sphere." In other words, the vampires are the right symbols for gay culture, because they're transgressive in a repressed society that attempts to tame the multifaceted sex drive.

In 1991, Jewelle Gomez published *The Gilda Stories.* An activist on several fronts, she broke some boundaries by devising a protagonist, Gilda, who is both black and a lesbian. Set in a variety of places from Louisiana to New Hampshire, the story begins in 1850. Gomez takes Gilda through several decades on a search for identity and family, with the intention of re-creating the vampire myth to fit her own needs— a central feature, as we've noted before, of vampire culture in the 1990s. We don't go to Dracula to make a carbon copy, but we deconstruct him and remake him (or her) according to who we are.

Gomez observed a central theme of desire in movies and films about vampires. The vampire tale wasn't necessarily about a creature that attacked people but about the quest to fulfill an intense need. Gomez had already noticed this undercurrent among those attracted to the vampire, but it was for different reasons during the 1980s than had previously been the case. Where once the desire embodied in vampire fiction was about power, sensuality, and charisma, there appeared to be an increasing interest in the vampire's spiritual and emotional resources.

Gomez wanted to push boundaries outward for women and for lesbians, and despite criticism from both camps that the vampire figure was negative and destructive, she continued to mine it for hidden ore. Recognizing the understated sexual energy in the early vampire tales, with bloodletting dominating the encounter between vampire and prey, she decided to make the latent overt. Thus she set about re-creating the vampire encounter as primarily emotional, and giving this aspect a central place in the lives of women. The vampire, as female, can have a social conscience and care about family.

Gomez penned eight heroic stories about Gilda, each set in a different era of U.S. history, and all addressing the question of what happens to a person who feels at odds with the rest of humanity. A central task was to strip away Christian superstitions and to make the tales more universally valid through recourse to ancient traditions.

"The changes came in two stages," Gomez explained. "I started writing the stories as an exercise to figure out what vampire lore would be like. It became clear that the character was going to dictate a different philosophy and mythology. I didn't feel comfortable with the idea of a vampire character killing people willy-nilly. In my memories of watching vampire movies, there was a haunting loneliness and isolation in the character. He was always trying to re-create a family."

She relied on memories of being raised by her great-grandmother. "So it started in a deeply emotional place. The vampire mythology, which is so passionate, was the perfect way to convey urgent longings, sadness, and need. I knew I had to create an investment in the character from whom Gilda was taking blood, and I required her to make an exchange.

"I wanted to shift vampires away from being totally evil and give them a power of will. In my story, some vampires are bad, but that's not the fate of all vampires. You can be seduced by it or you can take the high road and see yourself as part of the natural order, even in a preternatural way. You make your investment in sustaining the fabric of life and find pleasure in that.

"As a feminist, that's more interesting to me. I want to examine how we resist our meaner, smaller impulses and find ways to be satisfied by being part of a larger community, as opposed to focusing on ourselves as individuals. It's about how we contribute to rather than suck off the larger body. The idea that a character who has all the power in the world makes a choice not to subjugate others but rather to assist them, and sees that as her larger responsibility, that to me is interesting, because then you have tension with a character who resists natural impulses. You can also examine characters who don't resist that impulse to see how they spiral downward when their behavior has no checks and balances. The bad vampires are frozen psychologically, but the vampires in Gilda's family evolve. They end up having to learn to be immortal. They don't stay in one emotional place."

Gomez also gave a lot of thought to how she would work with the vampire's sexual reality. "In some novels, there's sensuality but vampires don't have sex. It bugged me. Why not? They say that the equipment doesn't work, but it works through the pulsing of the blood. And women don't need that. I think [vampires are] capable of having sex. It's counterindicated that vampires would have no sex. They have more blood pulsing through them than anyone else, and sensuality is key to the mythology."

While lesbian vampires have been part of both fiction and folklore for centuries, gay male vampires have not. Aside from some pornographic films and same-sex eroticism, gay males have been underrepresented until the 1980s, and there's still not much fiction available that describes gay sexuality that is specifically vampiric. David Lord Thomas has authored *Bound in Blood*, which features a gay male vampire, yet the encounters his character has with human males is fairly conventional. There is sex, to be sure, and descriptions of mutual male arousal, but like vampire romances for women, his novel offers typical gay erotica, with the addition of a bite. There's still plenty of room for someone to write truly creative gay vampire novels.

When role-playing became part of the vampire subculture, many gay men embraced it with abandon. Of all the people who got involved with vampire culture, perhaps gay males have identified the most specific attraction: there's power in the secrecy of the vampire just as there is in the dark, pulsing secrets that they themselves possess. Participants who've openly discussed the subject have provided bold accounts of their erotic activities as "vampires." Notably, they embraced the vampire's sexual permissiveness, its more experimental and promiscuous aspects.

"I erected a pole and told the boy to spread himself on it in the form of a crucified man, which he eagerly did. I then tied him to it and performed several erotic acts on him to work his desire into a frenzy of need. Then I picked up a sterilized razor blade and deftly sliced through his left nipple so I could suck his blood."

Many gay men have no traffic with mundane, conformist culture that preserves values of purity and uncomplicated sexuality. Yet it's the masses who protect these values who define what's normal and what's abnormal, so gay culture has historically been relegated to the margins or shoved into the closet. Yet, periodically, this has also freed them from the rigid mores of mainstream culture, allowing them more creativity and sexual experimentation. They can see the world in a different way, and if they can bear the loneliness, they may achieve a certain transcendent power. Those who grasp this know how to take what they want and can justify that behavior within a specific understanding of the human condition. That makes their shrewd vampirism even more threatening to the mainstream—and more seductive.

"The vampire *is* queer, by definition," says Michael Rowe in *Sons of Darkness*. "It is no accident that the public's fascination with vampires has always occurred at times of shifting sexuality and growing conservatism . . . They give voice to and form dark sexuality."

One gay male who identified himself as a vampire had made an art out of the many roles he'd taken on as a way to deal with people on many different levels. He viewed himself as a "frightening paradox," a person who could pretend to be a normal health-care provider by day and a vampire by night who stalked "prey" in gay bars. He drank blood, he admitted, as part of his sexual liaisons, though he could never admit this to his day-job clients or colleagues. So he viewed himself as a person who could adopt whatever identity he needed for a particular situation, none of which completely defined him. He could be whatever he needed to be for whomever he was with at the moment.

"The struggle I have," he admitted, "is achieving balance between my worlds. I end up feeling totally alone because no one really knows me or ever will. I can't be honest, yet to survive, I have to keep shifting from one thing to another. Since trust isn't really a factor in a vampiric relationship, it works. I can create and recreate myself for my prey— whatever works."

To him, the vampire requires this sort of recycling. It's not a static identity, but a dynamic that shifts with shifting needs and desires. "The vampire's charade is to appear harmlessly charming and erotic as a point-by-point response to his prey's every nuance. He seduces his victim through the lure of the mask, though enigma and mystery."

As a gay man and as a vampire, he is set apart. Being acutely self-aware, he and his cohorts in this scene mold their forbidden behaviors into seductive ideologies that embrace a dangerous soul.

Sex and Blood

What about AIDS?

That's among the questions most frequently asked about both vampire fiction and vampire role-playing. In other words, how does such a lethal blood-borne illness affect what goes on in the vampire world? Clearly, blood is not the life. Blood can mean death.

It was Dr. Lawrence Kahman who wrote the article for the *New York Times* about the unusual "cancer" affecting gay men in 1981. An internist at Bellevue Hospital, he knew of forty-one documented cases, but the backlash from the gay community against his attempt to warn showed that gay men did not want to believe there was something emerging that might shut down their recently won sexual freedom. Yet eventually the virus was isolated, and we learned that it was clearly transmitted by blood and bodily fluids involved in the most intimate embrace. Since vampires sucked blood, and since they were emblems of sexual energy and freedom, inevitably vampire fiction had to come to terms with this disease.

A number of authors have given this issue consideration, from using AIDS as a way to deliver to the vampire a powerful and disabling blow, to emphasizing their immunity, to giving them a preternatural sense about their potential victims. "AIDS became an issue while I was writing," Jewelle Gomez recalled, "and I had to think, if Gilda takes blood from people who are infected, what happens to her? I went back and rewrote the first chapter to account for physical disease in the blood, so readers would know that she could tell if someone was ill and make a decision not to touch that person." Some authors saw AIDS as a vampire metaphor: it struck through sexual contact and withered people slowly. Others ignored the disease altogether. Vampire tales, they felt, did not have to address real-world issues. They were fantasy.

Yet on the vampire scene, blood-borne diseases were another story. If they were cutting skin and drinking one another's blood, they had to respond to the threat. Four different responses formed among those who presented themselves as vampires:

1. The vampire is immortal, so we don't have to worry about AIDS; we're immune. (In other words, denial.)

2. We'll form safe partnerships with "donors" and make sure their blood is clean. (So they did in effect what people who were dating did.)

3. We'll become psychic vampires and only take the life force. (Sometimes a cop-out, sometimes a genuinely different manifestation of vampirism.)

4. We'll take the "glorious exit" and die young and beautiful, getting a fatal disease from a romantic activity. (Tragic but sincerely expressed by some.)

Rough Sex

Despite AIDS, or perhaps because of it, vampire club-goers began to frequent the fetish scene and to re-create themselves in light of its practices. In the 1990s especially, vampire culture adopted some of the practices of dominance and submission (D&S). It offered a way to experiment with sex and more fully explore the idea that the vampire is utterly open to possibility. In terms of sensuality, the philosophy was "anything goes," and if one identifies with the vampire, one may view the edginess of intense and even painful sex as a way to feel powerful and deadly. It gets closer to the vampire's aggression. As psychologist Thomas Moore, author of *Dark Eros: The Imagination of Sadism*, points out, "Sade the psychologist serves the soul by allowing it to embrace more and repress less." He's a specialist in the twisted paths that lead to inner cohesiveness and connection.

The aristocratic Marquis de Sade is considered to be the epitome of dangerous sex and has been hailed by some as the freest spirit who ever lived. He believed we should live according to our instincts, as nature intended, and for him that meant both promiscuity and aggression. During the latter part of the eighteenth century, he wrote explicit pornographic tales that in 1834 inspired the term *sadism*. They involved the enjoyment of inflicting pain and humiliation on others, holding them captive, and even killing them for personal pleasure and sexual gratification. His interest was in exceeding the boundaries of convention and social propriety. Arrested for sexual crimes, the Marquis was found guilty of multiple infractions from his numerous orgies. While serving time in prison, he wrote quite graphically about his sexual escapades, producing many novels and plays. His most famous novel was *Justine*, published when he was fifty-one; he declared it "a work capable of corrupting the devil."

Let's explore the psychology of dominance and submission.

Based on the idea that orgasm is both a "little" death and a merging with the gods in the feeling of losing one's boundaries, one can infer that the more intense the orgasm, the more engaged one is with the ultimate. Many people in the vampire scene consider themselves masochists seeking a dominant partner ("dom"), and while this is often misunderstood as someone who desires pain, the reality is actually much more complex.

The heart of sadomasochism (S&M) is dominance and submission, and the idea of D&S is to achieve a form of intimacy—or at least sexual satisfaction—that involves one person being assertive while the other surrenders to whatever is demanded. This is the feeling one expects from a vampire's embrace. While it appears that all the power collects on one end of the polarity, in fact there's a continuous exchange of power between the two partners. It's something of a choreographed game in which an illusion is developed. One person likes the feeling that he (or she) initiates the action and makes the decisions, while the other loves the sense of losing his or her will. A flow of energy is created that affects both, but in fact the two parties are aware that each needs to play the game according to the ritual in order for both to be totally pleasured.

Sadomasochism is an extreme form of dominance and submission, usually involving bondage, discipline, and consensual symbolic violence. The Master inflicts pain or humiliation to help the masochist, or slave, to experience the buildup of energy and achievement of emotional catharsis through the physical body. When consensual (and not the result of a sexually sadistic psychopath attacking a victim), both enjoy their roles. As they continue a partnership toward the end of perfecting their techniques, they strive for a form of authenticity. The rituals they develop are fueled by a specific co-created fantasy, and going through the motions as closely as possible make the images more concrete. Sadomasochism eroticizes mental and physical pain under the assumption that it fuses body, mind, and spirit.

The masochist seeks the dramatic loss of control that results from being bound and pushed through fear and anticipation toward a climax. It's a psychic orgasm via the obliteration of the self that he or she seeks, and that comes from the illusion of being at the mercy of another person. The stronger the passion they develop together, the more intense the experience, and part of the passion comes from the secrecy and sense of the forbidden. That's what's so appealing to vampire culture: the ideals converge and the rituals are protected by darkness, real or symbolic.

The idea is that sadomasochistic practices flirt with risk, and risk involves a form of fear-laden anticipation that can affect the body in such as way as to produce a radical transformation. In fact, it can push the participants toward an expanded experience, especially if the expression of cruelty is balanced with some affection. In short, masochism is all about being the center of another person's total focus (like a victim for a vampire), reveling in that, and deriving the greatest possible satisfaction from it. They strive for a completion of the soul, hoping to satisfy a demanding inner god (or demon) by shedding the small individual self. Supposedly with these extreme practices, conflicts of the soul diminish as limitations are shed. Masochists seek more than physical pain; they want to contact unknown dimensions of themselves by coming to terms with the paradoxes of joining discomfort to desire. Touching the inner mystery is tantamount to touching God, the supreme source of energy.

The ordeal of dangerous or painful sex gets spiritualized as a means for achieving a deeper psychological grounding. Masochists want to fully experience obedience, suffering, shame, and surrender as a way to mentally purge and achieve transcendence. That way, they may extend their psychological space. They become new people.

Then add the dimension of psychological conflict, which may occur with guilt over yielding to danger, eroticism, or evil. That, too, can heighten the sensuality of any physical experience, whether it's sex, mountain climbing, or murder. Psychophysical friction permeates the experience with intensity. In other words, the tension derives from playing with the paradoxes and exploiting the complexity of human psychology. It works according to the following truths about our psychology:

- We have the capacity to make a decision or initiate some action and then "forget" that we did so.

- We can so fully immerse in an activity that we achieve an altered sense of consciousness.

- We can intellectually entertain contradictory ideas, which means we can put them into play in fantasy.

- We can expand or change our understanding of ourselves through novel experiences.

■ We can participate in an activity without making covert thoughts or feelings clear to our consciousness.

Taken all together, this means we can consent to being "forced" into an act of surrender and come to believe that we are truly acting on the orders of another person, i.e., a Master. The surrendering partners covertly allow this person to push them to physical extremes so that they can explore their capacity for pleasure under these conditions—perhaps even move past them. Both partners recognize that the scenario works because they're playing with the illusion of force, though neither will call it that. Consent puts things into motion, but once the act is initiated, all awareness of consent recedes as the intense role-playing takes over. The pretense feels real and becomes real. While the captive did agree to it, under these psychological conditions, he or she can actually feel forced and thereby gain erotic benefits. If the captive is fully satisfied, then it becomes a form of luxurious sensuality and intense climax. It's fear and anticipation in the right measure that together produce the sexual stimulation.

People who are into S&M believe that the physical body has a wisdom all its own that's tapped only when pushed to its limits. Pleasure from the flesh can be merged with spiritual transcendence. Whatever makes one feel utterly alive is utilized within a safe framework devised by all participants involved in order to bring about the full exploitation of the erotic context. That may mean being tied up and blindfolded, it may mean whipping, it may mean being cemented into a tub. The goal is to defy the boundaries of the individual ego, whatever they may be, to help the person to flow into the feeling of something larger. Sensations involved in resistance and helplessness can aid in this process.

When one's identity is reduced to the suffering body, he can experience such intense immediate pleasure that he feels obliterated. Pain deconstructs the ego and allows people more latitude in their behavior. A practicing masochist can undergo an entire identity change. Dissolving oneself of responsibility and being guiding through feelings and acts that might otherwise seem inconsistent with the self facilitates a psychological breakthrough that would not occur were one left to choose to do these things on one's own.

Since the masochist (slave, submissive) desires to reach an ideal of perfection formed within some fantasy, the role of the dom is pivotal. Doms must be able to discern what it will take to reach that goal. It's often the case that a superior Master will have already experienced the role of a submissive. He will know with intricate fluency the submissive's fantasy, what percentage of firmness and discipline to exercise and what percentage of gentleness. Because this often involves exposing secrets, the relationship acquires an increasingly deeper intimacy. The Master must validate those images and desires that might otherwise embarrass the masochist, and that validation pulls out all stops: the slave can now go forward without psychological restraint. They can simply feel and stretch. Forced into their deepest needs and shame, they must locate inner resources to overcome their fears and embrace their desires.

Since arousal raises one's pain threshold, what might otherwise hurt can actually enhance pleasure. That means that what we fear might also evoke strong desire. The greater the risk, the greater the payoff, and the interplay of resistance and yielding can be highly exciting.

"I am in the hands of the unknown god
he is breaking me down to his own oblivion
to send me forth on a new morning, a new man."
—D. H. LAWRENCE

On a conceptual level, it seems that fear would inhibit desire, but both states are more complex than they seem. On one level of consciousness, the submissive knows that he is safe, but knowledge about the safety framework can dissolve in the experiential moment. Awareness blurs and allows for "believing" that one is really at risk. Enslaved souls who yield as if they have no real choice become more pliable, and a skillful master can maintain the illusion and guide the submissive to breaching inner barriers. The masochist can now contact his own most powerful source of stimulation. The goal of forced consent is to use the assistance of a willing partner to surpass apparent limitations for the heightened sensation that comes with having no other choice than to go all out.

Sadism, on the other hand, is the destructive side of the psyche—the murderer within us. It's an intoxication with power over another to the point of deriving joy from tormenting the other and feeling like God. The other person is just a thing to be played with for one's own sexual gratification. This is the essence of the "evil" vampire—the one who will exploit us for his own gain.

The vampire is the embodiment of the fine balance between surrender and power, between threat and utter rapture. There is always the possibility that danger offers enhancement and that the vampire's thrall holds the secret to a transformed existence.

The Goddess Rosemary, a vampire practitioner who's been on the scene since the 1960s and is an experienced dom, has seen a range of masochistic desires among her clientele. Her *Cirque de Erotique* rituals, derived from her research into blood and sex mythologies, were regularly performed at places like Manhattan's Vault and Hellfire clubs. She would present herself as a secretive vampire who only revealed herself onstage, working her audience into an intense unsatisfied desire for her, and then she would feed on their erotic need. She said their energy kept her young. She calls herself a fetish artist; vampirism is just one of her many erotic pursuits.

"I was exploring S&M for something I was trying to figure out in my own life," Rosemary explained. "In my rituals, I used branding, piercing, tattoos and scarification, because these practices bring one to new heights of sensual and chemical awareness. It's all about direct manipulation of physicality and about how the brain responds to things like sensory deprivation. I did studies of that."

Once she designed a mattress in which she enclosed a woman for thirty days who begged to be treated as an object. An "installation," she called it. She added a few fans for air circulation and fed the "thing," but otherwise ignored her. Then she had sex on top of the mattress. "They get vulnerable when you ignore them, so when they finally come out, they'll do anything you want. So I would think a vampire would have the same turnaround. Treat someone like an object and then get their complete devotion. It's always been fascinating to me to have adoring objects around me."

In an utterly vampiric gesture, she devised an intimate blood ritual.

People who are close to me that I wanted to bind to me, I would have drink my menstrual blood. That was their opportunity to partake of my vampire power. It was done in a ritualistic setting. It may seem backwards for a vampire, since they're drinking my blood, but it wasn't, because I was feeding off their fantasy. They liked it. It started with one person who had that as a fetish and it intrigued me that someone would request that. He'd make tea out of used tampons.

So I used the ritual to bind them to me. If they subjected themselves to that kind of offering, it cemented the relationship between the goddess and her followers. No one ever turned it down. With my blood, sometimes I laid the people on the floor and let it drip all over them. They'd say "Thank you, goddess." They'd feel a certain euphoria that's like sexual climax. It increased their endorphins and changed the serotonin uptake levels in their brains. It became a chemical cocktail of manipulating the senses. In sexual magic I like to manipulate the senses in different ways, whether it's with pressure points or energy rituals. I like getting the life energy out.

I also branded my followers with a hot branding iron, "S" for subject or "R" for my name. It was spiritual, not dark or evil. I wasn't going for the dark side. I'm more interested in ritualistic spiritualism. It's an extremity of human experience of the physical. It involves the intensity of touch and it seems natural to delve into the realm of S&M to observe and bring out the height of emotions, which is quite a vampiric practice in itself. In S&M, each emotion feeds on the other. There's no real definition as to which one is doing what. There's no clear line between them.

I don't like to tie them up because then I have to serve them. I like willing subjects who want to stay there. I don't *have* to tie them up. They want to be there. If someone is submitting to me, then it's their willingness to stay that's a turn-on. I don't use safe words [phrases that would stop a ritual because it's gone further than the masochist can bear]. I demand complete trust, and safe words aren't needed. I don't want to mess someone up and make them miserable. To me, it's more about sensuality. If they don't like it, what's the point? I don't like fear endorphins. They're like steak cooked too well.

When asked about the strangest fantasy request that someone had made to her, Rosemary offered the following:

The weirdest thing was a man who wanted me to turn him into a turkey, put him into a make-believe oven, check on him, baste him, and turn him around. I did it, but not just because he wanted it. Because of my vampiric nature and the way I feed off people in many different ways, I try to get into their fantasy and make it my own. I don't just cater to their fantasy, I twist it. I try to find something that fascinates me about it, and that one left a lot of doors open. So I'd go shopping while he was in the oven and then come in and set my packages down, open this fake oven door and use this paintbrush thing to baste him with butter, and he loved it. I didn't eat him or stuff him or anything, I just basted him. He'd arrive in a white Jaguar and he'd have a wonderful time playing turkey.

On a conceptual level, it may seem impossible that painful or humiliating experiences can be revelatory, but in reality the psyche opens up dark places that may prove that some taboos are only blocking the pathway to deep satisfaction.

Given the nature of sexuality and the many surprises it may bring, this chapter can't actually offer *everything* you ever wanted to know about vampire sex, because there are experiences about which we may yet know nothing. At least we've covered a lot of ground.

The wonderful thing about the vampire is that there are so many ways to experience its meaning. In fact, that's one of the secrets we'll explore in the next chapter.

TEN

Seven Secrets of Highly Sucksessful Vampires

✦—†—✦

In *Our Vampires, Ourselves,* a feminist look at the vampire as a cultural icon, Nina Auerbach states that because vampires are immortal, they are free to change incessantly. For vampires as fictional characters, I would say it's the other way around. Because they're malleable, they're at least long-lived in fiction, although we don't yet have the perspective to know if they'll be immortal.

It's always possible for a monster to get tiresome or be redefined in too many directions. The vampire image survives not only because it changes as the culture changes, but because no matter what changes it undergoes, it remains recognizably a vampire. There's a reason why Dracula has worked for so long: I think it's because while he's always familiar, we don't get to know him as well as we desire.

In keeping with the theme that opened this book—that our enduring myths are organic and are thus affected by forces that affect us—we can examine the vampire tale for truths not overtly articulated in a given narrative but nevertheless are implicit within it. Let's revisit physics first, and then psychology.

Dark Energy

We've already discussed how our ideas about reality have shifted into something more mystical, and how this shift has affected the structure of our narratives, including vampire tales. The study of the universe's fate is even more fundamental in that effect. It presents a profound possibility about why a vampiric image might endure—because it goes right to our bones: Our very notions about dark energies, dark entities, and parasitic forces may well be influenced by rhythms of the universe itself. In that case, the vampire does possess an eternal quality, but one that we fear and resist.

Let's start at the beginning and then skip to what's relevant. The theory of relativity introduced the idea that space-time might be warped by expansion and by the presence of matter (objects with mass, or the planets and stars). The real debate, however, is over whether the universe will expand forever, thus becoming less clustered and dense, or whether it will disappear in one big and horrendous crunch. Either possibility poses a problem for humankind, but a recent discovery indicates something vampiric at work.

When the universe began, cosmologists theorize, at first it expanded rapidly, but the gravitational pull of matter eventually slowed down the process. Some feared this pull might even stop the expansion and bring about a collapse. Yet observations throughout the 1990s indicate that celestial objects are farther away than original calculations suggested, which means the rate of expansion is faster than was once believed. Astronomers are puzzled by this phenomenon and some are also quite concerned.

This rate of expansion seems to mean that some invisible energy is offsetting the force of gravity. It's like tossing a rock into the air and watching it keep going up instead of returning to your hand. Something stronger than gravity has intervened, yet no one is sure what it means; hence the name "dark energy." It's unknown.

Whatever the energy is, it appears to be exerting an increasingly stronger influence. It inhabits what was once viewed as "empty" space and may be rather large in form. If it continues to push things away, eventually it will deplete the universe of the energy needed to sustain life. That certainly sounds vampiric, but let's look closer at how it appears to work.

Stars that implode under the force of their own gravity form a black hole in the universe. However, the negative energy of dark matter can transform gravity's pull into a push. This energy fills empty space and forces the universe outward. If it increases its force as it expands into space, then pushing the universe outward only feeds it. Scientists may be observing how the universe is vamping on itself.

Thus, if we're attuned to nature, and if consciousness and imagination are entwined with that attunement, then we may tell tales that express the subtle functionings of the universe. In that case, the vampire story appears to have parallels with dark energy, in that it sucks energy out of its host. As long as we're around, we'll resonate to Dracula.

Let's move on to what makes us crave more of the vampire, and for that we turn to psychology.

What We Don't See

We develop myths to address our desire for two things:

1. answers to the world's mysteries

2. enlarging ourselves spiritually

Often these two conflict. One is about closure and one is about keeping mystery and possibility alive, which means staying open. Within the same myth, it's a trick to achieve both. *Dracula* managed it, in part because what we know of the monster comes from indirect sources that may or may not be true. The information dispensed by

Van Helsing has the ring of authority and his rituals do seem to work, but there's always the feeling that there are things about the vampire we may not know. That's why so many movie sequels were possible.

We love mystery in part because it makes us feel that there are possibilities out there as yet unimagined. If we had all the answers, we could lose that sense—in particular the hope of encountering the extraordinary. The burgeoning corpus of vampire stories has pushed the boundaries of vampire lore well beyond anything Stoker envisioned and will likely continue to do so if such works both feed our hunger and keep an edge on it. That's really the trick: entice and satisfy to a point, but don't fill us up.

Creative imagination attuned to the social reality keeps the vampire symbol vital and relevant for any given period of time. It just needs the right elements: the vampire just beyond our reach, those who would try to destroy it, those who would want to become it, and those who unwittingly get caught in the scenario.

While we're always attempting to solve our mysteries and control all phenomena by categorizing and defining them, what really compels us is the vigorous puzzle of not solving something that appears to be solvable. The appeal of *Dracula* is that we know the monster through subjective perceptions, conjecture, and speculation. Van Helsing relies on legend and superstition to eliminate the vampire. But did he really succeed?

The fact that the creature no longer plagues the hunters after they "kill" it seems reason enough for them to believe that the danger is gone. Yet that's like saying that the arrest of a suspect in a series of murders that has ended means he's the guy—when in fact the killer could have just moved on, died, or been arrested for something else. The simplest explanation is often the accepted one, but good logic dictates that we consider all possibilities before jumping to conclusions. Dracula has dissolved into elemental dust more than once in the story and may well have done so again. Van Helsing believes that Dracula's powers diminish in the sun but he doesn't really know.

What we really want is for the game to continue. We love it when someone removes the stake from a vampire long ago dispatched and the creature starts up all over again. We want to believe that the vampire has some power that we don't yet understand that allows him to survive, despite our best efforts to figure him out and destroy him. We seek no final verdict on the vampire, even though we also strive to get it. We always want to believe that soon we'll finally get the job done . . . but not yet. It's that part—the not yet—that makes the whole thing so titillating. The vampire must be within our reach to make it exciting, yet always just beyond it.

This creature is an unfolding entity that conjures up primordial truths. He represents an eternal return that offers both danger and renewal. He punctures through our mundane lives with the possibility of knocking us off our feet. In short, he gives us the mythical moment, the promise of utter intimacy within a mystery that ensures we'll never have all the answers—which is exactly the answer we want.

How's that for a quantum koan?

That's why the vampire keeps changing. The narrative works best when it operates off the things we most crave, yet never allows us to fully possess them.

In 1989, folklorist Norine Dresser published *American Vampires*. She examined a culture in which the vampire flourished in many forms, and noted that vampire tales exploit the American obsession with sexual prowess, power, and youth. When asked over a decade later if she's seen anything to change her mind, Dresser responded with the following comments:

"Judging by TV fare and coming attractions for movies, I think the vampire will remain a standard cultural myth. Not too long ago, I attended a vampire-book signing at Dark Delicacies, a local horror bookstore. It was an exciting moment reentering that milieu. I was struck by the lure that has remained constant since the printing of *American Vampires*. The ages of the fans ran from young to old, and I was convinced that the lure of vampires would not die.

"Further, I still get letters and discover new kinds of vampire admirers—women who wish they were vampires so they could go out on the streets alone without fear of drive-by shootings or physical/sexual assaults; prisoners, who may be identifying either with being trapped in a nonliving existence or perhaps wishing for the power to escape prison life. It appears that new voyeuristic needs can be met by that legends-old creature.

"I haven't changed my mind about the vampires' fit with American ideals. We still admire sex, power, and youth. Look at our current media heroes and they are perfect examples—Julia Roberts in her own persona or as Erin Brockovich in a push-up bra. Roberts is the highest-paid American actress, and in the entertainment industry, studio executives put their money on those who bring in socko box-office receipts. The same goes for Tom Cruise and current heartthrob Russell Crowe. The popularity of these actors demonstrates what resonates with the public. All of them exemplify sex, power, and youth."

It seems that we've placed everything we desire into the single basket of the vampire narrative, and then made that image immortal yet accessible for a price—often one we don't fully understand. We get to have the vampire by reading or going to the movies, but then it dances enticingly away, making us want to go back for more.

Still, the vampire is about more than power and sex. It's also (usually) about death. That's what makes it edgy, and that's as much what fascinates us as the allure of the beautiful monster. Our most vulnerable feelings typically evoke the hottest pleasures, so we edge close to the diabolic in order to experience that which makes us feel alive.

As we've seen throughout this book, many individuals have attempted to crystallize in literary form humanity's fears. They recognize what the forces of darkness represent and they set out to mold our most basic desires—lust, aggression, greed—into seductive bloodsuckers that touch a powerful subliminal chord deep within us.

Vampires thrive in the dark. Part human, part monster, part deity, they inspire a multitude of passions. They disturb and enrich us. They keep alive in us the desire to transcend ourselves. As initiators into the secrets of physical transformation, they offer a doorway into another realm. Seeking new means of self-expansion, we keep reading vampire fiction and watching vampire movies for that rich metaphor of bewitchment and surrender that may birth us into our larger selves. Go for the rush, vampires urge, even if it means you die. Using the emotional tones of both life and death, vampire tales keep the rhythm of our lives in play.

Can There Be a Science of Vampires?

The paradox of bringing science to the vampire is this: the vampire works best when he defies our best attempts to pin him down. He presents much more than his surface suggests. He must have a charisma that's larger than life and that invites us into mystery, undefined power, and vividly disturbing possibilities that reach deeply into us. That means he can never be trapped inside clear-cut concepts, rituals, or rigorous analysis. He's a shapeshifter. We can't quite put the stake through the vampire without him disintegrating into elemental dust that can recombine elsewhere in a regenerated form, but we don't really want to. Despite the potential danger to ourselves, we hope to see the vampire's new form. Even as dark energy threatens to suck out our existence, we want to get close to its erotic aura.

And so the game goes on and the vampire remains a disquieting yet familiar enigma, attuned to our culture's primal fears and emerging in ever-more-provocative manifestations that show us our many facets, whether or not we want to see them. In many ways, a science of vampires reveals more about us than about them. But then, science, too, keeps shifting.

David Skal has examined the vampire's unfolding across many decades, and he offers a glimpse of what's to come:

"The future evolution of the vampire archetype has already begun, notably in alien abductor mythology, which is a kind of high-tech update on the medieval legend of the incubus. I was recently surprised to see an 'alien' mask in a Halloween store that had a stand-up Dracula collar already attached—clearly a pop-culture acknowledgment of the interdependency of two cultural nightmares."

So let's devise a vampire that can last for another century in our cultural imagination. What *are* the seven secrets of highly "sucksessful" vampires? From what we've seen, a vampire should show the following traits or behaviors:

1. Evolve with the culture but remain in its shadow, enacting those things we most fear and desire

2. Retain its larger-than-life aura

3. Maintain the tension between sex and death

4. Include in its presentation whatever makes us vaguely uneasy

5. Embody those goals that may threaten our souls but also promise new possibilities

6. Remain unpredictable

7. Be enticingly dangerous in its need

We want the vampire to live on, an image of our own desire for longevity, and there's no doubt the culture will inspire more visionaries who will deliver the monster to us in just the right measure.

"Mankind went one way, we another.
Their end is final, ours is not."
—MIRIAM BLAYLOCK,
THE HUNGER (FILM)

BIBLIOGRAPHY

Aldiss, Brian. *Dracula Unbound*. New York: HarperCollins, 1991.

Apter, Michael. *The Dangerous Edge: The Psychology of Excitement*. New York: The Free Press, 1992.

Auerbach, Nina. *Our Vampires, Ourselves*. Chicago, IL: University of Chicago Press, 1995.

Austin, James H. *Zen and the Brain*. MA: MIT Press, 1998.

Aylesworth, Thomas. *The Story of Vampires*. Middletown, CT: Weekly Reader Books, 1977.

Baden, Michael, and Marion Roach. *Dead Reckoning: The New Science of Catching Killers*. New York: Simon & Schuster, 2001.

Barber, Paul. *Vampires, Burial, and Death: Folklore and Reality*. New Haven and London: Yale University Press, 1988.

Begley, Sharon, with Anne Underwood. "Religion and the Brain," *Newsweek*, May 7, 2001.

Bell, Michael E. *Food for the Dead*. New York: Carrol & Graf, 2001.

Biondi, Ray, and Walt Hecox. *The Dracula Killer*. New York: Pocket Books, 1992.

Brite, Poppy Z. *Lost Souls*. New York: Delacorte, 1992.

Bunk, Steve. "The Molecular Face of Aging," *The Scientist* 16(10):16, May 13, 2002.

Bunson, Matthew. *The Vampire Encyclopedia*. New York: Crown, 1993.

"Can Wisconsin Law Stop Vampires?" *Herald News*, February 24, 2000.

Capra, Fritjof. *The Tao of Physics.* Boston: Shambhala, 1975, 2000.

Carlo, Philip. *The Night Stalker: The Life and Crimes of Richard Ramirez.* New York: Kensington, 1996.

Carter, Margaret. *Dracula: The Vampire and the Critics.* Ann Arbor, MI: U.M.I Research Press, 1988.

Castaneda, Carlos. *The Teachings of Don Juan: A Yaqui Way of Knowledge.* New York: Pocket Books, 1968.

Charnas, Suzy McKee. *The Vampire Tapestry.* New York, Pocket Books, 1980.

Clegg, Douglas, "White Chapel," *Love in Vein,* ed. Poppy Z. Brite. New York: HarperPrism, 1995.

Collins, Nancy. *Sunglasses After Dark.* New York: New American Library, 1989.

Copper, Basil. *The Vampire.* New York: Citadel, 1973.

Cowen, Ron. "A Dark Force in the Universe," *Science News,* 159:14, April 7, 2001.

Delbanco, Andrew. *The Death of Satan.* New York: Farrar, Straus & Giroux, 1995.

Dess, Nancy K. "Big News from Little Brains," *Psychology Today,* January/February 2002.

Dix, Jay and Robert Calaluce. *Guide to Forensic Pathology.* Boca Raton: FL: CRC Press, 1998.

"Doctors Say German Satanists Could Kill Again," Reuters, January 24, 2002.

Dresser, Norine. *American Vampires: Fans, Victims, Practitioners.* New York: W. W. Norton, 1989.

Dundes, Alan. *The Vampire: A Casebook.* Madison, WI: University of Wisconsin Press, 1998.

Everitt, David. *Human Monsters.* Chicago, IL: Contemporary Books, 1993.

Florescu, Radu R., and Raymond T. McNally *Dracula: Prince of Many Faces.* New York: Little, Brown, 1989.

Franz, Marie Louise von. *Alchemical Active Imagination*. Boston: Shambhala, 1997.

Gelder, Ken. *Reading the Vampire*. London/New York: Routledge, 1994.

George, Leonard. *Alternative Realities: The Paranormal, the Mystic, and the Transcendent in Human Experience*. New York: Facts on File, 1995.

Glut, Donald F. *True Vampires of History*. New York: HC Publishers, 1971.

Goldberg, Carl. *Speaking with the Devil*. New York: Viking, 1996.

Golden, Christopher, Stephen R. Bissette, and Thomas E. Sniegoski. *Buffy the Vampire Slaver: The Monster Book*. New York, Pocket Books, 2000.

Gomez, Jewelle. *The Gilda Stories*. Ithaca, NY: Firebrand Books, 1991.

Gordon, Joan, and Veronica Hollinger, eds. *Blood Read: The Vampire as Metaphor in Contemporary Culture*. Philadelphia, PA: University of Pennsylvania Press, 1997.

Guiley, Rosemary Ellen. *The Complete Vampire Companion: Legend and Lore of the Living Dead*. New York: Macmillan, 1994.

———. *Vampires Among Us*. New York: Pocket Books, 1991.

Guinn, Jeff, and Andy Greiser. *Something in the Blood: The Underground World of Today's Vampires*. Arlington, TX: Summit, 1996.

Hare, Robert R. *Without Conscience: The Disturbing World of the Psychopaths Among Us*. New York: Pocket Books, 1993.

Holder, Nancy, Jeff Mariotte, and Maryelizabeth Hart. *Angel: Casefiles*. New York: Pocket Books, 2002.

———. *Buffy, the Vampire Slayer: The Watchers' Guide*, New York: Pocket Books, 2000.

Holder, Nancy, and Jeff Mariotte. *Unseen*. New York: Pocket Books, 2001.

Holmes, Trevor. "Coming out of the Coffin: Gay Males and Queer Goths in Contemporary Vampire Fiction," in *Blood Read*, Joan

Gordon and Veronica Hollinger, eds. Philadelphia, PA: University of Pennsylvania Press, 1997.

"In Search of Extra Long Life," *New York Times,* January 6, 2002.

Iserson, Kenneth V. *Death to Dust: What Happens to Dead Bodies?* Tucson, AZ: Galen Press, 1994.

Jaffe, Philip D., and Frank DiCataldo. "Clinical Vampirism: Blending Myth and Reality." In Alan Dundes, ed. *The Vampire: A Casebook.* Madison, WI: University of Wisconsin Press, 1998.

Jones, Aphrodite. *The Embrace.* New York: Pocket Books, 1999.

Jones, Ernest. *On the Nightmare.* New York: Grove Press, 1951.

Kaplan, Steven, and Carol Kane. *Vampires Are.* Palm Springs, CA: ETC, 1984.

Karr-Morse, Robin, and Meredith S. Wiley. *Ghosts from the Nursery: Tracing the Roots of Violence.* New York: Atlantic Monthly Press, 1997.

Katz, Fred E. *Ordinary People and Extraordinary Evil.* Albany, NY: SUNY Press, 1992.

King, Stephen. *Danse Macabre.* New York: Berkley, 1981.

———. *'Salem's Lot.* New York: Signet, 1975.

Krafft-Ebbing, Richard von. *Psychopathia Sexualis: A Medico-Forensic Study.* F. S. Klaf, trans. New York: Stein & Day, 1965.

Lane, Brian. *Chronicle of Twentieth Century Murder, Vol. I and II.* New York: Berkley, 1995.

Lane, Laura. "Study Offers 'Radical Change' in Cellular Aging Concept," *CNN.com,* March 30, 2000.

Le Fanu, J. Sheridan, *Carmilla* (1872). In David Skal, ed., *Vampires: Encounters with the Undead.* New York: Black Dog and Leventhal, 2001.

Lester, David. *Serial Killers.* Philadelphia, PA: The Charles Press, 1995.

Leutwyler, Kristin. "Turning Back the Strands of Time," *Scientific American,* February 2, 1998.

Lewis, Dorothy Otnow. *Guilty by Reason of Insanity*. New York: Fawcett, 1998.

Linedecker, Clifford. *The Vampire Killers*. New York: St. Martin's Press, 1998.

Lord, David Thomas. *Bound in Blood*. New York: Kensington, 2001.

Lord Dunboyne, ed. *The Trial of John George Haigh*. London: William Hodge & Company, 1953.

Lumley, Brian. *Necroscope*. New York: Tor, 1988.

Madeline X. "How to Become a Vampire in Six Easy Lessons." New York: Dracula Unlimited, 1985.

Marcus, Jana. *In the Shadow of the Vampire*. New York: Thunder's Mouth Press, 1997.

Marigny, Jean. *Vampires: Restless Creatures of the Night*. New York: Abrams, 1994.

Martin, George R. R. *Fevre Dream*. New York: Poseidon, 1982.

Matheson, Richard. *I Am Legend* (1954). Reprint, New York: Tor, 1995.

McCammon, Robert R. *They Thirst*. New York: Avon, 1981.

McCully, Robert. "Vampirism: Historical Perspective and Underlying Process in Relation to a Case of Autovampirism," *Journal of Nervous and Mental Disease*, 139:5, November 1964.

McNally, Raymond T. *Dracula was a Woman: In Search of the Blood Countess of Transylvania*. New York: McGraw-Hill, 1983.

McNally, Raymond T., and Radu Florescu, eds. *The Essential Dracula*. New York: Mayflower, 1979.

———. *In Search of Dracula*, (1972) rev ed. New York: Houghton Mifflin, 1994.

Melton, J. Gordon. *The Vampire Book: The Encyclopedia of the Undead*. Detroit, MI: Visible Ink Press, 1994.

———. *Vampires on Video*. Detroit, MI: Visible Ink Press, 1997.

Miller, Elizabeth. *Dracula: Sense and Nonsense*. Westcliff-on-Sea, Essex, UK: Desert Island Books, 2000.

———. *Dracula: The Shadow and the Shade*. Westcliff-on-the-Sea, UK: Desert Island Books, 1998.

———. *Reflections on Dracula*. White Rock, BC, Canada: Transylvania Press. 1997.

Mitchell, Edgar. *The Way of the Explorer*. New York: Putnam, 1996.

Monaco, Richard, and Bill Burt. *The Dracula Syndrome*. New York: Avon, 1993.

Moore, Thomas. *Dark Eros: The Imagination of Sadism*. Dallas, TX: Spring Publications, 1990.

Morse, Melvin. *Where God Lives: The Science of the Paranormal and How Our Brains Are Linked to the Universe*. New York: HarperCollins, 2000.

Newberg, Andrew, and Eugene D'Aquili. *Why God Won't Go Away*. New York: Ballantine, 2001.

Niehoff, Debra. *The Biology of Violence*. New York: The Free Press, 1999.

Noll, Richard. *Bizarre Diseases of the Mind*. New York: Berkley, 1990.

———. *Vampires, Werewolves, and Demons: Twentieth Century Reports in the Psychiatric Literature*. New York: Brunner/Mazel, 1992.

Overbye, Dennis. "The Universe Might Last Forever, Astronomers Say, but Life Might Not," *New York Times*, January 1, 2002.

Page, Carol. *Bloodlust: Conversations with Real Vampires*. New York: HarperCollins, 1991.

Pauling, Linus, and E. Bright Wilson. *Introduction to Quantum Mechanics*. New York: Dover, 1985.

Pert, Candace. *Molecules of Emotion*. New York: Scribner, 1987.

Pincus, Jonathan. *Base Instincts: What Makes Killers Kill*. New York: W. W. Norton, 2001.

Pray, Leslie. "New Cells Thrive in Brain's Learning Center," *The Scientist*, 15(24):28, December 10, 2001.

Quinn, Andrew. "Could Rabies Explain Vampire Legend?" *www.skeptictank.org*, September 1998.

"Rabies: The Vampire's Kiss," *BBC News*, September 24, 1998.

Ramsland, Katherine. "Forced Consent and Voluptuous Captivity," in *The Anne Rice Reader*. New York: Ballantine, 1997.

———. *The Forensic Science of C.S.I.* New York: Berkley, 2001.

———. "Hunger for the Marvelous," *Psychology Today*, October 1989.

———. *Piercing the Darkness: Undercover with Vampires in America Today.* New York, HarperPrism, 1998.

———. *Prism of the Night.* New York: Dutton, 1991.

———. "Monster in the Mirror," *Magical Blend*, January 1991.

———. *The Roquelaure Reader.* New York: Plume, 1996.

———. *The Vampire Companion: The Official Guide to Anne Rice's The Vampire Chronicles.* New York: Ballantine, 1993.

Rein-Hagen, Mark. *Vampire: The Masquerade.* Stone Mountain, GA: White Wolf, 1991.

Ressler, Robert K., and Tom Shachtman. *I have Lived in the Monster: Inside the Minds of the World's Most Notorious Serial Killers.* New York: St. Martin's Press, 1997.

———. *Whoever Fights Monsters: My Twenty Years Tracking Serial Killers for the FBI.* New York: St. Martin's Press, 1992.

Riccardo, Martin. *Liquid Dreams of Vampires.* St. Paul, MN: Llewellyn, 1996.

———. *The Lure of the Vampire.* Chicago, IL: Adams Press, 1983.

Rice, Anne. *Armand.* New York: Knopf, 1998.

———. *Blood and Gold.* New York: Knopf, 2001.

———. *Interview with the Vampire.* New York: Knopf, 1976.

———. *Memnoch the Devil.* New York: Knopf, 1995.

———. *Pandora.* New York: Knopf, 1998.

———. *The Queen of the Damned.* New York: Knopf, 1988.

———. *The Tale of the Body Thief.* New York: Knopf, 1992.

———. *The Vampire Lestat.* New York: Knopf, 1985.

Rowe, Michael, and Thomas S. Roche. *Sons of Darkness: Tales of Men, Blood, and Immortality.* Pittsburgh, PA: Cleis Press, 1996.

Saberhagen, Fred. *The Dracula Tape.* New York: Warner, 1975.

Samenow, S. E. *Inside the Criminal Mind.* New York: Time Books, 1984.

Simmons, Dan. *Carrion Comfort.* Arlington Heights, IL: Dark Harvest, 1989.

Simon, Robert. *Bad Men Do What Good Men Dream.* Washington, DC: American Psychiatric Press, 1996.

Skal, David. *Hollywood Gothic: The Tangled Web of "Dracula" from Novel to Stage to Screen.* New York: W. W. Norton, 1990.

———. *The Monster Show: A Cultural History of Horror.* New York: W. W. Norton, 1993.

———. *V Is for Vampire: An A to Z Guide to Everything Undead.* New York: Plume, 1996.

———. *Vampires: Encounters with the Undead.* New York: Black Dog and Leventhal, 2001.

Somtow, S. P. *Vampire Junction.* Norfolk, VA: Donning Starblaze, 1983.

Stoker, Bram. *Dracula* (1897). New York: Signet, 1995.

Stolberg, Sheryl Gay. "Breakthrough in Pig Cloning," *New York Times,* January 4, 2002.

Strassman, Rick. *DMT: The Spirit Molecule.* Rochester, VT: Park Street Press, 2001.

Strieber, Whitley. *The Hunger.* New York: Pocket Books, 1981.

———. *The Last Vampire.* New York: Pocket Books: 2001.

Summers, Montague. *The Vampire: His Kith and Kin.* London: Kegan Paul, Trench, Trubne, 1928.

———. *The Vampire in Europe* (1929). New Hyde Park, NY: University Books, 1968.

Taylor, Karen E. *Blood Secrets.* New York: Kensington, 1993.

———. *The Vampire Vivienne.* New York: Kensington, 2001.

Vampyre Magazine, Issue #1, Fall 1997.

Varma, Devendra P., ed. *Voices from the Vault: Authentic Tales of Vampires and Ghosts*. Toronto, Canada: Key Porter Books, 1987.

Watson, Lyall. *Dark Nature: A Natural History of Evil*. New York: HarperCollins, 1995.

Weber, Renee. *Dialogues with Scientists and Sages: The Search for Unity*. New York: Routledge, 1986.

Wilson, F. Paul. *The Keep*. New York: William Morrow, 1981.

Wilson, Colin. *The Space Vampires*. London: Hart-Davis and MacGibbon, 1976.

Wilson, Jennifer Fisher. "The Nose Knows: How the Olfactory Influences Conduct." *The Scientist*, 15(24):22, December 10, 2001.

Wilson, John, and Tim Hunt. *Molecular Biology of the Cell*. Garland Publishers, 1994.

Wilson, Katharina M. "The History of the Word *Vampire*," in *The Vampire: A Casebook*, Alan Dundes, ed. Madison, WI: University of Wisconsin Press, 1998.

Withgott, Jay. "Bird Brain Transplants," *Science Now*, April 20, 2001.

Wolf, Leonard. *Blood Thirst: One Hundred Years of Vampire Fiction*. New York/Oxford: Oxford University Press, 1997.

Yarbro, Chelsea Quinn. *Hotel Transylvania*. New York: St. Martin's Press, 1978.

Youngson, Jeanne Keyes. *Private Files of a Vampirologist*. Chicago, IL: Adams Press, 1997.

———. "The Vampire in Contemporary Society via a Worldwide Census," a paper presented at the Transylvania Society of Dracula Conference, Romania, May 2000.

Zukav, Gary. *The Dancing Wu Li Masters: An Overview of the New Physics* (1979). New York: Bantam, 1994.

INDEX

Katherine Ramsland, Ph.D., has published nineteen books and writes forensic science articles for Court TV's *Crime Library*. She holds graduate degrees in forensic psychology, clinical psychology, and philosophy. Currently she teaches forensic psychology at DeSales University. Among her books are seven on Anne Rice and her novels, including a biography, *Prism of the Night*, and *The Vampire Companion*. She has also written a journalistic exposé, *Piercing the Darkness: Undercover with Vampires in America Today*, which took her into the vampire subculture for nearly two years, and her clinical expertise is in psychopathy and "vampire crimes."